SIGNIFYING FEMALE
ADOLESCENCE

SIGNIFYING FEMALE ADOLESCENCE

ADOLESCENCE

Film Representations and Fans, 1920–1950

Georganne Scheiner

Westport, Connecticut
London

Library of Congress Cataloging-in-Publication Data

Scheiner, Georganne, 1951–
   Signifying female adolescence : film representations and fans, 1920–1950 /
Georganne Scheiner.
      p.   cm.
   Includes bibliographical references and index.
   ISBN 0–275–96895–2 (alk. paper)
   1. Teenage girls in motion pictures.   2. Young adult films—United States—History
and criticism.   3. Motion picture audiences—United States—History.   I. Title.
PN1995.9.Y6S34   2000
791.43′652055—dc21   99–054651

British Library Cataloguing in Publication Data is available.

Library of Congress Catalog Card Number: 99–054651
ISBN: 0–275–96895–2

First published in 2000

Praeger Publishers, 88 Post Road West, Westport, CT 06881
An imprint of Greenwood Publishing Group, Inc.
www.praeger.com

Printed in the United States of America

(∞)™

The paper used in this book complies with the
Permanent Paper Standard issued by the National
Information Standards Organization (Z39.48–1984).

10 9 8 7 6 5 4 3 2 1

Copyright Acknowledgments

The author and publisher gratefully acknowledge permission for the use of the following
material:

IN BETWEEN, by Roger Edens
© EMI Feist Catalog Inc.
© Renewed
All Rights Reserved   Used by Permission
WARNER BROS. PUBLICATIONS U.S. INC., Miami, FL. 33014

Every reasonable effort has been made to trace the owners of copyright materials in this
book, but in some instances this has proven impossible. The author and publisher will be
glad to receive information leading to more complete acknowledgments in subsequent
printings of the book and in the meantime extend their apologies for any omissions.

To Anne and George Scheiner,
with love and thanks

Contents

Acknowledgments

I am grateful to many people who have helped this project along. A special thanks to Mary Rothschild, my "all-service" mentor, who guided the original version and edited the final draft. I am blessed by your friendship, encouragement, support and unfailing generosity of spirit. I also owe a special debt to Rose Weitz for her extensive comments on an early draft and her guidance. I also appreciate the valuable criticism of Kathleen Ferraro, Mary Felstiner and Vicki Ruiz of drafts of various chapters. Mike Willard's comments also helped enormously.

The support of the Women Studies Program at Arizona State University has been extraordinary. I gratefully acknowledge the two summer research grants as well as various mini-grants. I am particularly grateful for the patience and help of the Women's Studies staff, Jane Little, Debbie Tisdale and Angel Fletcher. Thanks also to my colleagues in Women's Studies including Mary Rothschild, Kathleen Ferraro, Amy Lind, Anne Hibner Koblitz, Alisa Klinger and Karen Leong for not only a rich intellectual environment but also their humor and collegiality. My research assistants—Peg Lamphere, Francine Valcour and Claudine Barnes—have helped this project considerably as well. I also appreciate the conversation and the chocolate from my Ya-Ya's in Study Group.

One of the delights of doing film research is having the opportunity to work in the various film archives. Charles Silver of the Museum of Modern Art's Film Study Center; Cathy Laughney and Madeline Matz of the Library of Congress; Barbara Hall, Dan Woodruff and Sam Gill of the Academy of Motion Picture Arts and Sciences; and Eleanore Tanin, Ed

Henry and Lou Ellen Kramer of the University of Southern California Film Archives were invaluable in helping me to locate many of the films and much obscure material. A special thanks to Kimberly Cooper of Twentieth Century Fox for not only allowing me access to archival material but also for her wonderful hospitality during my research trips. I was also fortunate to meet the late John Hampton of the Silent Movie Theater, who allowed me to see some rare prints from his private collection.

I am further blessed by a rich support system outside the university. I would like to thank my family, Helen and Bob Gillis, Rick and Gwen Scheiner, Joanne Jansen, Anne and Ken Gillis, and Margie and Tom Moss, for their interest and encouragement, and my Arcadia friends and neighbors for community. I owe my greatest debt to my parents, Anne and George Scheiner, for their unconditional love and support.

Finally, to my husband Marv Gillis, my deep appreciation for his love and emotional support, and to my private cheerleaders, my children Elizabeth and John. (I finally finished "my story," John.) To all of you who have sustained me during this project, my heartfelt thanks.

1

The In-betweens

There are two moments involving Judy Garland that capture for me the essence of female adolescence both on and off screen in the early twentieth century. In a rare musical interlude for an Andy Hardy film, making her debut in the series as Betsy Booth in *Love Finds Andy Hardy* (1938), Judy Garland plaintively sings a song called "I'm Just an In-between." The lyrics underscore the frustrations of this adolescent:

> I'm past the age of doll and carriage
> I'm not the age to think of marriage
> I'm too old for toys
> I'm too young for boys
> I'm just an in-between

Garland and her song capture the ambiguities and contradictions inherent in female adolescence. Adolescents are an in-between group—not quite children, not quite adults—trying to create their own identities, and often doing it through overt or covert rebellion. Adolescence is a difficult time for anyone, but especially for girls. At a time when all young people are trying to establish their identity and autonomy, girls are simultaneously taught to subvert their individuality to attain romantic relationships. What dilemmas does this present for individuals and for the society at large?

In the same year that Garland mourned that she was "just an in-between," she also had a cameo in the film *Broadway Melody of 1938*.

Alone in her bedroom, Judy takes out a photograph of Clark Gable, and sings "Dear Mr. Gable," a kind of musical fan letter to her favorite star, to the tune of "You Made Me Love You." Although she herself was a movie star, Garland is presented in the film as just another teenage girl with a crush on Gable. Garland is not only a representation of female adolescence, she is also represented as a fan and a consumer of the same popular images as other girls.

Today there are over thirty-one million twelve- to nineteen-year-olds in America, and it seems more than ever that the nation is fixated on the "problem" of youth. In the face of almost incomprehensible school violence, many teens feel increasingly alone and alienated, not only from their parents but from each other. They search for guidance, and often find it in the varied representations offered to them in both popular and peer culture, where brutality, sex and violence are common.

Since they first became a distinct demographic group early in the twentieth century, adolescents have cobbled out their own cultural space and created private codes of style and behavior designed both to signal membership in the group and to exclude and shock adults. Today, adolescent cultural products are probably harder than ever for adults to decipher, and the lives of adolescents are further complicated by new technologies.

Yet what has been most striking to me recently, as the popular media have dissected the American teen, is that gender is absent from the discussion.[1] The shootings in Pearl, Mississippi; Jonesboro, Arkansas; Paducah, Kentucky; Springfield, Oregon; Littleton, Colorado; and Conyers, Georgia were all perpetrated by adolescent males: Several of the shootings were directed specifically at girls. Popular representations of adolescent boys and girls have differed over time as well. Although they are marginalized in the current real discourse about teenagers, curiously since the 1920s girls in film have been generally constructed as powerful, dangerous, subversive and in opposition to the parent culture.

Although the term "teenager" is a post–World War II term, and although Americans typically think of the "problem" of teenagers as a postwar problem, in fact the perception that there is a problem predates the advent of the film medium. The earliest depictions of female adolescence on film simply echo previous characterizations of girls from popular novels and magazines as being both troubled and troubling. Films, then, can help to remind us of the continuities with the past. They can also provide us with a window into the cultural meanings of female adolescence and how those meanings changed over time. Similarly, by seeing how films of the decades between 1920 and 1950 defined the "problem" of adolescence, we can better understand something about the culture that produced it. Thus it is productive to use film to understand history, history to understand film, and both to understand adolescence.

Motion pictures have been one of the forces that have both shaped and reproduced adolescent femininity. Films not only reflect culture, they help to create it. So it is worth looking at films to see what messages they gave girls—and adults—about what girls were like and should be like. Historical interpretations of these film messages, however, must be expanded to determine what conclusions girls themselves reached from film. Girls are hardly passive consumers of images. Rather, they choose how to respond to the films they see. This is perhaps best illustrated through fan activities, where girls actively define what is important about films and film stars and create their own understandings of female adolescence through a particularly female form of popular culture.

This book looks at how female adolescence has been constructed in film, focusing on the period 1920 to 1950. I am concerned with the ways adolescence has been conveyed in film, and what films reveal about the period that produced them. I put portrayals of female adolescence in historical context by looking at the actual experience of adolescence in each period and by examining the material conditions and film industry processes that contributed to these portrayals. I look specifically at adolescent girls as fans to decode their responses to filmic representations of adolescence. An analysis of specific fan behaviors, such as writing letters or creating scrapbooks, helps us to determine the meanings generated by girls themselves. To specify how girls responded to film, I present a case study of a fan club. Taken together, I believe these ideas show how cultural and historical conditions create a context in which films with particular themes or character types predominate, how these films influence society and how girls respond to both society and films.

I begin this study in 1920 because I believe that is when a clear teen culture came into being, despite others' beliefs that "in the years prior to World War II, there were no teenagers, no teenage magazines, teenage music, or teenage culture."[2] Although a strong, identifiable teenage market is clearly a postwar development, there were signs of distinct teenage cultural activities in the early twentieth century, and to ignore them effaces the historical experience of American girls. Stuart Hall has commented on what he terms the "historical myopia" of youth studies because they have failed to compare the pre- and post-war situations of youth. Indeed, most of the work on adolescence in general, and on adolescence in film, has tended to focus on the post–World War II period.[3] To me, the period from 1920 to 1950 grounds virtually all our contemporary images of adolescence. Later films might use, amplify or amend representations of 1920 to 1950, but they do not substantially alter them. I believe it is impossible to understand current film depictions of female adolescence unless we start well before World War II.

This study also comments on the ways in which film narratives of female adolescence in specific historical periods are furthered by the conventions of genre. In the 1920s, film melodramas examined teenage sexuality, mediating it in both a public and private context. In the 1930s, the youth musical functioned ideologically to resolve the nation's fear of difference and to affirm the well-being of the community. Finally, through the coming-of-age comedies of the 1940s, adolescent sexual tensions could be conveyed in a safe, nonthreatening manner.

This is an historian's look at film and culture. I say that not to distance myself from the work that is being done in cultural studies but to justify a methodology that contextualizes cultural artifacts in a historical setting and looks at female adolescence as variable and changing over time. That is, I am interested in the ways girls' lived experiences and cultural practices are connected to cultural texts. As Angela McRobbie points out in her criticism of cultural studies and youth, "What is needed in the study of youth . . . is a research mode which prioritizes multiple levels of experience, including the ongoing relations which connect everyday life with cultural forms." Youth should not be viewed as an essentialist category. Instead, perhaps it is more useful to talk about what McRobbie terms "a range of youthful subjectivities." McRobbie also argues that there are "shared cultures of femininity" that allow adolescent girls to come together across ethnic, class, and racial backgrounds through various popular cultural forms.[4] This study brings an historical perspective to this unifying of backgrounds.

This does not pretend to be a definitive study of every film made about female adolescence in the first half of the twentieth century. Film lists were culled from the filmographies of the major adolescent stars of the early twentieth century, as well as from *The American Film Institute Index*. As with all film studies, serious investigation is restricted by the availability and quality of surviving prints. I have viewed nearly all the available films on adolescence, and the number viewed far exceeds the number identified by title. I specifically discuss a representative cross section of films from the particular historical periods, films that are exemplary of specific themes and characterizations.[5]

The films under discussion about adolescent girls are made by American filmmakers. The term adolescence will refer to the ages between twelve and nineteen, although occasionally girls may be slightly younger or older when films depict characters over time. Clearly, representations of adolescent girls in film do not even begin to reflect the diversity of the female adolescent experience. The dominant tropes of adolescence in film have been largely white, middle class, and homogeneous. Finally, the films under consideration include not only those that feature female adolescents as the main protagonist, but as supporting characters as well. So, for example, although the prolific Andy Hardy series turned on the activities of a male protagonist, the ancillary female characters provide a great deal of information about cultural attitudes and expectations of teenaged girls.

Finding sources that detail fan response for that era is a problem. Historically, the motion picture industry was hesitant about audience research. Eric Johnson, president of the Motion Picture Association of America (MPAA), once remarked that the industry knew less about itself than did any other industry. There are a number of reasons for this industry neglect, including complacence, shortsightedness, and fear and distrust of audience research by industry executives. That fear was partially warranted. Much of the early research undertaken by social scientists, such as the Payne Fund studies that I discuss later in this chapter, were motivated by pro-censorship forces. The few audience-response studies that do exist provide some useful data on the response of girls to films and film stars.[6] My primary interest, however, is in exploring sources generated by adolescent girls themselves. Fan mail sent to various stars would be the most useful sources for decoding fan preferences, but unfortunately, this evidence simply does not exist. The fan mail sent to studios is gone, but some fan mail is preserved through fan magazines, as well as in the publications of various fan clubs. Magazines such as *The American Girl* and *Calling All Girls* are also good sources of information about the fan behavior of girls. Finally, I look at untapped sources such as poetry and scrapbooks to try to tease out just what film representations meant to girls.[7]

Conditions in the nineteenth century resulted in a rudimentary youth culture that allowed girls to gain a greater sense of control over their lives in the twentieth century. By the 1920s, films seemed to be responding to the changing role of women in an expanding work force, increased voluntary activities for middle-class women, the decline in the birthrate, increased educational opportunities, the lure of Hollywood, the breakdown of organized religion, and the expansion of popular culture. Chapter 2 shows how films about female adolescents in the 1920s represented adolescence as a life stage requiring special control. Lack of control might result in sexual delinquency, and lax mothering was cited by films as one of the fundamental causes of screen delinquency. Girls themselves, however, seemingly rejected the hackneyed warnings of these exploitation films and chose to focus instead on more superficial aspects of screen teens in the 1920s.

The financial crisis of the Depression changed the ways girls were portrayed in film. Chapter 3 examines the image of girls as competent and capable, charged with "fixing" the problems of their elders. This competence reflected the increasing autonomy of adolescent girls both on and off screen. Through their fan activities, girls learned to assert their preferences and to respond critically to film representations of girls their age.

By the 1940s, adolescent girls had emerged as a separate subculture on screen, embodied by the bobby-soxer who had her own language, mannerisms, fashions, concerns, and style. Chapter 4 examines the bobby-soxer in film as a marker of generational change. As with the flapper films of the 1920s, fear of adolescent female sexuality crystallized around this new cultural stereotype. Yet in the 1940s, filmmakers disguised this anxiety by making the bobby-soxer into a comedic trope. There was, however, a subversiveness about this teen symbol who seemed intent on making her father miserable and in carving out her own cultural space.

This study ends with a look at the cultural agency of girls over the years from 1920 to 1950. Chapter 5 looks at fan activity through a case study of a specific fan club, the Deanna Durbin Devotees. I examine girls' responses to adolescent representations by focusing on the texts created by fans themselves. Girls used the discourse of fandom to make sense of the material conditions of the Depression and World War II. Fan-generated texts also helped girls to explore dimensions of female identity.

The rest of this chapter clarifies not only how the material condition of girls has changed since the nineteenth century but how the public, child-rearing experts, and contemporary scholars have interpreted these changes and the consequences of these interpretations for girls. This chapter concludes with a discussion of the unique nature of the adolescent viewing audience.

WHAT'S THE MATTER WITH KIDS TODAY?

Some historians have argued that the experience of adolescence was fairly consistent for girls from the preindustrial period to the industrial era, with the real change occurring late in the nineteenth century. Such a view is illustrated by Barbara Welter, "Adolescence in the nineteenth century was for most young girls a relatively brief, and stormy period, marked on the one hand by her first menstruation at fourteen or fifteen, and on the other by her marriage at eighteen or twenty."[8] During the nineteenth century the term "youth" was more generally used by child-rearing experts to refer to the period of adolescence. There were a number of popular books written early in the century that seemed to be responding to perceived "problems" of youth. These books taken together paint a picture of the time of youth as a "critical transition," and they represent the adolescent as emotional, vulnerable, suggestible and impressionable.[9]

Most historians agree that by the late nineteenth century this concern for youth, particularly for working girls, intensified as more young women began to work outside the home and began to experience longer periods of relative autonomy. Middle-class girls began to go to school in increasing numbers, and marriage and birth rates began to decline for the first generation of college women. Reformers began to worry about this "new girl," and the professionalization of motherhood among educators was essentially a backlash to some major changes taking place in American society. By the turn of the century, progressive reformers began to advocate a curriculum of sexual education or "sexual hygiene" as a way to control the sexuality of the "new girl." This evolved into a new legal category, the "sexual delinquent," and what was essentially two juvenile justice systems, one for boys and another for girls, which emphasized a strict standard of sexual behavior.[10]

The "invention" of adolescence is most often credited to G. Stanley Hall, who synthesized the work of educators, psychologists, social scientists, and reformers of the nineteenth century in his 1904, two-volume work, *Adolescence: Its Psychology and Its Relation to Physiology, Anthropology, Sociology, Sex, Crime, Religion and Education.* It is important to note that the very creation of the concept of adolescence further problemitized it. The work was largely a response to the forces of urbanization, industrialization, immigration, and increased opportunities for women. As some historians have argued, Hall was probably reacting to the increasing reality of a youth culture, that is, to the fact that youth were exhibiting discernible behavioral characteristics. Hall saw adolescence as a radical break with childhood, a time of "storm and stress." His theory created a clear delineation between childhood and adolescence and encouraged "the prolongation of a period of dependence and the segregation of youth from the pressures of adulthood." Hall devoted only one chapter to girls, and his conception of adolescence was essentially built on normative definitions of masculinity. Clearly reacting to the "new girl," Hall gathered a great deal of evidence to support his totalizing and essentialist views of women by warning of the dangerous consequences of higher education and touting traditional roles for women.[11]

Although Hall's reputation was short-lived and his influence declined among scholars after 1925, his paradigm continued to be the lens through which adolescence was viewed by most experts. Educators and reformers in the Progressive era warned parents that children needed a great deal of regulation and surveillance to help them to navigate the "storm and stress" of adolescence. Most professionals believed that girls, especially working-class and immigrant girls, were especially vulnerable to negative influences during adolescence. As Joseph Kett argues, the same mind-set that created the adolescent as a "type" created the delinquent as a "type." In both cases, "certain mental or physical mental traits were labeled appropriate or necessary correlatives of delinquency or adolescence, and then used to explain the behavior of young people."[12]

Clearly, motion pictures were perceived as being one of the most negative forces on children of the industrial age. From almost the beginning of the public discourse about film, there appeared to be a gendered assumption of spectatorship.[13] That is, film viewing seemed to pose a greater danger for women and girls than for men and boys. As Lea Jacobs points out, this criticism of Hollywood films and their scurrilous effects on females began as early as the teens. "At the most literal level, newspapers and magazines depicted Hollywood as a cause and potential site of female delinquency—luring girls away from their homes into tenuous and morally suspect professions."[14] Miriam Van Waters, one of the leading figures of female correction reform in the 1920s and 1930s, detailed the stories of sixteen-year-old Josephine and fourteen-year-old Clara, who had contracted venereal diseases after running away from home in their desire to work in the movies.[15] The popular press was filled with cautionary tales of girls like Clara and Josephine, and even the leading fan magazine *Photoplay* ran regular articles warning girls about the difficulties of finding jobs in Hollywood.[16]

In 1928, the Rev. William H. Short, director of the National Committee for the Study of Social Values in Motion Pictures, a censorship group, published *A Generation of Motion Pictures,* a summary of negative assumptions about films. In 1929, Short obtained a grant from the Payne Study and Experiment Fund, a foundation for the study of the effects of film on children and adolescents that resulted in the Payne Fund studies. From 1929 to 1933, the Payne Fund supported twelve research investigations by social scientists concerning the influence of motion pictures on youth.[17] The findings of the Payne Fund studies seemed to confirm the public's worst fears about the negative influence of this young medium on the youth of America and provided potent ammunition for the pro-censorship forces. There appeared to be quantifiable, scientific evidence that films were responsible for the moral decay of its young audience. Although flawed methodologically, the studies do contain some useful information through both interviews and questionnaires about the ways in which adolescent girls responded to screen representations.

Henry Forman, in *Our Movie Made Children*, the popular summary of the Payne studies, went so far as to conclude," for [adolescents] the movies constitute an education along the left hand or primrose path of life, to the wreckage of their own lives and to the detriment and cost of society. The road to delinquency is heavily dotted with movie addicts."[18] Girls seemed especially susceptible to the moral influences of film. Another Payne study by Blumer and Hauser looked specifically at the connection between films and delinquency and concluded that girls were much more suggestible than boys and, therefore, more easily lured into sexual delinquency.

Motion pictures may play a major or minor role in female delinquency and crime by arousing sexual passion, by instilling the desire to live a gay, wild, fast life, by evoking longings for luxury and smart appearance, and by suggesting to some girls questionable methods of easily attaining them, by the display of modes of beautification and love techniques, by the depiction of various forms of crime readily imitated by girls and young women, and by competing with home and school for an important place in the lives of girls.[19]

From 1910 until the outbreak of World War II, female delinquency turned on sexual activity (and the technical condition of the hymen), and a new category was constructed, that of the sexual delinquent. The delinquency of girls was confined chiefly to sexual misdemeanors, although truancy and running away were also considered delinquent behavior. In the same period some two million girls under the age of eighteen were described by one expert on juvenile delinquency as "coming to the attention of police." About 1 percent of the female population between the ages of ten and sixteen could be termed delinquent. One survey of children's court in New York City between 1902 and 1932 estimated that the ratio of delinquent boys to girls was sixty to one.[20]

Mary Odem argues in her study of delinquent girls in the Progressive period that girls became the focus of public concern about their sexuality and targets of intervention by the state. She details two phases of reform. The first dates to 1885, when girls were still viewed as being victimized by sexual predators. The movement to raise the age of consent in statutory rape began as a way to protect girls from male seducers. Yet by the turn of the century, girls increasingly were seen as agents in their victimization. Sexually active girls were no longer victims but "delinquents" who needed new policies of control and intervention. This anxiety about adolescent sexuality originated in changes in the lives of working-class girls that expanded their opportunity for autonomy. Urbanization and industrialization created new jobs that took young girls away from their homes into cities, where they were free of familial restrictions. Moreover, girls also had increased exposure to commercialized leisure activities, which allowed them a chance to explore relationships outside of marriage and away from regulation by parents. As Odem argues, the "extended period of relative autonomy was linked to a whole host of social problems—prostitution and vice, venereal disease, family breakdown, and out of wedlock pregnancy."[21]

Linda Gordon says of the discovery of female sexual delinquency, "That label blamed girls for things boys could get away with . . . girls who stayed away from home, came home late, who used vulgar language, rode in cars, drank or smoke, walked or dressed 'immodestly,' [were] liable to be declared delinquent." She also notes that girls were punished more severely than boys and were often sent to reform school. "Moral neglect" became a diagnostic category in the 1890s, and girls were labeled "morally neglected" for any sexual act, even if they did not commit an actual crime. Gordon underscores the part parents played in moral neglect:

Parental responsibility for children's misbehavior was at the heart of the meaning of delinquency for child-savers. To them delinquency was not just criminality in the young, it became in itself a form of child neglect, or more precisely, the prima facie evidence of the existence of neglect. Since girls' delinquency was usually sexual, it was evidence of moral neglect.[22]

This neglect was clearly blamed on mothers. In the 1920s, mothers were increasingly accused of inadequate supervision and regulation. Mothers were considered primary care-givers, and feminist Beatrice Forbes Robinson-Hale declared in 1923, "If there is anything wrong with our girls the fault lies in the soil, not in the plants." Another contemporary advisor, former actress Blanche Bates Creel, argued that it was not children who had changed, but the way they were being raised. "Children have always rebelled against parental authority . . . the only difference between today and yesterday is that our mothers were on the job and did not let us get away with it."[23]

Miriam Van Waters chose to hold both parents responsible, arguing that "selfish parental attitudes produce delinquency." In fact, the title of her 1927 book, *Parents on Probation*, reflected this belief. She editorialized on the term "delinquent" itself: "In terming children, we have failed to identity properly *Delinquent*, we have shifted the burden from adults to children. In contrast to primitive societies, civilized society places responsibility of delinquency on children."[24]

There was a clear double standard inherent in causation theories regarding delinquency. Mothers with "low standards" were perceived by child-care experts as being more harmful to girls than to boys. Thus both diagnostic definitions of delinquency as well as causation theories were gendered, and both turned on deviance from normative standards of femininity. The Payne Fund studies show the same bias: Movies were more harmful for girls than boys.

There were social scientists who looked for more-complex causes of delinquency, most notably Clifford Shaw and Henry McKay in Chicago. Shaw's work, *Delinquency Areas* (1929), summarized his work in the "Chicago Area Project." He, as McKay, theorized that the major cause of delinquency was the difficulty of immigrant groups adjusting to a new culture and the dislocations caused by urban and industrial life. Van Waters also recognized the problems of second-generation immigrant children caused by the dislocation of cultural traditions. She argued for the creation of more settlement houses to combat this problem.[25]

The public discourse on adolescence underscored the ambivalent attitude toward youth. Despite provocative titles as "The Destructive Younger

Generation," "The Problem of the Modern Girl," "How Wild Is Wild Youth?" and "The Flapper," some contemporary articles argued that fears about youth were overblown or exaggerated. A reflective article in *Ladies Home Journal* editorialized, "It seems to be an accepted axiom nowadays that our young people are going to the devil. Press, pulpit and publicist are agreed that youth is wild and getting wilder. . . . Most of this is lamentation . . . based on theory, not fact." Phyllis Blanchard and Caroline Manasses, in their book, *New Girls for Old*, added to the debate: "It's false to give the impression that all girls are committed to the new manners, when in fact we're talking about a relatively small number." A self-proclaimed "flapper" reacted to the furor over youth: "I read this book . . . [which] showed where they'd been excited about wild youth for three generations."[26]

Yet a series of opinion pieces from educators and social commentators on the adolescent girl that had appeared in *Forum* in 1923 concluded that "she was a 'holy terror' and that her conduct was directly traceable to the war, or the movies, or lack of parental discipline, or modern education." That view was underscored in a sensational book written by juvenile Judge Ben Lindsey, *The Revolt of Modern Youth* (1925). Generational fears crystallized around the cultural symbol of a young woman, the flapper, "whose ways, customs, purposes, vision, and modes of thought were as unknown to her parents . . . as the social customs of Mars." As Joe Austin and Michael Willard have argued, public debates about adolescence are useful windows into decoding how understandings of both the past and present are contested. Certainly, what seemed like the accelerated social change of the 1920s had its origins in the pre–World War I period. Historians have demonstrated that the flapper had probably been around since 1915. However, it seems clear that the acceleration of social change after the war added to the perception, at any rate, that the younger generation was very different from their elders. Moreover, the superficial aspects of change, such as short skirts and bobbed hair, which had begun to proliferate in the media, probably acerbated fears about youth.[27]

Historian Joseph Kett remarks that although generational conflict was not unique to the 1920s, nor particularly intense, a great deal of importance was attached to it. As Kett notes, "There was an odd mixture of alarm, tolerance, and plain curiosity, not to mention a substantial dose of voyeurism, underpinning the investigative curiosity about youth." He attributes this conflict to ambiguous standards of adults caught between Victorian and modern codes of behavior[28]

In the 1930s, sociologist E. B. Reuter rejected a biological basis for adolescence, arguing instead that adolescence was culturally determined. He defined adolescence as "a system of collective definitions that creates a world apart; it is a body of conception in regard to rights and privileges, an indigenous and self imposed system of standards, conventions and expectations that influence or determine behavior within the age group." In essence, he observed behavior that was socially determined and believed that adolescence was constituted as "whatever the group decides adolescence should be."[29]

By the 1930s, it seemed that adolescents themselves thought adolescence should be a time of increased freedom as they began to challenge traditional ideas of parental authority and respect. Grace Palladino has chronicled the efforts of adolescents to demand a degree of autonomy and to assert their right to behave the way they wanted to behave. Teenagers claimed the right to "choose their own friends, and run their own social lives, based on teenage notions of propriety and style, not on adult rules of appropriate conduct." This response prompted "professional character builders" and other youth organizations to find acceptable ways to channel adolescent energy. Even the federal government got into the act with the formation of the National Youth Administration, which targeted out-of-work youth.[30]

By the 1940s, the public discourse on adolescence once again focused on delinquency. During the summer of 1943, a Senate subcommittee on Wartime Health and Education convened, led by Claude Pepper. Expert witnesses placed the blame for delinquency squarely on working mothers, who they believed had abdicated their family responsibilities and had turned their children into delinquents. The solution to the breakdown of maternal care, argued Mark McCloskey, recreation director for the Office of Community War Services, and other youth experts, lay in more-careful engineering of the energy of youth into organized recreational activities.[31]

Although the reality of a youth culture has a longer history, the term "youth culture" was probably coined by Talcott Parsons in 1949. Parsons argued that a high degree of industrialization was a precondition for the development of the unique ways of behaving, the roles and values of adolescents. His notion of youth culture was expanded by Kenneth Keniston, who defined youth culture as the "special culture of those between childhood and adulthood, a culture that differs from both that of child and adult." Keniston argued that youth culture could manifest signs of both conformity and revolt simultaneously. He characterized youth culture as being "not always or explicitly anti-adult, but belligerently *non*-adult."[32] It was increasingly clear that adolescents were not rejecting the standards of the parent culture, they simply did not care about them, choosing instead to generate their own subcultural forms.

The study of youth cultures was further refined in the 1970s in Great Britain by Stuart Hall and Tony Richardson's *Resistance through Rituals*. They expanded Italian Marxist Antonio Gramsci's notion of hegemony to popular cultural forms, whereby cultural forms become sites in the struggle for and against the hegemony of the ruling interests. Scholars at the University of Birmingham's Centre for Contemporary Cultural Studies began exploring the ways in which various working-class, British subcultural groups both negotiate the dominant culture as well as resist the normalizing forces of popular cultural forms. *Resistance through Rituals* synthesized the initial work of the Centre's subcultural group, and the anthology focused on post–World War II, working-class, British youth, who they argued became potent signifiers of social change. These British scholars positioned youth as the locus between changing economic and institutional structures and dominant cultural values. Youth is privileged as a central site in these conflicts.[33]

In both scholarly and popular writing, teenage subcultures have often appeared to be a threat to the social order. Many of the fears and anxieties of the public, experts and scholars have been scripted into the Hollywood vision of the teenager, and these concerns are especially discernable for girls. Yet subcultural theory as articulated by the Birmingham scholars has consistently marginalized girls, and as Angela McRobbie points out in her 1970s critique of subcultural theory, girls may have become invisible because the term "subculture" has come to have such strong masculine connotations. In many ways, the early work of the Centre reinforced gendered notions of adolescence. Girls' culture has operated mainly within the private space of the home, within what McRobbie terms "the culture of the bedroom." Joan Jacobs Brumberg has argued that the bathroom has served as another important site of female adolescence, a place that afforded girls the opportunity for self-scrutiny. These private sites of girls' culture are often in opposition to the more public spaces of the street or the club of boys' culture. Another reason that girls' subcultural forms might have been marginalized is because they appear to lack political intent and do not appear to challenge the dominant culture. This is particularly true before the 1950s, when much of the cultural activity of girls revolved around consumption. Yet as McRobbie reminds us, consumption can be a political act and as much a part of the process of identity formation and meaning making as is production.[34]

The emphasis of the British scholars on class was increasingly replaced with an emphasis on representations of race and sexuality, and yet the issue of identity formation and youth culture continued to be ignored. As McRobbie says, "Identity is predicated on social identity, on social groups and populations with some sense of shared experience and history." Identity is tied to agency through cultural production. McRobbie calls for a move away from the binary approach of looking at the image versus the reality. Instead she suggests a new methodology that rests on the "relational, interactive quality of everyday life." Through such an approach, identity formation can be examined not only through cultural texts, but through the cultural practices of daily life and the way the two are related.[35]

As Wini Brienes argues, "a national, middle class, popular culture was a central event out of which girls constructed their feminine selves and to which they contributed." Although she is talking about the post–World War II period, the same could be said of the years preceding the war when the film industry helped to create a national cultural form. That an adolescent girl was usually white and upper middle class did not diminish her appeal to a diverse population. The fact is that film portrayals mattered to girls. They still do. Although today, women may have a love/hate relationship with the media, in the pre–World War II period there was no such ambivalence. Further, girls contributed to new definitions of femininity through their use of popular cultural forms.

I will be looking at a national youth culture, not in the sense that it was representative of the experience of all girls, but that it was universally disseminated and usually presented as being reflective of the experience of all girls. Adolescence is a useful concept insofar as it allows us to group on the basis of shared experiences of age, and adolescent girls can come together across class, racial and ethnic lines through cultural forms such as film.

THE FEMALE ADOLESCENT AUDIENCE

Historically, the teenage audience has been a unique group whose response to films has been remarkably different from either children or adults. While their economic power has certainly allowed them to influence the film industry, they have also been prey to media manipulation. Because teens are in the process of identity formation, films and film stars can be regarded as potent socializing agents. As David Considine notes:

The relationship between the young person and the film industry is thus a dichotomy. While the young viewer is capable of exerting an influence upon the product [s]he consumes, it in turn is equally capable of exerting an influence on [her]. While the search for self renders the adolescent susceptible to suggestion, there is evidence that at the same time, the young person is more perceptive and aware of film than at any other time.[36]

Since the early twentieth century, moviegoing has been an important social activity of adolescence. Movie attendance increased among teens in the 1920s, and the sociologists Robert and Helen Merrell Lynd found that the majority of high school girls in Muncie, Indiana went to the movies at least once a week. Film provided girls with potent models for behavior. In research undertaken by the Payne Fund to investigate the influence of motion pictures on youth, young girls indicated in numerous samples how much they admired and tried to emulate screen actresses. Girls took their dating and beauty cues from films as well. One researcher noted that "motion pictures provide patterns for dress and beautification and serve as one of the main sources of clothing and make-up." One fifteen-year-old lamented, "I have attempted to imitate the mannerisms, but I have never received satisfying results—I even bobbed my hair when I was only eight as a result of seeing someone in movies do likewise."[37]Henry James Forman in *Our Movie Made Children* (1933) concluded, "Motion picture scrapbooks, motion picture photographs of favorite stars decorating the lockers of high school girls and boys, motion picture conversation, motion picture imagery—what else is this for young people but a motion picture world?" The influence of films seemed undeniable. One high school student admitted, "The discussing of movies at school is an indoor sport."[38] By the 1920s, moviegoing had become an important social rite and avenue of consumption. In the 1930s, attending movies continued to be an integral part of the adolescent experience and a source of information about heterosocial behavior.

There is actually a debate among scholars as to the composition of early film audiences. Some early sociological studies of moviegoing found that by the 1930s, adult women were the chief patrons of motion pictures. As the Lynds note, "Especially in the better class houses, adult females predominate and as one producer remarked, 'set the kind of picture that will go.' " Sociologist Margaret Thorp noted that it was "the solid average citizen's wife who commanded the respectful attention of the industry." Sixty percent of the film-viewing audience in Muncie was comprised of women over the age of sixteen, with only 10 percent of the audience being under the age of sixteen.[39]

Yet Edgar Dale, one of the researchers of the Payne Fund studies, argued in 1935 that "there have been misrepresentations by motion picture organizations of the amount of child attendance. . . . Data have been presented in this report to show that children and youth the country over are regular patrons of motion picture theaters. Further evidence has been presented to show that they contribute a proportion of the total audience that is far greater than we have been commonly led to believe." Leo Handel, a social scientist who specialized in audience research for Metro Goldwyn Mayer in the 1940s, supported Dale's earlier findings. Disputing contentions that the majority of filmgoers were adult females, Handel instead found that the majority of the film-viewing audience was made up of ten- to twenty-four-year-olds.[40]

Whatever the case, girls were clearly able to wield some power over the representations of screen teens in their capacity as fans. By the 1920s, fans and adolescent girls were thought to be synonymous. Certainly, girls were a highly visible segment of fans. Social critics of the relationship between adolescence and fandom held real concerns and argued that "movie fans symbolized much that was vulnerable about the younger generation and dangerous about mass society." By the 1930s, the subscriber to the fan magazines was more than likely to be an adolescent girl who was apt "to shut herself up in her bedroom and proceed . . . to memorize its contents." She was able to interact with the film images with which she was presented through a kind of discourse with fan magazines and stars themselves. Editors knew what held her interest. "In dawning teenhood, she vaguely thrilled to the thought of becoming one of those gorgeous creatures, the stars." Fan magazines included star addresses, as well as "Fan Club Corners," where tidbits about favorite stars could be found. By the 1930s, fans operated as a powerful lobby group.[41]

One of the Payne studies by Frank Shuttleworth and Mark May actually attempted to discern whether there were in fact behavioral differences between adolescents who were movie fans and those who were not. They selected their subjects from some 1,400 high school students in New England on the basis of their frequency in moviegoing. They then created two control groups: those teens who were the most avid moviegoers and those who were the least frequent. Interestingly, in most of the comparisons made between the two groups, few significant differences were observed. The moviegoers did appear to be more social and were more apt to be chosen as friends. There is, however, no way of knowing whether these differences resulted from moviegoing or something else.[42]

Leo Handel discovered that adolescent girls were more likely than boys or adults to single out one or more movie stars for their "special attention." He also found that audiences preferred actors of their own sex, those with whom they could most readily identify. One adolescent girl in his sample, in discussing how she chose actresses with whom she could identify, said, "I think they are the kind of people I would like to know, or even be like." He admitted that only a small segment of the moviegoing public actually wrote fan letters, but he found that it was largely teenage girls who "seek this contact with their favorite stars."[43] Often their favorite stars were girls like them, girls who seemingly mirrored their lives.

David Considine, in his study of images of adolescence in film, is critical, however, of what he sees as the industry's inability to reflect adolescent concerns realistically. "The American film industry has been spectacularly unsuccessful in realistically depicting adolescence. . . . [T]he young people Hollywood has presented to us over more than half a century have seldom been representative of American youth as a whole."[44] The medium's ability (or lack thereof) to reflect reality is not the issue. The relationship between the lived experience of adolescent girls and a popular cultural form is the crucial issue. If adolescent representations have projected images at odds with experience, then the important issue becomes deciding why there is such incongruence and what that discrepancy says not only about the parent culture but about the culture of adolescent girls. There is a clear difference between female adolescence as a discursive subject in film and the lived experiences of adolescent girls.

Adolescence as a social construct has clearly influenced the cultural practices of adolescence. In the early twentieth century, G. Stanley Hall conceptualized a period of "storm and stress," a view that continues to frame popular perceptions of adolescence. Youth culture was already forming by the time of Hall's writing. Before the "birth" of the teenager in the 1950s, adolescents had an increased public identity built around their cultural forms, an identity linked to their consumption patterns.

Though it is often difficult to discern how many cultural practices were actually created by girls themselves, or suggested by the social conventions of the parent culture, it does seem clear that girls adapted popular practices to their own ends, sometimes subverting them in the process. Out of that evolved customs, fads and behaviors all their own. Film representations of female adolescence provided girls with a potent peer group, because they offered moviegoers certain standards and expectations for behavior. The process of adolescent identity formation can be viewed as the locus of struggle between the desire to conform and the desire to be autonomous.

There has been a renewed preoccupation in the 1990s with female adolescence, as evidenced by the success of several popular tracts on the subject.[45] As I have shown, this interest is hardly new. An examination of both film representations and popular discourse in the prewar period reveals a concern that transcends different historical periods and material conditions. Such concerns may also provide a way to understand that our preoccupation with female adolescence is part of an historical continuum. In singing to the ambivalence of adolescence, Judy Garland was not a miniature adult but a part of a vibrant and distinct subculture. The ways in which girls mediated the parent culture and their own is at the heart of adolescent representations in film before girls became "grrrls." From the flapper of the 1920s to the bobby-soxer of the 1940s, adolescent girls in film have been markers of generational, sexual and economic change.

NOTES

1. See "The Secret Life of Teens," *Newsweek*, 10 May 1999, 30–59.

2. Wini Brienes, *Young, White and Miserable: Growing Up Female in the Fifties* (Boston: Beacon Press, 1992), 94. For similar interpretations see also, Grace Palladino, *Teenagers: An American History* (New York: Basic Books, 1996); David Considine, *The Cinema of Adolescence* (Jefferson, NC: McFar-

land, 1985); Thomas Doherty, *Teenagers and Teenpics: The Juvenilization of American Film* (Boston: Unwin Hyman, 1988).

3. Joseph Kett's *Rites of Passage: Adolescence in America 1790 to the Present* (New York: Basic Books, 1977) is a gendered look at the experience of male adolescence. Grace Palladino begins her study in the 1930s, as does David Considine. Thomas Doherty argues that the 1950s began America's preoccupation with the screen teen. Stuart Hall and Tony Jefferson, *Resistance through Rituals: Youth Subcultures in Post War Britain* (London, Hutchinson, 1976), 17.

4. Angela McRobbie, "Different Youthful Subjectivities: Toward a Cultural Sociology of Youth," in *Postmodernism and Popular Culture* (London: Routledge, 1994), 178–179.

5. Kenneth W. Munden, ed., *The American Film Institute Catalog of Pictures Produced in the United States* (New York: R. R. Bowker, 1971). See also Richard Bertrand Dimmitt, *A Title Guide to the Talkies* (New York: The Scarecrow Press, 1963).

6. Bruce Austin, *The Film Audience: An International Bibliography of Research* (Metuchen, NJ: Scarecrow Press, 1983), xxiii–xxiv.

7. Jackie Stacey, *Star Gazing: Hollywood Cinema and Female Spectatorship* (London: Routledge, 1994), explores the role that American movie stars played in British women's memories of the 1940s. Stacey is also interested in analyzing fan behavior to understand audience reaction. However, instead of looking at the primary sources of fandom in the historical period under investigation, Stacey does an ethnographic study of fan memories and recollections of the cinema-going experience. Although it is an interesting and very useful method, I am more interested in the responses of fans at the time of production.

8. Barbara Welter, *Dimity Convictions: The American Women in the 19th Century* (Athens: Ohio University Press, 1976), 3.

9. John Demos and Virginia Demos, "Adolescence in Historical Perspective," in *The American Family in Social-Historical Perspective,* ed. Michael Gordon (New York: St. Martin's Press, 1978), 212–213.

10. Mary Ellen Odem, *Delinquent Daughters: Protecting and Policing Adolescent Female Sexuality in the United States 1885–1920* (Chapel Hill: University of North Carolina Press, 1995), 1–5; Joseph Hawes, " The Strange History of Female Adolescence in the United States," *The Journal of Psychohistory* (Summer 1985): 55, 60.

11. G. Stanley Hall, *Adolescence: Its Psychology and Its Relation to Physiology, Anthropology, Sociology, Sex, Crime, Religion and Education.* 2 vols (New York: D. Appleton, 1904). For his discussion of girls, see Chapter 7, "Adolescent Girls and Their Education," in vol. II, 551–647. John and Virginia Demos argue for the beginnings of a rudimentary youth culture in the nineteenth century in "Adolescence in Historical Perspective," 217. For a discussion of the "invention" of adolescence see Joseph Kett, 217– 244.

12. Steven Schlossman and Stephanie Wallach, "The Crime of Precocious Sexuality: Female Juvenile Delinquency in the Progressive Era," *Harvard Educational Review* 48 (February 1978): 82; Kett, 255.

13. Lea Jacobs draws these conclusions in "Reformers and Spectators: The Film Education Movement in the Thirties," *Camera Obscura* 22 (January 1990): 29–49.

14. Jacobs, *The Wages of Sin: Censorship and the Fallen Woman Film 1928–1942* (Madison: University of Wisconsin Press, 1991), 3–4.

15. Miriam Van Waters, *Youth in Conflict* (New York: Republic, 1925; reprint, AMS Press, 1970), 27–28. For a discussion of Van Waters, see Estelle Freedman, *Maternal Justice: Miriam Van Waters and the Female Reform Tradition* (Chicago: University of Chicago Press, 1996).

16. Jacobs, *Wages*, 4. See also, "A Warning for the Runaway Season," *Literary Digest* (16 July 1927): 29—30; "The Runaway Girl Problem," *Literary Digest* (10 May 1924): 31–32; and Vera Connolly, "The Girls Who Run Away," *Good Housekeeping* 85 (July 1927): 40–41.

17. For an excellent discussion of the Payne Fund studies see Garth Jowett, Ian C. Jarvie and Kathryn H. Fuller, *Children and the Movies: Media Influence and the Payne Fund Controversy* (New York: Cambridge University Press, 1996); and Robert Sklar, *Movie Made America: A Cultural History of American Movies* (New York: Vintage, 1975), 134–140.

18. Henry Forman, *Our Movie Made Children* (New York: Macmillan, 1933), 232.

19. Herbert Blumer and Philip Hauser, *Movies, Delinquency and Crime* (New York: Macmillan, 1933; reprint, Arno Press, 1970), 199.

20. Milton Barron, *The Juvenile Delinquent in Society* (New York: Alfred A. Knopf, 1959), 49.

21. Odem, *Delinquent*, 1–4. See also Kathy Peiss, *Cheap Amusements: Working Women and Leisure in Turn of the Century New York* (Philadelphia: Temple University Press, 1986); Constance Nathanson, *Dangerous Passage: The Social Control of Sexuality in Women's Adolescence* (Philadelphia: Temple University Press, 1991); and Ruth Alexander, *The Girl Problem: Female Sexual Delinquency in New York* (Ithaca, NY: Cornell University Press, 1995).

22. Odem, *Delinquent*, 138–139.

23. Beatrice Forbes Robinson-Hale, *What's Wrong with Our Girls?: The Environment, Training and Future of American Girls* (New York: Fred Stokes, 1923), xx; Blanche Bates Creel, "Job or Joy Ride," *Century* 115 (November 1927): 42.

24. Miriam Van Waters, *Parents on Probation* (New York: Republic, 1927). Van Waters, *Youth in Conflict,* 67, 146.

25. For an analysis of Shaw's work see James Gilbert, *A Cycle of Outrage: America's Reaction to the Juvenile Delinquent in the Fifties* (New York: Oxford University Press, 1986), 125; Van Waters, *Youth,* 58–59.

26. Maude Royden, "The Destructive Younger Generation," *Ladies Home Journal* 41 (March 1924): 31, 174; Aurelia Mary Reinhardt, "The Problem of the Modern Girl," *Woman's Home Companion* 55 (March 1928): 24, 135; "How Wild Is Wild Youth?" *New Republic* 46 (5 May 1926): 318–319; Frank Crane, "The Flapper," *Colliers* 74 (11 October 1924): 23; Phyllis Blanchard and Caroline Manasses, *New Girls for Old* (New York: The MacCauley Co., 1930), 13; "Flapper Jane," *New Republic* 45 (9 September 1925): 66.

27. The *Forum* issue was summarized by Elizabeth Adams, "What the American Woman Thinks," *The Woman Citizen* 8 (26 December 1924): 16. Ben Lindsey and Wainwright Evans, *The Revolt of Modern Youth* (New York: Boni and Liverlight, 1925), 25; Joe Austin and Michael Willard, eds. *Generations of Youth: Youth Culture in History and 20th Century America* (New York: New York University Press, 1998), 2; Henry May, *The End of American Innocence: A Study of the First Years of Our Time 1912–1917* (London: J. Cape, 1959); James McGovern, "The American Women's Pre–World War I Freedom in Manners and Morals," *Journal of American History* (September 1968): 315–333.

28. Kett, 263–264.

29. E. B. Reuter, "The Sociology of Adolescence," *American Journal of Sociology* (November 1937): 421, 423.

30. Palladino, 7–8, 45; Kett, 252–253 .

31. Gilbert, 33; Palladino, 82–83.

32. Talcott Parsons, "Age and Sex Grading in the U.S.," in *Essays in Sociological Theory, Pure and Applied*, ed. Talcott Parsons (Glencoe, IL: Free Press, 1949). Kenneth Keniston, "Social Change and Youth in America," *Daedalus* (Winter 1962): 145–171, emphasis added.

33. Stuart Hall and Tony Richardson, eds., *Resistance through Rituals: Youth Subcultures in Post War Britain* (London: Hutchinson, 1976).

34. Angela McRobbie and Jenny Garber, "Girls and Subcultures." In *Resistance through Rituals*, eds. Hall and Jefferson, 211. See also Angela McRobbie, "Settling Accounts with Subcultures: A Feminist Critique," *Screen Education* 34 (1980), and "Shut Up and Dance: Youth Culture and Changing Modes of Femininity," in *Postmodernism and Popular Culture,* 156, 160–61. Joan Jacobs Brumberg, *The Body Project* (New York: Random House, 1997).

35. Angela McRobbie, "Post-Marxism and Cultural Studies," in *Postmodernism and Popular Culture*, 58.

36. Considine, 3.

37. Robert Lynd and Helen Nerrell Lynd, *Middletown: A Study of American Culture* (New York: Harcourt, Brace and Co., 1929), 264. Cited by Herbert Blumer, *Movies and Conduct* (New York: The Macmillan Co., 1933), 37.

38. Forman, 160. Cited by Blumer, 37.

39. Robert Lynd and Helen Merrell Lynd, *Middletown in Transition* (New York: Harcourt Brace and World, 1937), 261. Sociologists Lloyd Warner and Paul Lunt in their study of "Yankee City" (Newburyport, MA) also found that movie patrons were predominantly female. See Lloyd Warner and Paul Lunt, *The Social Life of a Modern Community* (New Haven: Yale University Press, 1941), 110–111, 143. Margaret Thorp, *America at the Movies* (New Haven: Yale University Press, 1939 reprint, New York: Arno Press, 1970), 9–10.

40. Edgar Dale, *Children's Attendance at the Motion Pictures* (New York: Macmillan, 1935), 9, 73. Leo Handel, *Hollywood Looks at its Audience* (Urbana: University of Illinois Press, 1950), 99.

41. Lisa Lewis, *Gender Politics and MTV* (Philadelphia: Temple University Press, 1990), 89, 202–203. Richard Griffith, *The Talkies: Articles and Illustrations from a Great Fan Magazine 1928–1940* (New York: Dover Publications, 1971), v–vii, 179. Kathryn Fuller, *At the Picture Show* (Washington, DC: Smithsonian Institution Press, 1996), 147–148, 167.

42. Frank Shuttleworth and Mark May, *The Social Conduct and Attitudes of Movie Fans* (New York: Macmillan, 1933), 1–25.

43. Handel, 146–147, 149, 10.

44. Considine, 9.

45. See Brumberg; Mary Pipher, *Reviving Ophelia: Saving the Lives of Adolescent Girls* (New York: Ballantine Books, 1994); Naomi Wolf, *Promiscuities: The Secret Struggle for Womanhood* (New York: Random House, 1997); Sherrie Inness, ed., *Delinquents and Debutantes: 20th Century American Girls Culture* (New York: New York University Press, 1998).

2

Delinquent Daughters

Adolescent girls have been populating the screen from the inception of the medium. In their attempt to be topical, some of the earliest films telling a story at the turn of the twentieth century turned their attention to the "new girl." Titillating titles like *Why Girls Leave Home* (1909), *The Path to Ruin* (1914), and *A Danger Signal* (1915) offered blatant moral teachings and warned of the dangers inherent during adolescence.

By the 1920s, filmic representations of adolescence were increasingly problemitized as a life stage requiring special attention, and generational change seemed more than superficial. The breakdown of traditional forms of authority in both society and film appeared to spur an epidemic of sexual delinquency. There was a fine line separating the film flapper from the delinquent, and increasingly Hollywood crossed it. By the late 1920s, flapper-like behavior was labeled as sexually delinquent in a number of screen treatments. Sensationalized exposés and pseudo-documentaries produced by independent studios pandered to public perceptions and fears about "wild youth." Such depictions reinforced popular perceptions of delinquency on one hand, while erotizing female adolescent sexuality on the other. In both films and popular advice, the solution to a wayward daughter was a vigilant mother, and mothers were instructed to keep their daughters on a short rein. In this chapter, I discuss the material conditions of adolescence in the early twentieth century, examine the earliest representations of female adolescence in films and, finally, consider the ways in which girls reacted to these representations.

twentieth century. One educator bemoaned the extracurricular activities of girls who took piano and violin lessons, attended dancing school, went to parties and rarely were in bed before ten. He argued that all these extracurricular activities were making girls extremely "nervous."[1]

In the 1920s, school became further institutionalized for youth as compulsory school attendance and stricter child labor laws turned former workers into students. This removal from the work force precipitated more exposure to the peer group. Sociologists Robert and Helen Merrill Lynd discovered that high school was the center of teenage social life in "Middletown," their fictionalized version of Muncie, Indiana. High schools were crucial to new patterns of youth socialization by fostering homogenization and conformity. The Lynds actually argued that school constituted a subcultural form in Muncie. "The high school, with its athletics, clubs, sororities, fraternities, dances and parties, and other 'extracurricular activities,' is a fairly complete social cosmos in itself. . . . Today the school is becoming not a place to which children go from their homes for a few hours daily, but a place from which they go home to sleep." The backbone of the social life of the high school was the social clubs. These "clubs" were really illegal sororities and fraternities. The initiation rites of the social clubs were long and elaborate, but theoretically the students were not sorority or fraternity members until after graduation. Thus, under this ambiguous arrangement, these clubs could exist legally. One high school girl was asked to describe what made a girl eligible for a prestigious club:

The chief thing is if the boys like you and you can get them for the dances. Then if your mother belongs to a graduate chapter that's pretty sure to get you in. Good looks and clothes don't necessarily get you in, and being good in your studies doesn't necessarily keep you out unless you're a "grind."[2]

The chief precursor to popularity then appeared to be based on normative definitions of femininity, such as pleasing men and not being smarter than them. Social activity centering around sororities continued to be important well into the 1940s. In 1948, a female high school student in North Carolina likened sororities to the highest in social achievement, and admitted, "I'd have died if I hadn't been asked. . . . I never heard of a girl refusing."

The social life of middle-class African American girls closely paralleled their white counterparts in relation to sororities. The editors of *Ladies Home Journal* profiled one such group, the Iveyettes, of Chicago. Daughters of wealthy black doctors, realtors and businessmen, the Iveyettes held meetings once a month, "gave several small parties and one big dance a year, took in new members through a system of pledging and blackballing, and gave each pledge a traditional initiation."[3]

In the 1920s, school administrators viewed extracurricular activities as a way to "channel excessive adolescent energy." Students rarely controlled their own activities. Even school dances were seen as opportunities for "social engineering," events whereby adolescents could be inculcated in adult norms and values. School administrators were particularly opposed to sororities and fraternities because the secrecy of the clubs undermined adult surveillance. Between 1919 and 1922, administrators extended legislation outlawing these secret organizations. As Paula Fass remarks, "Teachers and deans were haunted by the specter of *sub rosa* youth life that was probably far worse than the reality."[4]

Vicki Ruiz demonstrated that schools were also potent agents of Americanization in the 1920s. Chicana girls were often pushed into vocational courses that then funneled them into low-paying jobs upon graduation. Girls soon became members of a family wage economy, contributing as much as 35 percent of a family's total income. Work was sometimes a liberator for these young girls, however, as it fostered the primacy of the peer culture organized around fads, fashions and movie stars. As Ruiz shows, celebrity personas were also Americanization agents. Through fan magazines and Hollywood gossip as perpetuated by publications like *La Opinion*, Mexican American adolescent girls were able to experience vicariously a middle-class lifestyle, which included stimulating a desire for consumer goods.[5]

Mexican American children who had entered the work force often introduced their families to various consumer goods, such as food or clothing. This new pattern of consumption sometimes clashed with traditional Mexican values, as in the case of Mexican American adolescents' desire for cosmetics or nylons. Second generation youth were usually the ones to introduce their families to motion pictures as well. There was a certain amount of conflict around the issue of spending the income earned by youth as girls affirmed the importance of social activities.[6]

There was a shift from an emphasis on homosocial to heterosexual networks as evidenced through the pages of *The American Girl* magazine, the official magazine of the Girl Scouts and one of the few periodicals catering to adolescent girls. In the early 1920s, the focus of the magazine was very much on the importance of female friendships and bonding. Most of the short stories took place in boarding school, and friendships were quite intimate. There was a real change by 1925, however, as the magazine began to look slicker. The young women presented on the pages of *The American Girl* took on the look and characteristics of the flapper. The emphasis shifted from the primacy of scouting activities and female friendships to beauty and dating, as relationships with boys began to figure prominently. This shift is reflective of larger changes in society as the "New Woman" of the early twentieth century gave way to the "Modern Woman" of the 1920s, with her emphasis on public sexuality and heterosocial relationships.[7]

Contemporary youth experts, Phyllis Blanchard and Caroline Manasses, believed that strict social prescriptions for virginity were loosening. In their 1930 book, *New Girls for Old*, they note,

[A girl feels] fairly certain that the man she marries will not inevitably detect any sophistication she may have acquired, unless she herself chooses to reveal her past. There is additional security also in the fact that men are becoming more tolerant on this point. There seems to be a consensus of opinion among young men, that while virginity is desirable in a bride, it is less necessary than other qualifications.

They were clearly not condoning premarital sex, however, and they indicated that most sexual experiences were oriented toward marriage. They argued that when a girl had a love affair, it was with "the unconscious hope that it will blossom into permanence."[8] The new medium of motion pictures was a major force in the changing social landscape.

FILM PORTRAYALS OF ADOLESCENCE

The earliest representations of adolescence on film took their subject matter from nineteenth-century forms of popular culture, such as stage melodrama, vaudeville, burlesque and pulp novels. Among the earliest actors for this new medium were adolescent girls, partly because stage actors were deterred from film work because of the stigma associated with film acting. Moreover, these young actors needed little training because early films were very short. There was also a technical reason for the use of young women. Because of the primitive early equipment, adolescent girls photographed well in the harsh lights. Lillian and Dorothy Gish, Mary Pickford, Norma Talmadge, Bessie Love and Blanche Sweet all began acting while in their teens.

The director who perhaps most embodied the Victorian consciousness that idealized girlhood and adolescence was D. W. Griffith, who remained fairly consistent in his portrayals of innocent, prepubescent girls well into the 1920s.[9] Griffith cultivated a repertory company that included a number of adolescent girls, including Mary Pickford, Mae Marsh, Carol Dempster, and Dorothy and Lillian Gish. His heroines seemed poised between girlhood and womanhood. Griffith described his "ideal" actress:

I am inclined to favor beginners. They come untrammeled by so-called techniques, by theories, by preconceived ideas. I prefer a young woman who has to support herself and possibly her mother. Of necessity she will work hard. . . . To me the ideal type for feminine stardom has nothing of the flesh, nothing of the note of sensuousness. . . . The voluptuous type, blooming into the full blown rose cannot endure. The years show their stamp too clearly. The other type—oh that is different![10]

Film scholars have often commented about Griffith's predilection for the child-woman not only in his films but in his personal life. Whether the result of his upbringing or a personal fetish, Griffith was clearly more comfortable with and less threatened by young women. The Griffith heroine was a girlish love object who was not allowed to fulfill her sexuality, such as Mae Marsh as "Little Sister" in *The Birth of a Nation* (1915) or Lillian Gish as Lucy in *Broken Blossoms* (1919). Both films juxtapose white virgins against men of color (who in both cases were played by white actors). Little Sister and Lucy are potential rape victims, although Griffith has them die before rape can occur, a death he clearly saw as preferable to interracial sex.[11]

The most enduring idealized representation of girlhood and adolescence from 1915 to 1930 was the one created by Mary Pickford. Pickford actually began her film career in 1909, when she was sixteen, already older than most of the parts she would play. She would continue to play children until she was in her mid-thirties. She ultimately became a prisoner of her own image. Together, Pickford and Gish represent two extremes of the Victorian paradigm. Gish was either the victim or the redeemer, whereas Pickford was the plucky tomboy who triumphed over adversity in films like *Rags* (1915), *Rebecca of Sunnybrook Farm* (1917), *Pollyanna* (1920), *Little Annie Rooney* (1925), and *Sparrows* (1926). Pickford managed to show great fortitude and courage in most of her adolescent roles. As Molly Haskell comments, "Even at her arch-angelic, Pickford was no American Cinderella or Snow White. . . . She was a rebel who championed the poor against the rich . . . she was a little girl with gumption and self-reliance, who could get herself out of trouble."[12]

Pickford's appeal, however, was not necessarily to children, but to working-class adults. Alexander Walker suggests that the Pickford trope seemed particularly suited to the working class because such audiences had little identification with the representations of flaming youth increasingly being portrayed on screen. The plots of Pickford's films turned on more-familiar themes of nineteenth-century entertainment forms, and Pickford was most often of the working class, herself, in her films. Moreover, as the champion of the underdog, Pickford's films offered an implicit critique of the rich. They usually contained elements of melodrama and were full of thrills and adventure. As Walker suggests, "Mary extracted an unhampered realism from her own curtailed childhood and her equally underprivileged fans sympathized with it intuitively."[13]

Major social and economic changes in the 1920s made idealized heroines passé. Screen audiences were increasingly looking to motion pictures to make sense of what appeared to be a new social order. Teenage audiences were particularly bored by sentimental portrayals. A 1927 survey of motion picture preferences among adolescents showed that both girls and boys were impatient with films with "too much sob stuff." Although girls in the survey liked films like *Lovey Mary* (1926), *Little Annie Rooney, Sparrows* and *Ella Cinders* (1926) a bit more than boys, they were still fairly dismissive of the genre and said that they "didn't care for fairy stories" and were critical of what they perceived as "kindergarten stuff."[14]

There was a real change in both the content and tone of films about adolescence after 1920, when, as Paula Fass points out, youth became "a media-dramatized minority." Although there were still idealized representations, increasingly the flapper began to replace the plucky orphan as the "heroine du jour." The change also coincided with a shift from working-class to middle-class patronage of motion pictures. Flapper films like *Prodigal Daughters* (1923), *The Wild Party* (1923), *House of Youth* (1924), *The Plastic Age* (1925), *Campus Flirt* (1926), *Our Dancing Daughters* (1928), and *Our Modern Maidens* (1929) helped to perpetuate the popular image of wild adolescence and youth run amuck.[15]

However, many critical studies of women in film representations of the 1920s dismiss the extent to which these female protagonists were really liberated. They argue, instead, that flapper films were really sensationalized morality tales that simply repackaged traditional gender roles and Victorian values. They argue that the "revolution in manners and morals" was overstated at best, because it stopped short with bobbed hair, scanty attire and petting, and it was still only marriage that legitimized a girl's sexuality in film. Sumiko Higashi sums up this view: "These heroines were basically conventional and after a brief experimentation with a freer life style, committed themselves to marriage."[16]

Though that may be true for many of the flaming youth films, films focusing on adolescence were often, in fact, very explicit in showing troubled teen behavior. In such films, the revolution in manners and morals was more than superficial: Screen teens smoked, danced, partied, petted and sometimes went "all the way" in films like *Port of Missing Girls* (1928) and *Road to Ruin* (1928). These young screen flappers often became sexual delinquents. For the most part, films about female adolescence in the 1920s problemitized female adolescence and offered a rather dark portrayal of youth. In films about female adolescents in the 1920s, the real threat appeared to be adolescence itself. It was represented as a life stage fraught with peril, and the greatest menace appeared to be the sexuality of adolescent girls.

Conventional wisdom held that films and the glamour of Hollywood were luring adolescent girls into prostitution and other forms of delinquency.[17] Several contemporary observers looked for the cause of delinquent behavior in girls and found a target in motion pictures. A judge in "Middletown" (Muncie, Indiana) listed movies as one of the causes of juvenile delinquency, believing that "the disregard of group mores by the young is definitely related to the witnessing week after week of fictitious behavior sequences that habitually link the taking of long chances and happy endings."[18] Sociologists Herbert Blumer and Philip Hauser, in their 1933 study *Movies, Delinquency and Crime*, found that of 117 girls in a state correctional facility, 25 percent indicated that movies were a direct contributing influence to their delinquency.[19] The sexual behavior of adolescent girls was increasingly a focus of films.

The number of films that dealt with female adolescence in the 1920s is admittedly small. *The American Film Institute's Catalog of Feature Films* made from 1921 to 1930 lists only fifteen feature films about adolescence and only five more about high school. Although that index is not definitive, the films that delineated an adolescent sensibility are limited. Film research is further hampered by the number of prints actually in existence. Nonetheless, there are enough portrayals to talk about a representative sample. I want to differentiate between flapper films that focused on the experience of young adults, such as those in college or socialites, and those in which the heroines are described by film titles as still being teens or in high school. Film adolescence, moreover, is a very short-lived period, a brief transition between childhood and marriage, a time marked by generational conflict with parents and other agents of moral authority.

Humor was strangely lacking in representations of female adolescence in the 1920s. One of the few films to actually show the lighter side of adolescence was *Harold Teen* (1928), the story of a farm boy who moves to the city to attend school. At Covina High, Harold meets virtually every trope of adolescence. Their introductory titles establish the dichotomy between the two female paradigms of adolescence: "The Class Flirt," Giggles Dewbury (Alice White); and "The Girl Next Door," Lillums Lovewell (Mary Brian). Giggles is introduced as

> The Perfect Vamp!
> Height . . . . . 5 feet 2 inches
> Waist . . . . . 25 inches
> Neck . . . . . Yes!

Giggles rolls her eyes, flutters her eyelashes, and puckers her lips imitating Clara Bow and other movie vamps. There are two routes to popularity for adolescent girls, and although Giggles is more fun to watch, Lillums' nice girl is positioned as being superior to Giggles' flapper.[20]

The Giggles character comments on the ways that teens were influenced by the movies. The girls at Covina High are truly "movie-made." In a twist on the "Hey, kids, let's put on a show!" theme, the students decide to make their own motion picture rather than perform a traditional play. In this hilarious film within a film, Giggles gets a chance to play a native hula dancer (à la Bow in the film *Hula* [1927]). The title informs the audience that Giggles too has "It," and she has clearly internalized the examples she has seen in the movies, where in this case, art imitates art.

The girls of Covina are preoccupied with being versed on the latest style. Their role as consumers of cosmetics and other personal products is emphasized through Pop Jenk's Malt Shop, a place where these new consumer goods are showcased. In the center of the malt shop is an abandoned jalopy, a spot where couples without a real auto can "neck." Screen teens of Covina High School have created their own cultural forms and fads, and the emphasis is on conformity and peer approval. The peer group has supplanted the family.

In fact, in another Mary Brian film, *Peter Pan* (1924), the peer group has become the family. Brian plays Wendy to Betty Bronson's Peter. Wendy is the quintessential surrogate mother, both to her brothers and later to Peter and the lost boys. As she plays house with Peter, she begins to awaken sexually. Her priggish, English schoolgirl countenance is contrasted with that of the other adolescent inhabitant of Neverland, the exotic Tiger Lily (Anna May Wong). Tiger Lily is racialized as being much more sexually aggressive than Wendy. As Wendy waits at home for a kiss from Peter, Tiger Lily is joyfully and sensuously teaching Peter to rub noses. Wendy is increasingly frustrated by Peter's sexual ambivalence. She confronts him about the nature of his feelings for her, and he innocently replies, "That of a devoted son." The totally asexual Peter is at a loss to understand the emerging sexuality of both Wendy and Tiger Lily. "You're so puzzling. Tiger Lily's just the same. There's something she wants to be to me, but she says it's not my mother." While Peter clutches at childhood, Wendy seems anxious to embrace adult status and responsibility.

If the influence of adults was negligible in *Harold Teen* and *Peter Pan*, when the family was portrayed in films of female adolescence, it was often in a negative way. The dysfunctional family was the butt of humor in Malcolm St. Clair's *Are Parents People?* (1925). Promotional posters asked, "Are fathers flirts? Are mothers merry makers? Are daughters dangerous?" Although a comedy, *Are Parents People?* dealt with the serious subject of the effects of divorce on a young girl. Betty Bronson plays Lita Hazlitt, who immediately becomes a pawn in her parent's impending divorce. Lita is sent to boarding school when she refuses to choose between her parents. At the Eldridge School for Girls, Lita's friend gives her a book, *Divorce and Its Cure*, which advises that parents can be reunited by a common concern for the welfare of their children. At school, she is befriended by Dr. Dacer, the young, handsome school doctor. Lita is soon expelled when she assumes the blame for her roommate for writing a suggestive love letter to a movie star. She sees expulsion as a means of bringing her parents together.

The Eldridge School is populated by rich, upper-middle-class girls, who are more concerned with their looks, movie stars and crushes than with their studies. While the girls are presented as silly and romantic, adults do not fare any better, as Lita's parents are childish and petty. Dacer chides the two, "You're so busy being incompatible, you haven't got time for your daughter." The film signals a real breakdown of the nuclear family. The social stigma of divorce appears to have disappeared with dire consequences for children. Lita metamorphoses from an innocent girl in a middy blouse and bloomer to an outrageous flirt. The only explanation for this change appears to be her desire for Dacer. In this film, Lita goes from schoolgirl to wife, and there is something insidious about an older man finding a child in his care sexually arousing.

Much of the comedy in this film turns on the mistaken notion of Lita's sexual activity. When she is expelled, Lita is told by the stern, mannish headmistress that "clandestine love affairs are strictly against the rules." Her roommate's love letter is taken as *prima facie* evidence of a sexual relationship with the star. Later in the film, Lita innocently spends the night in Dacer's apartment, unbeknown to him. Her parents are filled with recriminations as they ponder the loss of her virtue. The humor comes from the discrepancy between the real and the imagined, and the vehicle of comedy serves as a safe venue to release tensions about teenage sexuality.

As in *Are Parents People?*, many films about adolescents in the 1920s end with the promise of the early marriage of the girls, in many cases to older men. In the 1927 film *The Little Firebrand,* Edith Thornton is an unruly, motherless seventeen-year-old. Her father, multimillionaire Godfey Jackson, is unable to control her, so he appoints Harley Norcross, a junior member of his law firm, as her guardian while he is away. Norcross lays down strict rules of behavior, forbidding Dorothy to drink, drive, attend parties or see her boyfriend. She flaunts his rules by disobeying him, and predictably they fall in love. In the climax, Dorothy coerces Norcross into her car. Their joy ride ends in a crash. A grief-stricken and contrite Dorothy declares her love for the unconscious Norcross. What older man could resist?

One fan commented on the increasing trend of films to pair younger girls with older, worldlier men:

It isn't the vampire stuff that does the harm, it's the fact that the heroine, the center of interest of almost every film is a young girl—not a young woman, but a little, curly locked, immature, baby doll child. Most of these little girls are being pursued by some older man. . . . [They give] the impression that young girls are of extraordinary importance to older men.[21]

The early marriages of these adolescent heroines was one way to legitimize their emerging sexuality into sanctioned channels. For the most part, however, female adolescent sexuality was no laughing matter, it was delinquent behavior.

THE ROAD TO RUIN: FILMS OF SEXUAL DELINQUENCY

The earliest films about female delinquency in the 1920s actually denied the reality of delinquency for adolescent girls. The first appearance of an adolescent girl in a film treatment of delinquency appears to be that of Molly Moran in the 1921 film *As the World Rolls On*. Molly and her boyfriend are framed for robbery by Molly's jealous suitor, so technically she is not a bad girl at all. The same is true of the working-class heroine Alice Calhoun in the 1922 film *Angel of Crooked Street*. Alice works as a maid to support her mother. She is mistakenly accused of a robbery by her employer and sent to reform school. Although initially hardened by the experience, she is transformed and redeemed when she falls in love with the wealthy son of the woman who sent her to prison. *Handcuffs and Kisses* (1921) and *One Wild Week* (1921) are similar in their themes of nice girls wrongfully accused. By the mid-1920s, however, as films about "wild youth" began to proliferate, the representation of female adolescence became more pessimistic.

Mary Odem argues, "During the 1920s the intense public anxiety about female promiscuity began to subside. . . . The new sexual mores first evident among working-class daughters in American cities were increasingly adopted by middle-class teenagers in a somewhat tamer form and consequently appeared less threatening."[22] This is not true, however, if one looks to film as evidence of societal anxiety. Films about adolescents in the 1920s were very preoccupied with and threatened by middle-class female sexuality. Moreover, juvenile authorities began to collaborate with filmmakers to expose this threat. Juvenile authorities appeared willing to use the powers of the medium to advance their agendas.

A useful example and one of the first films to deal with sexual delinquency was *Lilies of the Streets* (1925). In this film the line between flapper-like behavior and delinquency is blurred. The writing of the screenplay was "supervised" by Mary E. Hamilton, a New York police matron, who had achieved the rank of captain by working with "wayward girls." Hamilton even had a bit part in the film, which told the story of a wild flapper (Virginia Lee Corbin) whose behavior is so overtly sexual that she is mistaken for a prostitute and ends up in jail.

Many of the films, then, became cautionary tales aimed more at parents than children. Delinquency films often played on social fears, real and imagined. From the teens onward, there was what Linda Gordon describes as "widespread panic" about girls being kidnapped and sold into "white slavery," or coercive prostitution. Although the term obscures the fact that not all the women forced into prostitution were white, in 1910 Congress passed the White Slave Traffic Act, later called the Mann Act, which prohibited the transportation of women for immoral purposes from state to state. Jane Addams spoke to the problem in her 1912 book *A New Conscience and an Ancient Evil*. The stereotype of the white slaver was an effective part of anti-prostitution campaigns. Many critics of the early nickelodeons charged that white slavers preyed on girls outside these theaters. This fear reflects the changing status of women, who were increasingly autonomous, especially in terms of their leisure activities. Several Broadway plays such as *The House of Bondage*, *The Lure* and *Damaged Goods* had focused on white slavery. The exploitive nature of both the plays and the films that would follow was camouflaged by the rhetoric of reform.[23]

The film industry capitalized on this fear in the 1913 film *Traffic in Souls*. Despite the crude melodrama, this film highlighted the vulnerability of working-class and immigrant women, and part of the film was actually shot on Ellis Island with real immigrants. *Traffic in Souls* was a huge money grosser, and a number of imitations soon followed. What makes this film particularly significant is the fact that the prostitution ring is controlled by a rich white man, alternatively identified as "The Do-Gooder" or the "Big Boss," who passes as a moral reformer. The film turns on the stories of two Jewish sisters, whose Hasidic father is an inventor. One of the sisters, Esther, is engaged to an Irish cop. Esther is kidnapped into prostitution by a kindly, white-haired gentleman. Shortly thereafter, her teenage sister Ruth gets a job as a receptionist for the "Big Boss." Ruth is not only brave but ingenious. She soon recognizes her boss's voice as that of the kidnapper. Using one of her father's inventions to record his voice, Ruth gets evidence against him. An angry band of immigrants, led by Esther's fiancé raid his houses and save the day. The film is unique in its portrayal of an ethnic coalition as heroes, while the WASPs are the villains. This film underscores the hypocrisy of those concerned with the morals of the working class. It not only impugns the motives of reformers but also reflects a deep suspicion of the Protestant elite.

On the heels of *Traffic in Souls* came *Inside the White Slave Traffic*, released just a few weeks later. The film was produced by Samuel London, a former government investigator, and featured actual scenes of girls being entrapped. Although this film carried endorsements of a number of suffragists, including Inez Mulholland and Carrie Chapman Catt, and played to "howling crowds," it was one of the first films raided by the police due to its incendiary content. Two weeks later, *White Slaver* was released about a young girl who barely escaped ruin. The film featured a live lecture by a Mr. E. A. Brown on the horrors of white slavery. One reviewer quipped that "girls seeing it who do not know that marbled palaces and liveried servants are incidentals of stolen virtue might find the picture a temptation instead of a warning." That observation would be true for many of the exploitation films of the decade.[24]

Sensationalized exposés and pseudo-documentaries produced by independent studios continued to pander to public perceptions and fears about adolescents and chide moral reformers to get their own houses in order. According to films dealing with female delinquency in the 1920s and 1930s, it was the middle-class family that had broken down. It was not really until the early 1930s with films like *Dead End* (1937) and *Angels with Dirty Faces* (1937) that films would begin to reflect the forces of poverty, acculturation and urbanization on the male delinquent.[25] In the 1920s, not only were female adolescents represented as a problemitized group, but increasingly, female reformers were blamed for the decline. One compelling trope of the period is the female reformer/clubwoman as bad mother. Inadequate mothering remained the major cause of delinquency for girls in films into the 1930s. Ironically, the motion picture mothers blamed for delinquency were the same reform-minded women who were at the forefront of both the film censorship movement and the moral reform movement.

An exemplary film was *Port of Missing Girls* (1928), Hollywood's take on teenage runaways and the effects of the white slave trade on the middle class. A provocative ad for the film in a trade paper asked, "75,000 girls in the past year were reported missing. Why do girls leave home? Where do they go? Who is to blame?" A contemporary source actually put the runaway girl figure at 80,000 girls a year, and numerous articles in the popular press kept the issue in the public consciousness. One author suggested that the problem of runaway girls was "one of the biggest problems" facing law enforcement, a problem that came "within the scope of the policewoman, who has already proved her value."[26]

The film focuses on sixteen-year-old Ruth King, who is lured into prostitution. The opening shot immediately establishes the cause of her delinquency: Ruth's marginality in her mother's life. A close-up of a newspaper headline, "Mrs. Cyrus King will lecture at Women's Clubs," leads to the next shot revealing Mrs. King checking off a list of "Cities to be visited: Cleveland, Toledo, Columbus: Get Railroad Tickets." Mrs. King is an upper-middle-class clubwoman and philanthropist, whose introductory film title reveals that she heads "The League for Improving Conditions among Working Girls." Mrs King serves as a trope for the white, middle-class, female moral reformers who assumed the authority to prescribe appropriate codes of behavior and morality for working-class girls. She is so busy legislating morality for other people's children that she neglects that of her two daughters, Ruth and Catherine.

Mr. King, a successful attorney, is much like his wife in putting his own concerns above his family's and in his self-righteousness. In the opening moments of the film, he discovers that his young niece, who has been staying with the Kings, has spent the night with her lover. It is at this point that we meet Ruth King, the youngest daughter and the youthful protagonist. As she bounds exuberantly down the stairs, Ruth is stilled by her father's tirade to her cousin, during which he accuses her of "contaminating his house" and throws her out. Like his wife, for a man seemingly concerned with the morality of others, he shows little interest in the activities of his own daughters.

If Ruth's parents are not "watching" Ruth, then strangers are. In the next scene we see Ruth through the eyes of two "white slavers" parked outside the high school to "check out the local crop." The shot suggests that vague, unknown dangers may be lurking even outside such "safe" institutions as schools. Their sales pitch for their "Rehearsal School" is interrupted by the arrival of Buddy Larkin, Ruth's older boyfriend. Buddy is an odd "hero"— not only is he older and worldlier than Ruth, he is a bootlegger as well. Without the moral guidance of her mother, Ruth has been attracted to the "wrong sort." Buddy may not be a prototype of Jack Armstrong, All-American Boy, but Ruth hardly appears the paradigm of virtue. She seems to be the sexual aggressor. After a visit to a local speakeasy, Ruth says to Buddy, "Let's say it with moonlight," and they go to Buddy's car. Although the dissolve is ambiguous to appease the censors, subsequent actions reveal they have spent the night together and have had sex. The next morning, a point-of-view shot establishes Buddy's one character flaw that Ruth cannot forgive, he is a womanizer—shown by the numerous women's names that have been written and crossed out on Buddy's ukelele case.

With her father's condemnation of her cousin fresh in her mind and her own virtue gone, Ruth falls easy prey to the owners of the "Rehearsal School," a front for prostitution. This phony actor's school might have played on public anxiety about star struck daughters as well. When the Kings discover Ruth has run away after spending the night with Buddy, they immediately blame each other. Mr. King accuses his wife of being "a business manager instead of a mother," while Mrs King chides him for his "lack of love and sympathy." Their daughter, Catherine interrupts,

You are out of step with the times. You have no idea what's going on around you. Suppose I told you that I smoke and drink and petted. We do this behind your backs because we don't think we could confide in you. Poor Ruth, she probably didn't think you'd understand.

The fault is not with the girls, but with the parents. The condemnation is not of smoking, drinking, petting or even sex, but with the lack of parental availability and surveillance. Mr. King has been too rigid, and Mrs. King has failed to provide maternal guidance. Rather than being shocked by Catherine's revelations, her speech is an epiphany for her parents.

In the conclusion, a reformed Buddy and Mr. King go off to rescue Ruth, but she has already been saved from the clutches of a rich, lecherous playboy by the police. In a twist from the usual formulaic movie ending, it is not the handsome hero who gets to save "his girl." Because of both Buddy and the Kings' moral ambivalence, they are not capable of "saving" anyone. Buddy finally finds Ruth in church piously praying for forgiveness. The white rays of the sun filter in through the church window, bathing her in light and born again virginity. The light illuminates one part of the aisle. Buddy and Ruth approach each other, but she pulls back, not trusting Buddy. A close-up of Buddy reveals a look of contrition and love. Ruth's face relaxes as she registers the change in her wayward lover. They move slowly toward each other in the beam of light as she holds out her hand to Buddy, symbolizing a forgiveness that is both personal and divine.

Although Ruth has transgressed the rules of sexual propriety and is imperiled for her moral laxity, her fall is not irreparable. The redemptive power of love will allow Buddy to control his sexual desires and confine them to one woman. Ruth has hurdled over adolescence and delinquency into adult female status as symbolized by her implied marriage to Buddy, a marriage that legitimizes her sexual activity.

A trade paper announced that *Port of Missing Girls* had been endorsed for all viewers by the National Board of Review. "[It] unanimously passed without change by a large review committee, and was recommended to family audiences including young people of high school ages. . . . Themes hold unusual interest both for parents and their growing daughters."[27] Another review moralized,

The theme is the waywardness of the modern girl. It teaches a wholesome lesson and is none the less entertaining because it is propaganda. It definitely establishes the fact that it is better business for a girl to behave herself than it is for her to drift down the pathway of pleasure. One thing it stresses . . . is that when a girl leaves home it is the parent's fault.[28]

Variety, another trade publication, was not as generous in its praise, noting that at the preview, "the hip audience found cause to snicker." The paper discounted the film as being suitable for large theaters, "but those changing twice daily can look it over." The *New York Times* sarcastically played upon Catherine's speech in their review noting, "If instead of 'smoking, drinking, and petting' [Ruth] had gone more often to the movies she never would have trusted [the head of the Rehearsal School]."[29] The review underscores the power of films to influence the behavior of girls and the increasing sophistication of teen audiences.

What message did girls themselves get from what appeared as the hackneyed warning of the film? Perhaps not the message that filmmakers had intended. One sixteen-year-old girl said that it gave her "some ideas about the freedom we should have. For instance . . . the wildest girl always tames down and gets the man she loves—why not in real life?" One seventeen-year-old argued, "I think a girl of seventeen should be allowed to go anywhere. I think she knows what to do and how to act." Another seventeen-year-old high school senior spoke to the film's ability to induce feelings of rebellion against parental control:

I remember one picture that showed the effects of being too strict which I will always remember. There was a young girl who had some strict parents. They did not allow her any privileges. . . . The girl slipped out with a fellow that her father did not know anything about. She and the fellow went so far that she was afraid to go home. She would have gone with the fellow, but she found out he was a bootlegger. . . . She did not go home, but instead went to some place where girls were supposed to get on stage. In reality they did anything the manager wanted them to do. . . . I think parents should take a lesson from that picture. I wished my mother had seen it. Maybe she would not be so strict on me. . . . I think a girl of seventeen should be allowed to go anywhere. I think she knows what to do and how to act. She should have the right ideas about right and wrong if she has had the right training.[30]

This is a useful example not only of the difference between a discursive subject and an historical spectator, but the way spectators create their own meaning. Ruth ended up in the *Port of Missing Girls*, not because of the strictness of her parents, but because of their lack of regulation and involvement in her life. Her father's stern inflexible attitude and self-righteousness certainly contributed to Ruth's running away, but he did not seem to regulate her activities. Moreover, it was Ruth herself who initiated sex with Buddy. She did not balk when she found out that he was a bootlegger; rather, it was evidence of his sexual liaisons with other women that sent her to the Rehearsal School. Girls seemingly appropriated a representation of gender and reinterpreted its message based on their conflicts with their own parents. This is a clear example of a resistant reading of a film, whose real warnings appeared to be to parents and not adolescent girls. These fans' confusion is hardly surprising in light of the contradictory discourses of femininity and adolescence that stress both sexual attractiveness and sexual passivity.

In both reel and real life, girls seemingly balked at adult restrictions. In the 1921 film *Short Skirts*, seventeen-year-old Natalie Smith resents being treated as a little girl by her mother's fiancé, Wallace Brewster, the reform candidate for mayor. Natalie is vindictive and spoiled and clearly ambivalent about her mother's remarriage. She falls easy prey to the opposition candidate's son, who convinces Natalie to get some documents incriminating Brewster of some illegal dealings. She soon regrets her act, retrieves the documents and finds that they were falsified. After a tearful confession, Natalie and Brewster are reconciled. Although her rebellion is short-lived and easily resolved, the bid for attention and autonomy has been a consistent feature of representations of girls since the 1920s.

Sixteen-year-old Cynthia Perry (Helen Foster), the protagonist of the 1928 *Sweet Sixteen,* also wants to grow up too fast. She falls for an older, worldlier man, Howard DeHart, despite the repeated warning of her sister Patricia. Patricia takes it upon herself to break up the romance. She risks her own reputation by being alone in DeHart's apartment and almost loses her own boyfriend to protect her silly sister. These screen teens are rash, self-absorbed, willful and anxious to grow up.

Resentment of adult control seemed to be a part of the adolescent experience. One sixteen-year-old girl said, "Of course the movies make me want to rebel against my parents' supervision. . . . I think that girls should be treated the same as boys by their parents. I resent parental restraint especially in the matter of how late I stay out and where I go." Adolescent girls clearly were questioning whether parents really did know best and were asserting their own right to autonomy. Another adolescent underscored this attitude, "The problem of whether mother does know best is being discussed universally just now, and [movies] make me feel that maybe if a daughter did get a word in edgewise once in awhile, parents and children would not be having so many difficulties."[31]

Another film that served as a dire warning for parents instead of a behavioral model for girls was the 1928 film *Road to Ruin*. Made cheaply for $2,500 in ten days, it grossed over $2,500,000. The film affected a pseudo-documentary tone about juvenile delinquency. Although it is surely one of the raciest films made about female adolescence, the film was sponsored by juvenile authorities as an exposé of delinquency, and it was shown by them in high schools. Surprisingly, at the same time, *Road to Ruin* was also banned in a number of cities. Nevertheless, it was popular on the road-show circuit, where it was often shown to men and women in separate audiences. Segregating audiences by gender was quite common well into the 1930s, whenever film content was deemed too inflammatory by film exhibitioners. In such cases, theater owners often had a physician standing by to answer women's questions after a screening, as was the case with *Road to Ruin*. Film exhibitors must have believed that this film would be consumed differently by males and females, and that women needed extra "protection" while viewing sexually explicit material.[32]

The film opens with a close-up of a grave man sitting behind a desk. He is introduced by the title as "Captain Marden of the Los Angeles Police Department," and indicates the film we are about to see is based on a "true case." He warns the audience,

During the World War the need for conservation of food and the necessities of life was brought home to us. Today we face a graver need—the conservation of our youth. Our police and juvenile authorities are making every effort to combat the present day menace—Juvenile Delinquency.

Both the opening title and the film itself suggests that the real menace is adolescence, a time fraught with hidden dangers. The film forewarns of the inability of families to deal with this problem alone and valorizes the social institutions that can help them.

The opening shot of seventeen-year-old Sally Canfield (Helen Foster) reveals her involved in girlish chatter with her best friend, Eve Terrell, in front of the high school. After Eve asks Sally to spend the night, Sally returns home to ask her bridge-playing mother for permission. Mrs. Canfield and her friends represent three different approaches to rearing adolescent daughters. Mrs. Canfield quickly assents, hardly glancing at Sally, and one friend asks, "Do you think it's wise to let daughters spend the night away from home?" (Obviously it is not.) Another woman, the "modern" permissive mother, symbolized by her smoking a cigarette, adds, "I have found with my own girl that you can't deny these youngsters their freedom or they become rebellious." Mrs. Canfield replies firmly, "I trust Sally implicitly," words she will eventually regret.

Regulation is the key to the successful rearing of adolescent girls. The message is hammered home in the next scene, as later that evening at Eve's house, the Terrells prepare to go out. The Terrells and their friends are guzzling cocktails, smoking furiously, and gyrating wildly to jazz music. They soon leave the girls without adult supervision, and Eve quickly models her parents' behavior for Sally by introducing her to the vices of smoking and drinking. Eve warns Sally that she must let boys kiss her "or they won't bother with you if you don't." Through Eve, Sally later meets Jimmy, a high school boy, who drives a jalopy full of graffiti, smokes, drinks from a hip flask, and plays the ukelele, all the filmic trappings of flaming youth. Exposed to such influences, Sally succumbs to the next step to ruin, sex with Jimmy. Sally's fall is represented by a close-up of an empty canoe, strewn with clothes on a moonlit lake. There is a quick counter shot that reveals Mr. Canfield in a car kissing some woman.

In the next scene, Mrs. Canfield is anxiously waiting for Sally to return from her date with Jimmy, when Mr. Canfield comes home from his evening of womanizing. He dismisses his wife's worries, "We were young once." Sally sneaks in later, and the title sternly comments, "This was the first of many such evenings made possible because Mrs. Canfield knew Sally and trusted her implicitly—and blindly." Mrs. Canfield tends to have a blind spot as far as her husband is concerned as well.

Soon Sally is a full-blown flapper. She frequents an illegal roadhouse where she meets an older, worldlier man, Don Hughes. Sally has sex with Don almost immediately, and as the title proclaims, "And so Sally has passed another milestone on the Road to Ruin [sleeping with more than one man] from which intelligent guidance could have saved her."

A few nights later, Sally and Eve get into a strip poker game at Don's apartment. The close-up lingers sensuously on Sally face flushed with excitement and desire. The audience is positioned voyeuristically, as we see the scene through the eyes of a passerby standing outside an open door. Within a short time they are all in their underwear, but before it turns into a full-blown orgy, they are apprehended by the police. Sally and Eve are taken to Juvenile Hall, where they are told they will be examined by a doctor. When a tearful Sally asks why, she is told, "It is the rule of the Police Juvenile Bureau that all girls brought in under suspicion of delinquency be examined by our physician." The scene of Juvenile Hall fades, and the title announces that Eve has "tested positive" [for venereal disease] and will be "detained for treatment."[33]

Sally is taken home to her mother by the social worker, who presumably must tell Mrs. Canfield about the condition of Sally's hymen. Instead of being upset at Sally, Mrs. Canfield's anger is directed to the messenger. The lovely, refined social worker is the voice of moral authority as she tells Mrs. Canfield,

You are like ninety percent of the mothers with whom we deal in our work. We are not condemning your daughter, only asking your cooperation to prevent mistakes like this from being repeated. . . . It is the duty of parents to protect their children by intelligent instruction and advice on the subject of sex.[34]

Instead of disciplining Sally, Mrs. Canfield promises not to tell her father. Not only has Mrs. Canfield been too trusting, she has not warned Sally to control her sexual desire until marriage. The social worker's words go unheeded. Sally continues down the road to ruin. Shortly after her arrest, she discovers that she is pregnant, and the title moralizes "Those who transgress the moral laws must pay the bitter price." When she tells Don she is "in trouble," he refuses to marry her and arranges a back-alley abortion with a seedy doctor.

Although she is very ill after the abortion, Sally consents to going to a party given by Don's boss. What Sally does not know is that Don's boss runs a house of prostitution. She is immediately ushered into a back bedroom, where her would-be client turns out to be her father. Sally loses consciousness when confronted with the fact.

In the final scene, Sally, near death, begs for her mother's forgiveness, but Mrs. Canfield tearfully replies, "I am the one to ask forgiveness—I have failed you—I should have watched over you and told you what all mothers tell their daughters." Sally then dies in her grieving mother's arms. Even though the doctor has told her father that "a botched operation coupled with a great shock" is the cause of death, the mother appears more accountable. Although the father is not only a lax parent, but an immoral man, it is still the mother who must shoulder most of the blame for Sally's fate.

The director, Norton Parker, had the idea of adding the ending title, which proclaims, "For the wages of sin is death, but the gift of God is eternal life through Jesus Christ Our Lord." The religious ending is very incongruous. Although the film clearly offers a moral, it is also quite suggestive and titillating. Sensationalism and sex are supposedly camouflaged by religious sermonizing. Because *Port of Missing Girls* is similar in the religious overtones at the conclusion, the religious endings can best be explained as an effort to appease the censors.

It is astonishing that this film had the support of juvenile authorities and that it would be shown in schools. One woman who remembered seeing the film as a young girl said,

I suppose it would be considered an X-rated movie by today's standards, and it was advertised with lurid billboards emphasizing "No one under sixteen admitted." My girlfriend and I were so intrigued that we "borrowed" our mothers' lipsticks and hats and high heels, and managed to get past the ticket taker. . . . And there we sat in the darkened movie house, our eyes as big as saucers as we watched Helen Foster's virtue being destroyed by Grant Withers.[35]

It seems reasonable to assume that juvenile authorities hoped teens would be frightened by the horrible consequences that befell the film's heroine, yet it appears they were titillated instead.

One of the Payne Fund studies examined the deterrent effects of films on juvenile delinquents. Blumer and Hauser concluded that pictures meant to be deterrents did not always have such an effect. Among reasons cited were peer pressure, the discounting of films that punished the offender, the lack of a vivid depiction of punishment, and sympathy for the protagonist. They argued, "Because of the frequent inclusions in such pictures of entrancing scenes, such as those of a life of gaiety, wild life, luxury, adventure . . . the deterrent aspects may be confused." One delinquent girl illustrated their contention when she said, "When I see pictures about women who 'go wrong' it only makes me wish I was in their place . . . because I do know what thrills and pleasure they get going wrong." While 50 percent of delinquent girls in state training schools responded that girls pay a price for a good time, they obviously did not take that message to heart as they were all being detained as sexual delinquents.[36]

Films of the 1920s had become quite suggestive as a result of competition among film companies. In addition, a number of scandals had rocked the film industry. In an effort to appease pro-censorship forces, film magnates formed a trade association, the Motion Picture Producers and Distributer's Association (MPPDA), and hired Will Hays in 1922 as its first president. The purpose of this new organization was the regulation of the morals of the film industry and films themselves. Hays, a Presbyterian elder, had once been chair of the Republican National Committee and had served briefly as Warren Harding's postmaster general.[37]

Will Hays initiated a number of reforms, among them the insertion of morality clauses in performer's contracts, which permitted cancellation if actors were accused of immorality. In 1927 he appointed Jason Joy, formerly of the War Department, to read screenplays and to advise producers of potential problems with local censorship groups. He synthesized rules from censorship boards throughout the country and introduced "The Don'ts and Be Carefuls," in an attempt at self-regulation. Producers were advised to avoid nudity, profanity, sex perversions, white slavery, venereal disease, abortion, and sex hygiene. Two years later, both *Port of Missing Girls* and *Road to Ruin* would blatantly ignore such proscriptions. They seemed to do so under the pretext of realism, and as contemporary chronicler Frederick Lewis Allen noted, the Hays Office made "moral endings obligatory" and "sexy pictures were smeared over with platitudes." Ironically, the same can be said of the actual vice reports of delinquents themselves. Girls' lives were scrutinized, and juvenile reports could be very titillating and even pornographic. Female delinquency became fetishized both on screen and off.[38]

Films about adolescents in the early Depression continue to echo themes made popular in the 1920s. An exemplary film, *High School Girl* (1933) could have easily been made in the 1920s, so similar was it in its theme of the breakdown in communication and the need for surveillance between girls and their clubwoman mothers. The film looks very much like the exposés of the 1920s, such as *Port of Missing Girls* and *Road to Ruin*. Although *High School Girl* again focuses on the result of parental neglect on an adolescent girl, it goes even further than earlier films and becomes a blatant polemic for sex education not only in the home but in the school as well.

Beth Andrews (Cecilia Parker, who would gain fame later in the decade as the sister of the screen's most famous teen, Andy Hardy) is a lonely, confused teenager with little or no guidance from her busy parents. Her mother, not surprisingly a middle-class clubwoman, self-righteously preaches about the evils of leaving children alone, while she neglects her own daughter for her voluntary activities. The first shot of

Beth reveals her sitting at her desk, dreamily writing love poems. Beth clearly romanticizes love and relationships but gets no practical advice on the subject.

She begins dating a young man, Phil, who pressures her for sex. She turns to her mother for advice on the facts of life, but her mother is embarrassed by Beth's frankness and dismisses her concerns. Beth is forced, instead, to turn to the Andrews' African American maid for sexual advice. The maid, in typical "Mammy" fashion, is Beth's surrogate mother and the only person parenting Beth. She is nurturing and compassionate and stands in sharp contrast to Mrs. Andrews. Worried about Beth's interest in sex, Mrs. Andrews' solution is to forbid Beth to leave the house. Beth is thus forced to sneak out of the house to go to a party with Phil. Beth and Phil leave the party, gaze at the moon, and then there is an unambiguous dissolve. Inevitably, Beth gets pregnant, presumably because she was both unaware of the consequences of sex and because she did not know how to say no.

The film turns on the efforts of the high school biology teacher to wage a campaign for "moral hygiene." He is constantly haranguing his students for the need of "scientific instruction to correct ignorance." When Beth and Phil find out that she is pregnant, they turn not to their parents but to the sympathetic biology teacher, who arranges for them to go out of town to have the baby. The teacher is fired, however, for his stand on sex education, and in his polemic before the school board he warns that "boys' and girls' lives have been ruined because parents refuse to tell them the truth." Although sex education is an ambiguous term at best in the film, it clearly means instruction on abstinence.

In the climax, the teacher confronts Beth's parents for not doing their duty, "Most girls want to be good, but they must be told more than that." Beth has her baby and gets a marriage proposal from Phil at the same time. Mrs. Andrews sees the error of her ways and not only gets the school board to reinstate the teacher but also begins her own campaign for the teaching of moral hygiene in the schools. Her new "cause" is sanctioned by the film because it relates to the middle-class adolescent instead of the working-class one. The film ends in the biology classroom, with the teacher instructing his pupils about the facts of life, the triumph of science over ignorance.

A contemporary review in *Variety* did not take the film very seriously and dismissed it by saying, "The kids at whom it is aimed may snicker at it."[39] However, kids were not the target of the film's message. In many ways, *High School Girl* is a natural conclusion to the reasoning first presented in *Port of Missing Girls*. If parents (read mothers) are going to abdicate responsibility for sexual instruction, then social institutions must fill the void. The film also underscores the continued anxiety over middle-class girls' sexuality. Yet, *High School Girl* is almost alone in its depiction of female adolescent sexuality in the 1930s. From the intense preoccupation of the 1920s, for the most part, sex and the teenage girl was a topic that was virtually ignored in the film universe of the 1930s.

Another theme that emerged in the 1930s was concern for juvenile treatment facilities. One of the first films to look at this theme was made in the late 1920s. Cecil B. DeMille's *The Godless Girl* (1928) was meant as an exposé not only of the evils of juvenile reformatories but also of the high school atheist clubs that began appearing in the 1920s. Actually, DeMille was also politically motivated in his campaign against atheism. He saw an essential link between youthful Godless societies and the Communist threat.[40] At base, however, De Mille's film is a harsh indictment of the juvenile penal system. He spent $200,000 and over eight months had a private investigator uncover conditions in reform schools throughout the country. Supposedly every incident in the film was based on fact. His researchers found evidence of everything from leg chains, manacles, human restraint gloves, and straitjackets to stockades. The film did lead to some reforms and stoked the fires of moral outrage by a number of prison reformers.[41]

The film opens with Judy Craig's forming a club called "The Godless Society" in her high school. A vigilante group arrives to break up the meeting. A riot ensues, and a young female atheist is accidentally killed as a result. Both Judy and Bob, the leader of the vigilantes, are held responsible for the accident and sent to the state juvenile reformatory, where inhumane treatment is meted out by sadistic guards and matrons. The reformatory is introduced in a title that claims that conditions in the film reformatory truly represent conditions in some institutions.[42] Further, ironically and perhaps unwittingly, DeMille eroticizes the sadism of the guards toward the female inmates, filling his film with scenes of bondage and writhing female bodies.

Before the film was released, DeMille added dialogue to the climax to try to attract an audience that was rapidly becoming fascinated by talking pictures, but his gimmick failed to attract patrons to this melodrama. The heavy religious undertones of the film were ponderous and dull, and the film was both a critical and commercial failure. The *New York Times* dismissed the film. "It is filled with vapid religious admonitions and strange heavenly warnings." *Picture Play* declared it as unreal "as life on another planet."[43] Girls were clearly not interested in DeMille's vision of their lives and concerns.

Exposés of the penal system continued in the 1930s, as in the 1938 film *Girls on Probation*. Connie Health's domineering, authoritarian father drives her from her home. She falls in with the wrong crowd, is wrongfully accused of a crime, and is sent to a penal institution where conditions are abysmal. Instead of turning to her father for help, she goes to jail rather than "giving him the satisfaction of knowing that he was right and I was bad all along." She ends up marrying her attorney, thereby ensuring her re-entrance into respectable society.

A theme that continued in films about teens in the 1930s was the clear abdication of parental authority and responsibility. In *Rebellious Daughters* (1938), a girl is driven from her home by unsympathetic parents. The title of another 1938 film, *Delinquent Parents*, placed the blame squarely on parents for the actions of their children. David Considine comments on this trend. "The evidence of parental absence or impotence on the screen is so overwhelming that it cannot be ignored. Over and over one witnesses youthful figures, devoid of parental guidance, left to their own devices."[44]

Considine is talking about parental neglect chiefly in the context of delinquency films of the 1930s, but what is particularly surprising is the extent to which this theme pervades film comedies about youth as well. Considine further argues that Andy Hardy notwithstanding, the overwhelming representation of male adolescents was a negative one. Moreover, the nuclear family was almost nonexistent in the 1930s on screen. Films focused instead on dysfunctional or "fractured families."[45] This was not, however, a new trend, just a continuation of ones started in the 1920s, when many filmic girls lived in dysfunctional families. Pessimistic portrayals of adolescent girls continued as well.

By the 1930s, reformatories were depicted as more benevolent institutions. This is illustrated by the 1938 film *Beloved Brat*. Like screen delinquents of the 1920s, Granville's Roberta Morgan is upper middle class, but unlike them, she is simply incorrigible not sexual. The cause of her delinquency has not changed, however, as it is still the fault of her busy businessman father and her clubwoman mother, who spends her days lecturing other women about how to raise children. Parental neglect is signaled by Roberta's thirteenth birthday party, attended only by the servants. Her parents are too busy to even remember.

Roberta's only friend, Pinkie, in a rare example of an interracial friendship in film, is played by Stymie Beard, who had already crossed the color line in the "Little Rascal" shorts. His loving mother, Mrs. White, a surrogate to Roberta, is positioned as the superior parent as she coos, "Taking care of my babies is the most fun of my life!" As in *High School Girl*, African American women are more maternal and loving. In contrast, Roberta's mother constant refrain is "What did I ever do to deserve such a difficult child?"

Roberta is a fierce and loyal friend. After she brings Pinkie home for dinner and the servants refuse to wait on him, she physically assaults the butler, Jenkins, in anger over the slight. He threatens to take her to reform school and hauls her to the car. A freak accident ensues because Roberta continues to hit Jenkins, and a man is killed. Her false testimony convicts Jenkins of manslaughter, but she eventually confesses her perjury. Roberta is sent to reform school by a judge who echoes Miriam Van Waters in the 1920s when he tells the Morgans, "Reform School should be for parents, not the children."

In the 1930s, however, reform school is not the harsh penal institution of the 1920s. It is staffed by capable, efficient, trained social workers, and looks more like a boarding school for upper-class girls. At the Lawndale School for girls, Roberta is guided by another mother surrogate, the compassionate superintendent. Through her love and understanding, Roberta is rehabilitated—and so are her preoccupied parents. The film ends with Roberta's integrated fourteenth birthday party, as she is surrounded by many playmates and her proud parents. Jenkins has been replaced by a black butler, and Mrs. White is now a servant in Roberta's house. As in Shirley Temple films of the period, the races can come together in the context of a clear social hierarchy. In *Beloved Brat*, Roberta's rebelliousness is not sexual, and it is only temporary, easily solved by parental love and attention.

Locating themselves in the tradition of realism, many films about delinquency in the 1920s and 1930s have a gritty, documentary feel and make inflated claims to topical realism. Their surface reality tries to obscure the sensationalized, far-fetched plots. Delinquency is situated firmly within the white middle class, and sexual activity is in and of itself evidence of delinquency. As Hollywood fought a running battle with traditional guardians of morality over censorship, clubwomen, often at the head of censorship groups, became the "cause" of screen delinquency in girls. Perhaps this represented the real anxieties of middle-class reformers, or perhaps it was a way ethnic filmmakers could take aim at middle-class reformers for targeting motion pictures. Such films transmit a real hostility against the Protestant elite and the traditional guardians of morality.

If these films indicate the breakdown of the family because of the expanded role of women in activities outside the home, then they also valorize the social institutions that must pick up the slack. From the police in *Port of Missing Girls* who "save" Ruth before Buddy and her father can, to the social worker in *Road to Ruin,* to the high school teacher in *High School Girl,* moral authority has shifted from families to institutions. Yet sometimes, social institutions themselves fail delinquent girls, as is the case in *Lilies of the Streets, Godless Girl*, and *Girls on Probation,* and need reform.

That delinquency itself is gendered is important. Films make it appear that girls need more moral guidance and regulation so that they will not drift down the "pathway of pleasure." Popular discourse stressed regulation and surveillance. Moreover, girls must be protected from the detrimental influences of films themselves. Female spectators were positioned by industry watchdogs as being not only more vulnerable to film influence but more suggestible as well. Girls and their mothers were offered cautionary tales and even shown them in separate spaces as was the case with films like *White Slaver* and *Road to Ruin*.

Filmic discourse outlines boundaries of normative definitions of femininity by using delinquency as a site to define conflicting notions of gender, notions that in turn subvert the discourse of adolescence. Girls must be sexually desirable and attractive, but they must not be sexually active. There is, however, an implicit recognition of adolescent girls' sexual desire. Even though acting on these feelings is labeled "delinquent," the films do not uniformly condemn these sexual desires. Instead, filmic condemnation is of parents' failure to offer moral guidance. Films about sexual delinquency do not simply mirror existing norms of sexual behavior, they also reveal the limitations of the double standard and of social prescriptions about sex. This is not, however, a world of moral polarities. There is a great deal of moral ambiguity. Ruth and Judy might have transgressed moral law, but their fall from grace is not irreversible. Sally pays with her life, but at least there is the promise of divine forgiveness.[46]

Family melodramas underscored middle-class anxieties about the forces of urbanization and immigration. Delinquency was situated within a private sphere and mediated within the home. As Susan Hayward argues, "Melodrama reflects the bourgeois desire for social order to be expressed though the personal." In that sense, melodrama is very nostalgic, invoking desire for a simpler, idealized time. Ideology within melodrama is expressed through a series of binary oppositions that reinforce gender divisions. Teen sexuality is constructed as good/bad (delinquent); motherhood is also dichotomized into good/bad (someone with interests and concerns outside the home).[47]

MOVIE-MADE GIRLS

Many films about girls in the 1920s and 1930s seemed to employ a "scared straight" approach. That is, their lurid plots emphasized the consequences of making wrong choices. All of this begs the question: Were girls buying it? Some of the best evidence can be found in the Payne studies. An analysis of several of these studies indicates that even though films appeared to be moralizing against the wild life, many adolescents were, in fact, taking these images at face value. As one adolescent girl said, "I think the movies have a great deal to do with present day, so-called wildness. If we did not see such examples in the movies, where would we get the idea of being hot?" Another girl learned from films that "The bad and pretty girls are usually more attractive to men than the intelligent and studious girls." Though films about wild youth might have been pandering to adult anxieties, girls themselves seemed to enjoy them. As one girl explained, "I like to see men and women fall in love in the movies, and go out to parties. . . . I also like to see them kiss, drink, smoke, and make love to each other." Blumer and Hauser admit, "The discrimination of the observer may be confused and [her] subsequent difficultly in keeping apart the different 'motifs' may result in a failure to get the deterrent import of the picture."[48]

In sample after sample, girls indicated that their clear screen preferences were for Clara Bow and Joan Crawford. They seemed to embody the spirit of the generation. In fact, the laureate of the jazz age, F. Scott Fitzgerald, even referred to Crawford as "the best example of the flapper . . . a young thing with a talent for living."[49] One African American girl lamented,

Oh to possess what Miss Bow has—that elusive little thing called IT! After seeing her picture by that name, I immediately went home to take stock of my personal charms . . . and after carefully surveying myself . . . I turned away with a sigh thinking that I may as well want to be Mr. Chaney. I would be just as successful.[50]

One girl cited in the Payne study said of Bow and Crawford:

The heroines are generally the life of the party, and I believe that when you are in Rome, do as the Romans do. I used to think just the opposite, but after seeing *The Wild Party* and *Our Dancing Daughters,* I began to think this over, and I found out that this is the best way to act.[51]

Another adolescent agreed, "I have learned from the movies how to be a flirt, and I found out that at parties and elsewhere the coquette is the one who enjoys herself the most."[52]

Perhaps the film that most captured the imagination of female adolescents in the 1920s was *Our Dancing Daughters* (1928). One fourteen-year-old girl called it "an educational picture . . . clothed in modernism." Joan Crawford as Deana Medford is a very different kind of screen heroine and set what Mary Ryan has called "a new standard of movie virtue."[53] The film tells the story of three young women poised between adolescence and adulthood. Although Deana has taken on all the trappings of wild youth and is uninhibited, flirtatious, exuberant, vivacious and beautiful, she is still a "nice girl."

The film is most interesting in terms of how it comments on parental relationships. Deana's parents are the same parents who might have produced a sexual delinquent in another screenplay. Although Deana enjoys a close relationship with her parents, it could more accurately be termed a "companionate" one. They are more like good friends than authority figures. After sharing cocktails with her parents as Deana leaves for a party, she breezily says to them, "See you at dawn," words that in another film would clearly mean she was on the road to ruin. Her relationship is in sharp contrast to that of her friend Beatrice (Dorothy Sebastian). Beatrice's mother's attitude toward child-rearing can be summed up by her observation about children, "Keep them on a short rein and they'll behave." She dismisses Deana as being too "wild" for her daughter, yet it is Beatrice, not Deana, who has had premarital sex. A tight rein, then, may not be the best form of parenting. The third teen is Ann (Anita Paige) whose mother is a gold-digger, who has clearly inculcated those values in her daughter, advising her that "a rich man wants his money's worth."

Both Deana and Ann vie for the affection of Ben Blaine, football hero and multimillionaire. Ben is both attracted and repelled by Deana's lust for life and wild abandon, and ultimately he questions whether she is the kind of girl he should bring home to his mother, "A man has to be sure of the girl he marries." Ben is easily manipulated by Ann, who pretends to be virtuous: "I'm not modern, I want a husband and a baby." Her performance wins Ben, and he marries Ann. A heartbroken Deana turns to her parents, "What's wrong with me, I'm not a liar, a cheat. I've been decent."

Ann quickly tires of married life, and begins drinking and cheating on Ben. She conveniently falls down the stairs in a drunken stupor and dies, paving the way for Deana's marriage to Ben. Although they end up together, Deana confronts his hypocrisy, "Because I was a woman, not a lying imitation, you thought I was unworthy." Though the film clearly upholds the sanctity of sex within marriage, nonetheless the range of permissible behavior for women is enlarged in this film. Further, although Beatrice's fiancé says he forgives her for her sexual transgression before their marriage, ultimately, he does not. It hangs between them, and he becomes consumed with her other sexual partner. She pays big for her mistake. Deana, too, appears to pay for her honesty for a time. Men appear hypocritical and immature, and Deana emerges as the healthiest of all the characters.

Speaking of this film, one female Payne respondent said that Crawford was "the embodiment of the true spirit of the younger generation":

No matter what happened, she played fair. She even lost her man . . . but Crawford showed that even in a crisis, she was sport enough to play fair. And fair play is really the motto of the younger generation. I hope that many of the women who are scandalized at the actions of the modern miss saw that show—and if it did not change their beliefs after seeing it, well then, it does not mean that the movie was a failure, but that they are the failure, not to recognize a truth so obvious.[54]

There is a clear indication that this fan was asserting a new code of behavior. While adhering to traditional notions of virginity, both Bow and

Crawford showed that that did not mean prudery. These women just wanted to have fun. As Mary Ryan points out, *Our Dancing Daughters* emphasized "Crawford's gusto and liveliness, rather than eroticism. When the dancing Crawford ripped off her skirt, it was as if to remove a constricting garment, to facilitate freedom of movement and release of energy, not to entice male admirers."[55]

After the release of *Our Dancing Daughters*, letters poured into MGM from girls who wanted to be "just like Joan Crawford." Crawford answered every one by hand. By the early 1930s, however, the flapper had become an anachronism. While Crawford's roles matured as she did, Bow, both on screen and off, was a kind of "flapper age Peter Pan." In 1930 a *Photoplay* magazine lambasted Bow's hedonism, and asked, "Will the immortal flapper learn self-discipline? Or is she fated to dance her way to oblivion?"[56] The tastes of filmgoers in the 1930s was clearly changing, and new paradigms of youth would emerge in the next decade.

Films about adolescent girls in the 1920s and into the 1930s respond to discourses about the changing role of women due to an expanding work force and increased voluntary activities, increased educational opportunities for women, the lure of Hollywood, the breakdown of organized religion, and the fear of the effects of the media itself. Both adolescence and delinquency are considered temporary or transitional stages to be navigated and "moved out of," unlike femininity, which is something to be acquired. On the one hand, filmic representations of adolescents reinforced popular perceptions of delinquency, all the while erotizing female adolescent sexuality on the other. It was perhaps the latter message that girls internalized.

NOTES

1. Joseph Hawes, "The Strange History of Female Adolescence in the United States," *The Journal of Psychohistory* 13 (Summer 1985): 51–63; John Demos and Virginia Demos, "Adolescence in Historical Perspective," in *The American Family in Social-Historical Perspective,* ed. Michael Gordon (New York: St. Martin's Press, 1978), 212–221; Joseph Kett, *Rites of Passage: Adolescence in America 1790 to the Present* (New York: Basic Books, 1977), 51–63; Irving King, *The High School Age* (Indianapolis: Bobbs-Merrill, 1918), 184.

2. Paula Fass, *The Damned and the Beautiful: American Youth in the 1920s* (New York: Oxford University Press, 1977), 211; Robert Lynd and Helen Merrell Lynd, *Middletown: A Study in American Culture* (New York: Harcourt, Brace and Co., 1929), 215–216.

3. Maureen Daly, ed., *Profile of Youth* (Philadelphia: Lippincott, 1949), 223, 183.

4. Fass, 212–216.

5. Vicki Ruiz, "Star Struck: Acculturation, Adolescence and Mexican American Women 1920–1950," in *Small Worlds: Children and Adolescents in*

America 1850–1950, eds. Paula Petrik and Elliott West (Lawrence, KS: University of Kansas Press, 1994), 64–67.

6. George Sanchez, *Becoming Mexican American: Ethnicity, Culture and Identity in Chicano Los Angeles, 1900–1945* (New York: Oxford University Press, 1995), 173.

7. For a discussion of heterosocial relationships among women, see Carroll Smith-Rosenberg, "The Female World of Love and Ritual: Relations between Women in Nineteenth Century America," *Signs: Journal of Women in Culture and Society* 1 (1975): 1–30. For a discussion of the categories of twentieth-century women, see Mary Logan Rothschild's unpublished typology, "Towards a Typology of Twentieth Century Women," Arizona State University, 1985.

8. Phyllis Blanchard and Caroline Manasses, *New Girls for Old* (New York: The MacCauley Co., 1930), 238–239.

9. See Paul O'Dell, *Griffith and the Rise of Hollywood* (New York: Castle Books, 1970); James Hart, ed., *The Man Who Invented Hollywood* (Louisville: Touchstone, 1972); Robert Henderson, *D.W. Griffith: His Life, His Work* (New York: Oxford University Press, 1972); and Lillian Gish, *The Movies, Mr. Griffith and Me* (Englewood Cliffs, NJ: Prentice Hall, 1969).

10. Quoted in Kevin Brownlow's *The Parade's Gone By* (New York: Ballantine, 1968), 97.

11. See Marjorie Rosen's *Popcorn Venus: Women, Movies and the American Dream* (New York: Avon, 1973), 44–58.

12. Molly Haskell, *From Reverence to Rape: The Treatment of Women in the Movies* (New York: Penguin, 1974), 60.

13. Alexander Walker, *The Celluloid Sacrifice: Aspects of Sex in the Movies* (New York: Hawthorne Books, Inc., 1966), 52.

14. Mary Alice Abbott, "A Study of Motion Picture Preferences of Horace Mann High School," *Teachers College Record* 28 (April 1927): 830.

15. Fass, 126. For a discussion of flapper films, see Sumiko Higashi, *Virgins, Vamps and Flappers: The American Silent Movie Heroine* (Montreal: Eden Press, 1978).

16. Higashi, iii. See also Mary Ryan, "The Projection of a New Womanhood: The Movie Moderns of the 1920s," in *Our American Sisters: Women in American Life and Thought,* 2nd ed., eds. Jean S Friedman and William G. Shade (Boston: Allyn and Bacon, 1988), 501–518; Rosen, 75–97; and Haskell, 42–89.

17. Lea Jacobs, *The Wages of Sin: Censorship and the Fallen Woman Film 1928–1942* (Madison: University of Wisconsin Press, 1991), 3–4.

18. Cited by Robert S. Lynd and Helen Merrell Lynd, *Middletown: A Study*, 268.

19. Herbert Blumer and Philip Hauser, *Movies, Delinquency and Crime* (New York: Macmillan, 1933; reprint, New York: Arno Press, 1970), 80.

20. Interestingly the stereotypical roles that Alice White and Mary Brian would play in *Harold Teen* would set the stage for the rest of their screen careers. White was considered a second-rate Clara Bow, and Brian would spend her career playing "nice" girls. John Springer and Jack Hamilton, *They Had Faces Then* (Secaucus, NJ: The Citadel Press, 1974), 40, 253.

21. Quoted by Frederick L. Collins, "Are the Boys Better Than the Girls?" *Colliers* 73 (9 February 1924): 16.

22. Mary Ellen Odem, *Delinquent Daughters: Protecting and Policing Adolescent Female Sexuality in the United States 1885–1920* (Chapel Hill: University of North Carolina Press, 1995), 188.

23. Linda Gordon, *Heroes of Their Own Lives: The Politics and History of Family Violence* (New York: Penguin, 1988) 220; Jane Addams, *A New Conscience and an Ancient Evil* (New York: Macmillan, 1912); Kevin Brownlow, *Behind the Mask of Innocence* (New York: Alfred A. Knopf, 1990), 70– 79; Terry Ramsaye, *A Million and One Nights: A History of the Motion Picture* (New York: Simon and Schuster, 1926), 613.

24. Ramsaye, 618. See also "Inside the White Slave Trade," *Variety*, 12 December 1913, and "A White Slaver," *Variety*, 1 January 1914, in *Variety Film Reviews 1907–1920* (New York: Garland, 1974).

25. One of few films of female delinquency to deal with working-class girls was *Girls under 21* (1940). A woman married to a gangster breaks it off and reunites with her former sweetheart, a poor, inner-city teacher. Because she is now reformed, he hopes she can convince his charge to give up petty thievery. When a young would-be gang member is accidentally killed during a robbery, they are convinced to go straight.

26. "A Warning for the Runaway Season," *Literary Digest*, 16 July 1927, 29.

27. *Exhibitor's Herald and Moving Picture World,* 3 March 1928, 8. AMPAS Clipping File.

28. *Film Spectator,* 10 December 1927. AMPAS Clipping File.

29. *Variety,* 1 August 1928. AMPAS Clipping File.

30. Herbert Blumer, *Movies and Conduct* (New York: Macmillan, 1933), 152, 159–160.

31. Ibid., 158, 152.

32. See Brownlow, *Mask*, 175; "The Road to Ruin," *Variety,* 30 February 1934, 3; My thanks to Sam Gill, film historian and reference librarian at AMPAS for his discussion of the practice of segregating audiences by gender.

33. There is some evidence that the strip poker scene was shot with full nudity that was either removed later or never included in the final cut. The wife of the director remembers his telling her that "Helen Foster was a lovely, innocent, blue eyed brunette and he used to have to keep a case of gin on the set and keep her half smashed so she would take off her clothes in the strip poker scene" (see Brownlow, *Mask*, 176, 527fn.).The marker of "ruin" was the loss of virginity. It was standard procedure for juvenile authorities to do pelvic exams on girls suspected of delinquency. During the exam, physicians specifically checked the condition of the hymen to determine whether "ruin" had taken place (see Gordon, 216). As Mary Odem argues, "The federal government used Progressive institutions and the services of professionals to carry out a discriminatory program of compulsory examination and incarceration of women and girls suspected of moral offenses" (186).

34. To the modern viewer this may seem like a plea for sex education. However, as Steven Schlossman and Stephanie Wallach point out ("The Crime of Precocious Sexuality: Female Juvenile Delinquency in the Progressive Era," *Harvard Educational Review* 48 [February 1978]: 90), the main goal of sexual

educators was not to offer information on birth control or sexual practices but to instill "inhibitions against sexual gratification" and to "discipline lust and to channel it to conventional ends."

35. Quoted by Brownlow, *Mask*, 175–176. The woman recounting her story subsequently married the director, Norton Parker.

36. Blumer and Hauser, 199–200.

37. Leonard Leff and Jerold Simmons, *The Dame in the Kimono: Hollywood, Censorship and the Production Code* (New York: Grove Weidenfeld, 1990), 4.

38. Frederick Lewis Allen, *Only Yesterday* (New York: Harper and Brothers, 1930), 84; Schlossman and Wallach, 74.

39. *Variety*, March 1935. AMPAS Clipping File.

40. See Brownlow, *Mask*, 182. Ironically, when DeMille visited Russia in 1931, he found *The Godless Girl* was so popular that he was hailed as its creator. He was very surprised until he found out that the last reel detailing the heroine's conversion had been cut out of the film. The film enjoyed widespread popularity in Russia well into the 1950s. DeMille's concern about the spread of atheism in the schools hardly seems warranted. Homer Croy, a journalist investigating the spread of atheism in the schools found that the American Association for the Advancement of Atheism had succeeded in establishing chapters in twenty colleges and preparatory schools and had founded a Junior Atheistic Movement. There was even a Godless Society at Hollywood High. The protagonist of *The Godless Girl*, Judy Craig (Lina Basquette), was probably a compilation of two real teenagers, Christine Walker and Queen Silver. Walker was the eighteen-year-old national secretary of the National Atheist League. Silver, a seventeen-year-old California girl who published her own newspaper, was the western leader of the Junior Atheistic Movement. See Homer Croy, "Atheism Beckons to Our Youth," *World's Work* 54 (May 1927): 18–26, and "Atheism Rampant in Our Schools," *World's Work* 54 (June 1927): 140–147.

41. Brownlow, *Mask*, 176–180.

42. For a discussion of actual conditions earlier in the century, see Barbara Brenzel, *Daughters of the State: A Social Portrait of the First Reform School for Girls in North America 1856–1905* (Cambridge: M.I.T. Press, 1983).

43. "Godless Girl," *New York Times,* 1 April 1928, 22. Cited by Brownlow, *Mask*, 181.

44. David Considine, *The Cinema of Adolescence* (Jefferson, NC: McFarland, 1985), 15.

45. Ibid., 13–33.

46. For a discussion of the contradictory discourses of adolescence and femininity, see Barbara Hudson, "Femininity and Adolescence," in *Gender and Generation*, eds. Angela McRobbie and Mica Nava (London: Macmillan, 1984), 31–44.

47. Susan Hayward, *Key Concepts in Cinema Studies* (London: Routledge, 1996), 202. See Christine Gledhill, ed., *Home Is Where the Heart Is: Studies in Melodrama and the Women's Film* (London: British Film Institute Publishing, 1987).

48. Henry Forman, *Our Movie Made Children* (New York: Macmillan, 1933), 167, 166, 224; Blumer and Hauser, 200.

49. Bob Thomas, *Joan Crawford: A Biography* (New York: Bantam, 1978), 57.

50. Forman, 141.

51. Blumer, 165.

52. Forman, 147.

53. Blumer, 184; Ryan, 504.

54. Forman, 165.

55. Ryan, 504.

56. Ryan, 514; Leonard Hall, "What about Clara Bow?" *Photoplay*, October 1930, 24.

3

Babes in Arms

The 1936 film short *Every Sunday* marked the film debut of both Judy Garland and Deanna Durbin. It was the only time the two stars ever appeared together on film. The plot revolves around the efforts of two girls to save the job of Deanna's grandfather, whose orchestra performs in their town's bandstand. Due to declining attendance, the town fathers have decided to hire a new band. Judy and Deanna leap into action trying to marshal support for the orchestra. Ultimately, it is their own unique talents that save the day. Deanna's impromptu aria and Judy's spirited scat are what bring audiences back to the band concerts. *Every Sunday* is significant for a number of reasons. It features the two actresses who would become the biggest adolescent film personas of the 1930s and underscores their distinctive singing styles. Moreover, it also highlights the theme that would predominate both Durbin's and Garland's adolescent characterizations: adolescent girls as saviors.

Going beyond the problematic, sexual teens of the 1920s, by the late 1930s, adolescent girls were idealized as competent, almost magical beings, capable of solving the problems of all around them. A partial reason for this shift is the emergence in the late 1930s of a number of strong adolescent stars who needed tailor-made vehicles through which to showcase their talent. For the first time, actors who represented adolescence on screen were really adolescents themselves. At perhaps no other time in the history of film have adolescent personas been as distinctive as in the 1930s. Durbin, Garland and other stars who represented youth in the 1930s such as Bonita Granville, Anne Shirley and Ann Rutherford were clear signifiers of the female adolescence experience. In this chapter I examine the historical condition of female adolescence during the Depression and the ways in which the experience was represented in film. Finally, I try to discern what this meant to girls themselves.

ADOLESCENCE AND THE DEPRESSION

By 1930, 60 percent of American teens of school age were attending high school. Some social commentators have argued that the impact of the Depression on high school girls was less than on their parents and their male counterparts. As the Lynds said of girls in Muncie, "Although there has been less money to play with, cars have not been so new, more dresses have been made at home . . . the social pace has continued." Perhaps the greatest factor in the extension of teenage subcultural form was the near universality of high school enrollment by the late 1930s. The Depression forced many teens to stay in school because unemployment rates for teens were so high. In fact, the Depression actually served to reinforce adolescent subculture. The youth culture of Muncie as described by the Lynds, however, was hardly the world of the Hardy family. The Lynds comment on "increased sophistication" and the pronounced increase in teenage drinking. "They know everything and do everything openly—and they aren't ashamed to talk about it." At one point the situation was so severe that the high school had to bring in ministers and other youth workers to confront the "drinking and immorality."[1]

Middle-class girls (or the "Business Class," as the Lynds called them) continued to set the social pace at the high school through their social clubs or thinly disguised sororities. The most exclusive sorority in Muncie was the "Sewing Club." The quaint title belied the fact that the club had little to do with traditional female domestic arts. Although mothers of the girls in the club tried to curtail the cost of social functions (such as importing Guy Lombardo for a sorority dance), the daughters overrode their mothers' protests. School officials also seemed to have little control over the activities of club members and illegal pledging. Moreover, as the Lynds noted, some mothers actually encouraged social ambitions in their daughters, thus undermining the authority of the school policy against sororities. So influential were the middle-class girls that the high school tried to channel the pressure to conform into their domestic science classes. For example, they had the girls stage a "Style Show" in February of 1933 to feature graduation attire. The girls would decide on the style and they could spend the rest of the school year making their graduation dresses in home economics class to save the less affluent families money.[2]

Grace Palladino has documented the active, social side of teenage life in the 1930s and the prerequisites of popularity for middle-class youths.

The Lynds reported that some poorer students actually would use only the side entrance to the school to "avoid the steps crowded with richer students looking you over." One study of Los Angeles schools in the 1930s found that 53.7 percent of Mexican girls and 43.7 percent of Mexican boys dropped out of school by the time they were sixteen. Many cited financial hardship as the reason; however, about 13 percent said they dropped out because no one encouraged them to stay. Some said that their curricular needs were not being met, while others cited racism by teachers. The school environment was clearly not hospitable to minority students. Only 11 percent of African American school-age children were enrolled in high school, due in large measure to the school and teacher shortages, particularly in the South. In rural southern counties, the National Youth Administration taught black adolescent girls grooming and encouraged them to emulate white middle-class styles. Certainly these standards were not attainable by most working-class, immigrant, racial or ethnic groups, but all groups still managed to carve out cultural space.[3]

Although Mexican American girls may have adopted some new cultural forms, these forms did not undermine their cultural identity as Mexican Americans. Youth agencies and community organizations helped to promote cultural pride and traditions through encouraging use of the Spanish language in the home, family trips to Mexico to visit relatives, family stories and youth groups like Logia Juventud Latina and El Congresso De Pueblos Que Hablar Español. That is not to suggest that there were no intergenerational conflicts. Such conflicts most often arose over the appearance of adolescent girls. While *La Opinion* might idealize the image of white, middle-class cultural icons such as the flappers in advertisements and articles, daughters and their parents were often at odds over short skirts, bobbed hair, and makeup. At the same time, there were numerous barrio beauty pageants sponsored by community groups. Another source of conflict between Mexican American girls and their parents revolved around dating. Certainly the rules governing dating behavior were much more stringent than those of their Anglo counterparts, as many Mexican American girls were required to be chaperoned. Girls might rebel, however, by marrying early or resorting to subterfuge to meet a boy. Even going out alone with other girlfriends was not allowed among some families until the 1940s.[4]

By 1935, if sex was increasingly taboo in films, in reality the Lynds found more permissiveness in teenagers' attitudes toward sexuality in Middletown, patterned to a large extent on behavior they had seen in the movies. One high school boy said of teenage girls,

They've been getting more and more knowing and bold. The fellows regard necking as a taken for granted part of a date. We fellows used to get slapped for doing things, but the girls don't do much of that anymore.

The Lynds found teenagers to be increasingly "sophisticated" in matters of sex. There was also a rise in teenage drinking that forced school administrators to confront what they described as widespread "immorality." John D'Emilio and Estelle Freedman also point to an expansion of permissible codes of sexual behavior among teens in the 1930s. They cite one study of teens in St. Louis that found that teens were actually more tolerant about sexual matters than about smoking and drinking. Freed from parental supervision, teens believed that petting was a natural part of a date.[5]

Girls continued to be encouraged by prescriptive sources to orient their identity around the primacy of heterosocial relationships, and were fed a steady diet of advice on the importance of being popular, being attractive and getting and pleasing a boy. Yet an examination of *The American Girl* magazine in the 1930s reveals that gender prescriptions might not have been so narrowly defined. Although *The American Girl* featured standard prescriptions of behavior, it also offered girls models of career women and emphasized the importance of economic independence.[6]

In the 1930s and well into the 1940s, girls' adolescent fiction was also populated with a number of adolescent girls with unlimited options and aspirations. Author Ruth Wheeler introduced young readers to the glamorous professions of actors and flight attendants in books like *Janet Hardy in Hollywood* and *Jane, Stewardess of the Air Lines*. The Beverly Gray series, begun in 1934 by Clair Blank, included four books about Beverly's adventures in a small women's college and were followed by twenty-one books that chronicled her career as a journalist. Although Beverly had a number of suitors throughout the series, her romances were secondary to her career. Judy Bolton, the fictional detective of a series written between 1932 and 1950, began solving mysteries when she was only fifteen and continued to be actively involved in professional detective work even after her marriage to an FBI agent. The quintessential girl sleuth, of course, was Nancy Drew. Nancy seemed particularly indifferent to romantic attachments, her longstanding beau, Ned Nickerson, not withstanding. In fact, Nancy seemed happier in the company of her two "chums," the "plump" Bess and the "boyish" George. Following popular teen novels, the process of fictionalizing adolescent stars, such as Deanna Durbin, Bonita Granville, and Jane Withers, and turning them into detectives was quite common in the 1930s and 1940s. While these fictionalized star series served as shrewd marketing techniques for the stars' films, they were also significant in that they represented the stars as normal teens with the same interests, concerns, and mannerisms as other adolescent girls. These books also allowed for another form of fan activity.[7]

Attending movies continued to be an important part of the adolescent experience and a source of information about heterosocial behavior. The Lynds described an exchange at the local soda fountain:

Joan Crawford has her amateur counterparts in the high school girls who stroll with brittle confidence in and out of Barney's, the soft drink parlor, 'clicking' with the 'drug store cowboys' at the tables; while the tongue-tied young male learns the art of the swift, confident comeback in the face of female confidence.[8]

The art of the "line" appeared to be *de rigueur* for adolescent girls. One mother bemoaned the fact that her daughter and her friends actually wrote out their repartee beforehand. She was particularly shocked by what she considered the rude behavior of girls to the boys in their lives. When she confronted her daughter, she was told, "But Mumsey, he expects it! All the girls treat the boys like that! Naturally we don't want the boys to think we like them!" "Mumsey" also had difficulty accepting the imitative behavior of adolescent girls, which she found "appalling, they dress alike, imitate speech and even diction and inflection." Another mother, upset by the fact that the primary activity among her daughter's high school set was "messing around," decided to send her adolescent to boarding school. "She was becoming too rapidly absorbed . . . in a social life which seemed to consist mainly of impromptu parties organized by the youngsters themselves, usually unchaperoned and offering a rough and tumble beer and spaghetti joint type of entertainment which was making no contribution to a healthful social development."[9] Even middle-class parents were troubled by an increasing lack of control over and regulation of their daughters' behavior, a behavior that was beginning to garner much more media attention.

Palladino argues that teens created a "public identity" around swing music, which forced adults to take note of their music, their dress, their language. Swing is said to have originated in 1935 with Benny Goodman and his band at the Palomar Ballroom in Hollywood. By 1938, teens literally stopped traffic in front of New York's Paramount Theater, as police were called in to contain 3,000 screaming teens waiting to see Goodman. The *New York Times* worried that the swing craze was out of hand and wondered about the "dangerously hypnotic influence of swing" on the youth of America. Dedicated swing fans could follow the exploits of their favorite bands in trade journals such as *Downbeat* and *Metronome*. The swing craze also generated its own language, a language not instantly decipherable to adults. As Palladino says, "The concept of a separate teenage generation was beginning to gain ground."[10]

REPRESENTATIONS IN THE EARLY DEPRESSION

David Considine argues that the overwhelming representation of male youth during the Depression was a pessimistic one. The Andy

Hardy series, far from being representative of the portrayal of teens, was more of an aberration from the more pervasive films of delinquency and dislocation in films such as *Wild Boys of the Road* (1933), *Dead End* (1937), *Girls on Probation* (1938) and *Angels with Dirty Faces* (1938). A preponderance of "fractured" and dysfunctional families populated the screen. In fact, although Andy Hardy himself was a very positive representation of youth, often ancillary girl characters in his films were used to signify the effects of the breakdown of the family. Several of the girls Andy would consider "fast" were portrayed as the children of divorce. It was girls in these films who were used to represent all that was "wrong" with youth. In many ways this was just a continuation of the delinquency films of the 1920s and was the context in which screen teens tried to claim autonomy in the Depression. Such films focused on the ways in which the American family had broken down and the absence of parental authority and regulation. Instead, the peer group became a substitute for the family.[11]

Compared to the erotically charged films of adolescence in the 1920s, films about girls increasingly portrayed girls as asexual in the 1930s. There were, however, films about teenage girls in which sex is equated with violence. Girls were most vulnerable to threat of sexual predators. *Wild Boys of the Road* (1933) first introduced this topic in the story of homeless teens who ride the rails. The vulnerability of young women is underscored when one of the teens, Rochelle Hudson, is raped by a lecherous railroad official, who forces the teens off the train and then preys on the homeless girl. The film is extraordinary in its sympathetic look at violence as a way to achieve ends as the teens turn into an angry mob and retaliate against the evil official. In *They Won't Forget* (1937), a film about vigilante justice and lynching, the rape and murder of a young secretarial student (Lana Turner) in a small Southern town causes the unjust imprisonment of a Northern man. Implicit in these films is the recognition that legitimate institutions had failed and could no longer protect the young.

In the 1930s, the chief genre form for representing the female adolescent became the musical, which was often utopian in its visioning of American life and culture. When youth was portrayed positively as in the films of Deanna Durbin or Rooney and Garland's "Hey, kids, let's put on a show!" musicals, as opposed to negatively as in juvenile delinquent films, youth autonomy was subordinated to the larger task of making the world a better place during a time of crisis and economic hardship. In the case of the Depression, youth was one more identity that was preserved within coalitions of difference in opposition to big business and the state. In the case of World War II films, youth was enlisted in the "American" effort to help win the war.[12]

Though representations of juvenile delinquency continued in the 1930s, as discussed in the previous chapter, for the most part these troubled teens of the 1920s turned into either mischievous rascals or in some cases forces of real evil. The trend might be attributed to the success of Jane Withers, a fresh antidote to some of the sweetness and light of the period. Withers was the bratty little girl with the good heart. She was not evil, just mischievous. The real representative of female adolescent malevolence in the 1930s is surely Bonita Granville. Although she did act in some lighthearted comedies, she got her start playing brats. She was born in Chicago in 1923. Her mother, Bunny Granville, was a Ziegfeld girl. Granville went on stage when she was three and made her first appearances in film at the age of seven in *Westward Passage*. Her first adolescent portrayal was as the chilling Mary Tilford in *These Three* (1936). Based on Lillian Hellman's play *The Children's Hour*, the lesbian theme had to be discarded for the screen adaption as a concession to the censors. The screenplay, however, was written by Hellman and remains faithful to the spirit of the play. Mary, a student at a small private school, spreads a rumor that one of the headmistresses is having an affair with the school doctor, who is spotted leaving her room one night. This lie ultimately ruins the lives and reputations of the headmistresses and the doctor as well.

Granville is very effective as the vicious sociopath. She forces another student, played sympathetically by Marcia Mae Jones, to back up her story. Mary's threats reduce Jones to absolute terror. In no time, the school has lost all its students, and even a libel suit fails to clear the victims' names. Their livelihoods are irretrievably lost and even the "happy ending" cannot obscure the tragedy of the situation. An adolescent girl is empowered by the rumors she spreads, she is powerful enough to destroy the lives of adults. Although Granville was only twelve years old when she made the film, it remains her best performance and a superb characterization of an evil bully and her victim. In fact, Granville was nominated for a supporting actress Oscar for this role in the first year of the category. The pure malevolence of the leading character is jarring in the guise of this beautiful young girl, a feat not repeated until *The Bad Seed* (1956).

Granville followed Mary with another vicious teen, the hysterical witch accuser in *Maid of Salem* (1936), which is also a representation of a girl with an enormous amount of power over the adults in her town. The threat from adolescent girls is no longer purely sexual. Granville's evil is finally contexualized in the 1938 film *Beloved Brat*. Yet she was often evil, simply for evil's sake, such as in the film, *My Bill* (1938). Although Granville had the perfect mother played by Kay Francis, she once again reprised her malevolent alter ego as the spoiled daughter of a widow, trying to hold her family together.

The trope of the vicious, conniving teenage girl would be played by a series of adolescent girls including Helen Parrish, Marcia Mae Jones, June Preisser and Ann Rutherford. They were situated against the "good" heroines and often tried to undermine them with their jealousy, hatefulness and self-centeredness. Torn between adult standards and their desire for an independent identity, these brats ganged up on other girls in their own search for autonomy. In the process, they were often cruel. Their anger seemed to lurk beneath the surface of their ladylike veneers. Clearly the malevolence of these screen brats documents the real cruelty of youth. They are also a permutation of the delinquent, albeit without the sexual sting. That girls were allowed an outlet for their anger, however, was remarkable. Their unbridled viciousness could be quite liberating. While set in opposition to good girls, they certainly subverted normative definitions of femininity in the process, without being sexual. The representation, however, did not have much staying power.

Even Granville could not maintain her evil persona. She traded her meanness for goodness when she became the film personification of one of the most popular adolescent heroines, Nancy Drew. It was really a casting switch. Granville was a great deal perkier and enthusiastic than the more mature and somewhat conservative fictional counterpart. Ted Nickerson (as opposed to Ned) was her less-than-adoring boyfriend and reluctant accomplice. Granville had gone from bitch to problem solver by the end of the decade.

SAVIORS AND MATCHMAKERS

Many film historians have commented on the trend to mythologize children and adolescents during the Depression. Though not all children were endowed with such magical qualities, films of the 1930s offer some of the most idealized portraits of children and adolescence. Marjorie Rosen argues that children were turned into "good fairies." Dick Moore, a child star of the 1930s himself, comments on this trope in his autobiography, "Important to Hollywood's economy and to the public's need to escape, each of us were the representation of a cliché. . . . [We] were irrepressible little adults who could accomplish more than real adults and solve their problems."[13]

Certainly the element of fantasy and escape in Hollywood films coincided with a stricter enforcement of the Production Code in 1934. In 1930, the informal "Don'ts and Be Carefuls" of film censors was superseded by the more rigid Motion Picture Production Code, the brainchild of Martin Quigley, a devout Catholic and publisher of *The Motion Picture Herald*. He hired Father Daniel Lord, a St. Louis University professor, to write the new code. As with earlier attempts at self-regulation, this was also mainly a public relations gimmick. Early films of the Depression continued to evade the Code.

Conventional wisdom holds that a new sense of caution was forced upon the film industry in 1933 with the formation of the Catholic Legion of Decency, a pressure group charged with reviewing and classifying films according to moral content for Catholics. Parishioners were told to stay away from "objectionable films," and soon Jewish and Protestant organizations joined in a boycott aimed at forcing Hollywood to terminate some of the excesses of earlier films. In some larger cities, movie attendance did decrease.[14]

As a result of such pressures, in July 1934, Will Hays and the Motion Picture Producers and Distributors Association (MPPDA) established the Production Code Office. Joseph Breen, another prominent Catholic and former Chair of a public relations firm, the Studio Relations Committee, was placed at the head of the new regulatory department. Yet the power of the department was questionable. Despite contentions that industry censors could actually block a film's exhibition, Lewis Jacobs found that censors could not actually refuse to release a film that did not have a seal of approval. Instead, the Production Code Office exercised the most power during preproduction.[15] Although films about adolescents were often likely to be in trouble with censors in the 1920s, by the 1930s they had become a safe topic.

Idealizing children is also credited to the public's desire to "escape" into an idealized world during the Depression. Kathy Jackson underscores this point of view. "As Americans endured their economic struggle, they looked two ways: to the past for the security of tradition and to the future for hope in a better world. Children, who are a continuation of past generations and the key to future ones, represented both of these comforting perspectives." Other film historians have argued that it was the election of Franklin Roosevelt and the quick introduction of New Deal relief measures that added to this trend toward escapism in film:

After Roosevelt's inauguration, people were determined to believe . . . that happy days were here again and equally determined no longer to be afraid of the big bad wolf. It was not only a matter of moral reform. . . . Audiences wanted to believe in goodness and happiness again.[16]

In her study of the role of movie stars in women's memories of wartime and postwar Great Britain, Jackie Stacey points out that few film scholars have taken the time to theorize the pleasures of escapism, especially the gendered meaning of escape. She argues that escapism is one of the three key processes of spectatorship, along with identification and competition. Moreover, studying escapism requires looking at more than the narrative conventions of specific film texts, but also at the moviegoing experience. Certainly, the pleasure filmgoers found in the elaborate movie palaces must be considered in evaluating the parameters of escape. An evening out becomes as important as the films themselves. The sense of a "shared group identity" was also part of the appeal of the process. That is, the collective nature of seeing a film heightens its pleasure. Finally, it is not only important to detail what spectators are escaping "into," it is also important to look at what they are escaping "from."[17]

Certainly filmgoers were escaping from the realities of life in the 1930s. After all, escapism is a form of problem solving. I also believe the key to understanding both escapism and the theme of children as saviors is the star personas themselves. As Stacey writes, "Stars were as important for cinema spectators as the narrative of the film in which they appeared." They were already worshiped and deemed mythic by their fans. It is a short jump to believe in the same powers in film. Perhaps stars of the "golden age" were not any more talented than at any other time. What was different was the process of myth making. As one fan admitted,

I think in those eras, we were more inclined to put stars on a pedestal. They were so far removed from everyday life, they were magical. . . . These days stars are so ordinary—the magic has gone. Hollywood will never be the same again![18]

In the 1930s, stars were created by the studios and their huge publicity departments that controlled every aspect of their image. Studios had absolute power over the lives of those under contract to them. Actors were optioned by studios for six months to a year, and then the studio might offer them a contract, which usually ran for seven years. Stars were not allowed to break their contract for any reason and had to accept all the roles offered to them. If they refused, they were suspended without pay. This practice did not end until 1944, when Olivia De Havilland won a court battle against Warners. Stars also had to submit to morality clauses in their contracts, which covered both professional and private conduct. Alexander Walker has characterized the studio system as a "star serfdom," so stringent was the control of the studio. Star personas were carefully constructed, nurtured and perpetuated by the studios. As Edgar Morin said, the "fabrication of stars" was the most important facet of the studio system.[19]

More children than ever before came to Hollywood, fueled by the desire of families who saw stardom for their children as a way out of their own economic hardship. Hedda Hopper wrote of this new breed of "stage mothers" and compared their children to "a flock of hungry beasts driven by gale winds of their pushing, prompting, ruthless mothers. One look into the eyes of these women told you what was on their minds: 'If I can just get this kid of mine on screen, we just might make it big.' " These parents themselves seemed to believe in the children-as-savior theory as well.[20]

This mania was fueled by the fact that one child did "make it big." Shirley Temple was perhaps one of the biggest stars of all time. She was the reigning box office figure between 1935 and 1938. Temple was an anomaly; never before or since has a child star been as successful. Kathy Jackson posits that Temple allayed adults' guilt over the lack of material comforts they were able to give their children during the Depression. "[Temple's] affirmation of the happy childhood may have better enabled Americans to believe that even though their own children were making sacrifices, they were nonetheless content and optimistic." That does not explain why children and adolescents found such pleasure in her films, as well, however. Jackson dismisses the notion that talent alone was enough to account for Temple's phenomenal success, yet I believe that her talent goes a long way to explaining her appeal. Temple was an extraordinary presence, and what is most significant is that she achieved her success when she was only four. By the time she was six, she had been dubbed "Little Miss Miracle." She seemed too good to be true.[21] Her popularity and her fortunes, however, began to decline by the time she was about ten. She simply was not that cute any more, nor that remarkable.

I believe we must look to Temple's success as the key to the child-as-savior trope of the decade. Temple was the first and foremost good fairy of the Depression. Temple's films repeated the themes made popular a decade earlier by Mary Pickford, yet in the 1930s, the roles were filled by someone who was actually the same age as the roles she played. Temple was often an orphan, charged with her own care. She was capable, decisive, and efficient in solving the problems of the adults around her. Marjorie Rosen argues that Temple's age "allowed her to meddle in the business of all concerned. As a child, therefore a neuter, she possessed tremendous latitude; her opinions counted in areas where no adult woman would dare venture much less be heeded."[22]

One fan writing in the monthly "Boos and Bouquets" column of *Photoplay* underscored this attitude toward female child stars:

We should be grateful to motion pictures for making us realize . . . how completely appealing small girls can be. . . . I do hope that movies will give us many opportunities to watch the development of these adorable infants, because I know that millions of admirers will be anxious to know how they all "turn out."[23]

Later in the decade several adolescents would gain stardom. In vehicles tailor-made to their unique talents, filmmakers would simply repackage the formula made successful by Temple for teens like Durbin and Garland. It had worked before, it would work again. Although children and adolescents were idealized, the world around them was not.

Their screen universes were marked by dislocation, death, divorce, poverty, parental neglect, incompetence, and impotence. There was a lot of work for these adolescent girls to do.

NOSTALGIA AND GIRLHOOD

Perhaps the apogee of idealized girlhood during the Depression was the 1933 film *Little Women*. Amazingly faithful to the book, the film lovingly recreates the nineteenth century frame by frame. The camera continually captures the March sisters in frozen shots, gathered around Marmee, grouped around the piano or knitting by the fire, so that they actually look like lithographs of the period. Joan Bennett, as Amy, first appears standing on a bench in a schoolroom with a sign around her neck, "I am ashamed of myself." She is the sister least able to reconcile herself to the family's genteel poverty, as she continues to put on airs and alienate others with her affectations. Her snobbery is emphasized by her frequent use of malapropisms; yet it is difficult to resist her girlish charm. The ever-dying Beth (Jean Peters) is canonized even before her lingering finish, and Meg (Frances Dee) appears the quintessential "True Woman."

The most dynamic portrayal of the film is Katharine Hepburn's Jo. It is as if Louisa May Alcott actually had her in mind when she wrote the book. Hepburn's Jo is full of passion and exuberance. She literally gallops through the film as she cries, "Look at me world, I'm Jo March and I'm so happy!" She functions as the surrogate father while her own is at war. Jo captures the essence of girlhood dreams in her aspiration to be a "scribbling woman." Her passion for meaningful work is so great that she sublimates romance with her beloved Laurie for her goal. When she learns that Laurie has left for Europe without saying good-bye, and that Aunt March is taking Amy to Europe instead of her, Jo's expression is a study of pain and disappointment. It remains one of the most memorable portraits of adolescence and womanhood in film and an enduring representation of an independent and willful girl.

Another actor able to play nostalgic roles was Anne Shirley. She was born Dawn Evelyeen Paris in 1918. Her stage name was Dawn O'Day, and she appeared in a number of silent and sound films under this name, but changed it in 1934 to Anne Shirley to fit the heroine of the title, *Anne of Green Gables*. In this film of an orphan in a small town in Nova Scotia, adopted by a kindly brother and sister, Anne ages from fourteen to seventeen. Shirley is a whimsical Anne, with an exaggerated sense of the romantic and dramatic. Her childhood sweetheart warns, "I think you read too much," and her adoptive father advises, "I've come to the conclusion that too much imagination is not a good thing." No one can put a damper on Anne's enthusiasm, and Shirley's performance is warm and honest, never cloying or sentimental. With her long braids, straw hat, and quixotic temperament, she merges with the fictional character and she creates the identity that her name change suggests. RKO quickly cast her in a series of similar adolescent roles, *Chatterbox* (1936), *M'liss* (1936) and *Make Way for a Lady* (1936).

A representative film was *Girls' School* (1938). Anne Shirley played Natalie Freeman, a student who plans to elope after her senior prom with a moonstruck youth. The film faithfully re-creates the mounting excitement of the girls as they prepare for the prom, whisper of elopements and wait for the arrival of their young men. In a twist at the end, it is not Natalie who elopes, but the most popular teacher. Her students exclaim at the film's ending, "Who'd elope with her?" *Variety* noted, "Refreshing also is that there are no pillow fights, or other antics generally injected into boarding school yarns, and not one box of candy was passed among the girls."[24] Boarding school stories were popular both on film and in the juvenile fiction of girls' magazines like *American Girl* and *Calling All Girls*, with readers often writing in to ask for "more stories of boarding school life." The boarding school setting provided a rich context against which to study the different adolescent types, as in *Finishing School* (1934) and *Girls' Dormitory* (1936), and offered a rich glimpse into adolescent girls' culture.

Shirley was cast as the adolescent daughter of the coarse and vulgar *Stella Dallas* (1937). It is the quintessential story of mother love and sacrifice so common to the period. Barbara Stanwyck in the title role plays a lower-class girl from a small town who marries above her station. The union produces a daughter, Laurel, but it is not enough to keep the mismatched couple together. Although Stella is a caricature in every sense, the film offers a positive portrayal of a loving relationship between an adolescent daughter and her mother. At an age when young girls are often embarrassed by the most normal of parents, Laurel remains loyal to her grotesque mother, while struggling to control her own aversion to her mother's crudeness. In a particularly poignant shot, a close-up reveals the pain and concern in Laurel's eyes as she overhears some of her friends making fun of her mother, knowing that Stella hears the derogatory comment as well. The film moves to its inevitable conclusions as Stella realizes that she is not good enough for her daughter and selflessly removes herself from her daughter's life. It features the ultimate tear-jerking scene as Stella watches her daughter get married as she stands outside the window in the rain.

Perhaps the apogee of the self-sacrificing mother was Louise Beavers as Deliah in the 1934 film *Imitation of Life*. In many ways this film is the natural progression to the trope of the maternal black woman in films like *High School Girl* and *Beloved Brat*. *Imitation* tells the story of two mothers, one black and the other white (Claudette Colbert), who build a life and fortune together selling Deliah's pancake recipe. It is also the story of their daughters, Jessie and Peola, raised as sisters. From the time she is a child, Peola struggles with her identity as a light-skinned African American. When Jessie calls her black, Peola hysterically cries "I'm not black, I'm not black!" Her own self-hatred is projected onto her dark-skinned mother. "It's your fault, it's 'cause you're black that makes me black," she accuses her mother. Her light skin allows her to "pass," but her attempts at passing are foiled inadvertently by her mother, once when she shows up at Peola's classroom. Peola tries to hide behind a book, as her teacher kindly tells Deliah, "I'm sorry, but there aren't any colored children in my class." Deliah spots Peola, and reveals her identity to her horrified classmates.

Peola turns into a sullen, embittered adolescent, played by Fredi Washington, who continues to rail against her identity. "I want to be white because I look white!" she cries to Deliah. She runs away from her all-black college, and tries to pass again as a cashier at a fashionable restaurant. Once again, Deliah foils the attempt by showing up looking for her "baby." Finally Peola, determined to have her own life away from her mother, tells her mother that she must go away. "You mustn't own me or claim me, even if you pass me on the street." This proves the death-knell to Deliah, who essentially dies of a broken heart. A grief-stricken Peola shows up at her mother's funeral, throwing herself on her mother's coffin and begging for forgiveness.

The white mother, Bea, fares little better with her daughter. Their close relationship is threatened when Bea becomes engaged to a man to whom her adolescent daughter is also attracted. Jessie is not shy about declaring her love to the fiancé despite her mother's feelings. When Bea must choose between Jessie and the man she loves, she selflessly chooses her daughter. Although recognizing the hard work and sacrifices their mothers have made on their behalf, both daughters want to carve out an identity separate from those of their mothers.

Yet this is not only a film about mothers and daughters, this is a film about race. The only other film of the decade that would address this issue was *Show Boat*. The trailer for *Imitation of Life* focused on the superb portrayals of Beavers and Washington; Colbert was not even mentioned. Most fans and critics sympathized with Peola's desire to pass and in her desire to enjoy the privileges of being white. They also believed Beavers was too smothering and self-effacing. In fact, although touted as the apogee of films about maternal sacrifice, *Imitation of Life* actually is one of the few films to problemitize the selfless mother.

DEANNA DURBIN

Although largely overlooked by serious film historians, Deanna Durbin was one of the major screen presences of the 1930s and 1940s. She, like Judy Garland, was able to bridge the transition successfully between adolescence and adulthood on screen. Often depicted as a savior in her films, Durbin actually played that role in real life. Deanna Durbin has often been credited with single-handedly saving Universal Studios from bankruptcy. Although that claim is exaggerated, her film grosses accounted for 17 percent of the studio's entire revenue in the late 1930s, and her presence attracted some major stars to Universal. Within a year of her screen debut in 1937, Durbin had completely eclipsed the other major stars of the period, including Shirley Temple and Jane Withers, to become one of the biggest box office stars of the period. In 1939, at the eleventh annual Academy Awards, Durbin received a special miniature Oscar for "bringing to the screen the spirit and personification of youth, and as a juvenile player, setting a high standard of ability and achievement."[25]

Like an earlier "America's Sweetheart," Mary Pickford, Durbin was really a Canadian. She was born Edna Mae Durbin in 1921 in Winnipeg, Canada, to British parents. The Durbins moved to Los Angeles when she was a baby. Edna Mae's singing talent was apparent from an early age. While performing in a recital in 1936, she was spotted by an MGM talent scout and signed to an optional contract. While at MGM, her name was changed to Deanna, and she was teamed with newcomer Judy Garland in a short, *Every Sunday*. Her option was dropped, and it was soon picked up by Universal. Her early film career at Universal was guided by producer Joe Pasternak and director Henry Koster, who oversaw her first feature film in 1936, *Three Smart Girls*. Her film career was relatively brief, spanning only the next eleven years.[26] In 1948, when her contract with Universal was up, Durbin embarked on an extended stay in France. She was only twenty-seven but already had two failed marriages and an infant daughter. In France, Durbin refused all film offers, choosing instead to live modestly in Paris. In 1950, she married French film director Charles Henri David. Madame David and her husband settled in a Paris suburb, had a son, and she has lived with her family in relative obscurity ever since.[27]

In many ways, Durbin's film representations appear to go against the dominant ideology of femininity. Durbin's comedic skills have been overlooked by film historians in favor of her singing talent. Yet the Durbin persona in virtually all her adolescent characterizations is witty, sarcastic, mischievous, outspoken, argumentative and bossy. She has no compunctions about standing up to the adults in her life—cab drivers, butlers, industrialists, society matrons, bachelors, teachers, symphony orchestra conductors—who are all leveled by her determination. She is the general deploying troops of grown men. Nothing intimidates her.

Universal, once the prosperous studio of Carl Laemmle, Hollywood pioneer and creator of the star system, was facing bankruptcy in 1935. A group of New York bankers came in to try to salvage the ailing studio, which had produced a number of successful horror films in the early 1930s, including *Dracula* and *Frankenstein*. Shortly after the takeover, two Europeans, Joseph Pasternak, a Hungarian producer, and Henry Koster, a German director—both of whom had been hired by Laemmle before the takeover—arrived at the studio. They were grudgingly given office space by the new president, Charles "Buddy" Rogers, and charged with coming up with a story idea. They told Rogers that they wanted to make a film about three sisters, but it appears that they had little in terms of a story idea. From that inauspicious beginning, Universal screenwriter Adele Commandini created a screenplay that would become Durbin's first feature film, *Three Smart Girls*.

Durbin came to the attention of Pasternak and Koster by a former MGM executive who had recently been hired by Universal. He told the two men about a talented girl with an operatic voice who had been dropped by MGM. Durbin had been a student of the Metropolitan Opera baritone Andre de Segurola. In her first meeting with Pasternak and Koster, she reportedly "never said a word; she refused to talk when spoken to; she was obviously scared stiff." Her screen test was no better as Durbin broke down in tears and cried, "I don't want to be an actress, you're all torturing me!" The filming of *Three Smart Girls* was postponed for two weeks, while Pasternak and Koster tried to break down her reserve and prepare her for her film debut.[28]

It was clear almost immediately to studio executives that they had a star in Durbin. The budget for the film was raised from $150,000 to $300,000, and Durbin's role was increased to highlight her singing talent. *Three Smart Girls*, released in 1936, was enormously successful, earning Universal in excess of $2 million. The film would set the formula for the rest of Durbin's adolescent characterizations. All showcased her singing. Many of Durbin's films involved fractured families: She was either an orphan or the daughter of a single parent scheming to create a nuclear family. They also turned on a relationship to an older, less capable man.

Three Smart Girls revolved around the efforts of three upper-class girls to foil the marriage of their father to a gold digger and to reunite their divorced parents. Parental ineffectiveness is revealed by their mother who, although divorced for ten years, still cries for her ex-husband, choosing to hide away with her daughters in Europe. The mother is too passive and ineffective to do anything other than cry, albeit in a very dignified, stiff-upper-lip manner. The family learns of their father's impending nuptials from a newspaper. Their mother collapses from the emotional stress. It is up to the girls, spearheaded by Penny (Durbin), the youngest, to break up the engagement. Penny is clearly smarter, more savvy and forceful than her older sisters. Unbeknownst to their simpering but dignified mother, they rush to New York. Their absentminded, befuddled, millionaire father does not even recognize his daughters, as he has not seen or communicated with them for ten years. Mr. Craig may be a successful businessman, but he is too stupid to recognize that his predatory fiancée is only after him for his money, something Penny figures out instantly. Penny engineers the plot to destroy the engagement and reunite her parents, all the while confidently deploying the troops around her.

In the sequel, *Three Smart Girls Grow Up* (1939), the Craigs have not improved their parenting skills. Mrs. Craig, rebounding nicely from the years apart from her husband, has slipped easily back into the role of Mrs. Judson Craig, busy society matron. After raising her daughters alone for ten years, she now passes responsibility on to her husband, but Mr. Craig remains befuddled and preoccupied with matters other than his family. Because no one appears to be in charge, it is up to Penny to parent herself and look out for her sisters. She is left to her own devices. Penny must once again utilize her matchmaking skill as she schemes to marry off her sisters. Penny thinks that they are paired with the wrong men, so Penny simply reshuffles them. Her enthusiasm, impudence, and sarcasm stands in sharp contrast to her rather humorless sisters. She finally confronts her busy father. "Nobody ever listens to me," she cries. Defensively he replies, "I have to work to give you, your mother, and sisters the things you need." Penny says, "We don't need things, we need someone to help us when we're in trouble, and listen to us, not to be a million miles away." Finally, her father shares her burden and helps her to orchestrate the right relationship for his daughters. The girl, who might have turned into a sexual delinquent in the 1920s because of parental neglect, has become a comedic trope by the 1930s.

The theme is repeated in *Mad about Music* (1938), as Durbin plays the fourteen-year old daughter of a glamorous movie star mother. Convinced by her manager to hide her daughter from the press to maintain her glamour-girl reputation, her mother leaves Gloria (Durbin) in a Swiss boarding school. Gloria invents an exciting, explorer father to impress her boarding school friends and then commandeers a stranger, Richard Todd (Herbert Marshall), to play the part when her classmates question his existence. Mom feels bad about hiding Gloria (she cries a lot and speaks lovingly and in hushed tones of "her little girl"), but the bottom line is that she has put her career before motherhood. Of course the nuclear family desired by Gloria comes about when Richard Todd and Gloria's mother actually do fall in love. In *It's a Date* (1939), Durbin spars for the affections of Walter Pidgeon with her single, actress mother. Although she's never positioned seriously as the romantic object, the man becomes the focal point of the healthy competition both women have with each other. Again, these films show seriously dysfunctional parents, yet their daughters are not only none the worse for their neglect, they are, in fact, wonder kids. They seem to efface the role of the parent in shaping the adolescent personality. Perhaps this is due, in part, to the enormous dislocation of the American family by the economic crisis.

Perhaps the most representative Durbin role was in *100 Men and a Girl*, released in 1937. Durbin plays Patsy Cardwell, the daughter of an unemployed musician (Adolphe Menjou), who must convince the noted conductor Leopold Stokowski to conduct her father's orchestra of unemployed musicians. Grown men are rendered impotent by the economic crisis, but the Depression makes Patsy more capable and effective. Her kindly father is simply not as savvy as his adolescent daughter. Early in the film, Patsy stumbles into a society party, where she instructs the rich folks about the plight of the out-of-work musicians. The hostess, Mrs. Frost (Alice Brady), makes an off-hand comment that she will ask her industrialist husband (Eugene Palatte) to sponsor an orchestra of the unemployed on his radio show, but she leaves for Europe without informing her husband of her promise. In the meantime, Patsy has assembled the musicians, giving them hope of employment. She becomes the organizer, agent, manager and promoter. Frost initially refuses to honor his wife's promise, but he later concedes that he might reconsider if they can get a famous conductor. Patsy must overcome numerous obstacles to convince the great Stokowski to conduct, including assembling the orchestra in his foyer, where, moved by their playing, he begins to conduct them in Liszt's *Second Hungarian Rhapsody*. Patsy, the adolescent girl, has single-handedly engineered the employment of 100 men. During the concert finale of the film, Stokowski brings her on stage for an "impromptu and unrehearsed" aria from *La Traviata*, thus ensuring not only the orchestra's success but her own as well.

This film can be situated in relation to the work of Lary May, who has challenged the dominant view of historians who argue that a "constant commitment to liberal capitalism and consumerism informed the popular arts from the 1930s through the 1950s." Instead, May concludes that the "American Way" was really not formed until World War II. May challenges the vision of Hollywood as a monolithic entity that produced a "classic American cinema." Instead, May sees Hollywood as part of a "competitive civic sphere," where myths, symbols and national ideologies were contested. When Hollywood films are explored as an arena of competing ideologies, May finds a significant number of films critical of the American Way. Films critical of the status quo were not the only films made during the 1930s. Certainly, there were numerous films that "promoted escapism and reinforced the myths and symbols of liberalism, individualism and conformity." Yet, as May posits, films critical of the American Way were films that featured coalitions of class, ethnic and sometimes racial difference. Such films did not champion an American consensus, an overriding deference to authority, business or the state. Films of the 1930s that preserved class and ethnic differences showed groups "tied together in reciprocal social environments." Films of the 1930s that challenged established "American" values did not privilege authority but rather portrayed mutual cooperation and reciprocity, which, in turn, preserved class, ethnic and regional differences.[29]

100 Men and a Girl was clearly critical of the status quo, particularly the role of big business. The gravelly voiced Palatte is in sharp contrast to the melodious tones of Durbin and her orchestra. He is the heartless industrialist motivated by money, with little thought for human suffering. Moreover, he remains unmoved by the entreaties of the darling Patsy, further proof that he is not worthy of deference. *100 Men and a Girl* features a reciprocal cross-ethnic coalition of musicians who meld together to form an orchestra, and a cross-class alliance between the unemployed and the rich. Patsy is an empowered, autonomous adolescent girl, who asserts her independence not in the domestic sphere, but in the public sphere. Durbin's film characterizations of the late 1930s have much in common with those of Shirley Temple, in terms of her being a savior who fosters cross-class coalitions, which either implicitly or explicitly critique the rich, the state or big business. The difference is that Durbin employs high culture, while Temple employs popular culture, whose characters were more often associated with the vernacular.[30]

There does appear to be a change from cross-class alliances to consensus in Durbin's films of the 1940s. Perhaps it was her high-culture status that made a switch to patriotic support of consensus possible. By the early 1940s, Durbin's roles also began to change as she matured from a child star to an ingenue, and even though she could no longer be depicted as child-as-savior, she was still working miracles. A representative film is *It Started with Eve*, made in 1941. Although the film was released shortly before the United States entered World War II, there are still signs of a change toward consensus. As May argues, films of the 1940s labeled 1930s counternarratives of difference as subversive. Many 1940s films featured plots where a character underwent a conversion from an animosity toward the state and big business to a deference for authority and organized institutions that subordinated "class and ethnic consciousness" on the one hand to patriotic effort in service to the nation on the other. There was a shift from the critical stance of reciprocity to a rejection of that stance in favor of patriotic conformity. Although these 1940s films of consensus still featured ethnic, racial, class and regional differences, these differences were melted into a common American consensus.[31]

Such is the case in *It Started with Eve*, the plot of which turns on a case of mistaken identity. As rich industrialist Jonathan Reynolds

(Charles Laughton) lays dying, his last request of his playboy son Johnny (Bob Cummings), who has been in Mexico on vacation, is to meet his new fiancée. Unfortunately, she is not immediately available, and with time at a premium, Johnny finds a quick replacement in the hatcheck girl at the hotel, Anne Terry (Durbin). The elder Reynolds is instantly taken with the young woman, and instead of dying, he makes a full recovery, forcing Johnny and Anne to continue the charade.

Anne is initially disdainful of the upper-class patrons who frequent her hotel, as she complains that they are "diming her to death." She is clearly not intimidated or impressed with the wealth of the Reynoldses. Yet, unlike Eugene Palatte in *100 Men and a Girl*, Laughton's Reynolds is the industrialist without the sting. Inside this gruff curmudgeon is a pussy cat, whose role is simply to show Johnny and Anne that they were made for each other. From Anne's initial disdain for the rich, there is a conversion to a deference for authority. Early in the film, Anne is focused on manipulating Reynolds to further her own career as an opera singer. Her continued participation in the charade is motivated not only by her sincere kinship with Reynolds but also by the fact that Reynolds is good friends with Leopold Stokowski (the constant references to the invisible Stokowski serves as a sort of inside joke for Durbin aficionados). Yet by the end of the film, Anne's self-aggrandizing behavior gives way to altruism as she is no longer motivated by personal gain but by her love for both of the Reynolds men. Big business, in the guise of the lovable Jonathan Reynolds, is rendered benign, paternal and all-knowing. Father really does know best. Class lines are blurred in *Eve*. Although Anne initially appears to be working class, this is no ordinary hatcheck girl. Her work is simply a means to an end, earning money for singing lessons so that she can achieve her goal of being an opera singer.

Although Durbin's screen characterizations changed according to the material conditions of the 1930s and the 1940s, both Durbin's adolescent and young-adult film characterizations appear to go against the dominant ideology of femininity. Durbin's screen representations have a certain power over adult men, a theme that would take on new meaning in the 1940s. It is much like the power the young Shirley Temple displayed in her films. Durbin demands respect and attention from men. That same single-mindedness of purpose is apparent in *100 Men and a Girl* as she literally wills the orchestra into being and gets not only one man but a hundred to do her bidding. In *Mad about Music*, she gets a man to go along with the charade of being her father, a role he soon internalizes. In *It Started with Eve*, she bulldozes Reynolds into arranging an audition with Stokowski and foils Johnny's efforts to get her out of his father's life. She is more agile physically and mentally than Johnny, and even though they are the romantic leads, it is clear that Anne and the elder Reynolds are the true soul mates, and Anne will never be a docile wife. Durbin's films did not position spectators as passive objects of the male gaze. Instead, spectators were given agency, an agency that corresponded to their fan activities, as I demonstrate in the last chapter.

JUDY GARLAND

Judy Garland represented a differing experience of adolescence in the 1930s. To her studio, MGM, Garland was not an adolescent but a valuable box office commodity. Like Durbin, Garland had a tremendous talent, "a trembling vocal style that somehow managed to combine womanly pathos and childish innocence." Studio publicity for Garland constructed a picture of all-American girlhood. A movie magazine commenting on the Rooney-Garland team gushed,

Off screen Judy and Mickey are normal, happy, young people who enjoy the sort of thing that the kid around the corner likes. . . . Both are close to their mothers for they realize that if it were not for maternal efforts they might not be on the top of the movie heap today. They consider themselves too young for serious romance and laugh at gossip columnists who try to pair them.[32]

By age twenty-one, Garland had made twenty films, had two failed marriages, was visiting a psychiatrist regularly and was living on pills to which she had become addicted to lose weight at MGM. Born Francis Gumm in Grand Rapids, Michigan, Garland was a vaudeville performer at age five. Her father died when she was twelve, leaving her and her sisters with the quintessential stage mother. Garland bitterly remembered that her mother was "no good for anything except to create chaos and fear. She was the worst—the real Wicked Witch of the West."[33]

The details of her personal life are testament to her extraordinary talent. MGM picked up Garland's option after the short *Every Sunday*, in which Garland is the more charismatic of the two juvenile performers. She made a brief appearance in *Pigskin Parade* in 1936. She stole the film *Broadway Melody of 1938*, as she sang a plaintive rendition of "You Made Me Love You" to a photograph of Clark Gable. She played her first savior in *Everybody Sing* (1938). In the film Judy is the daughter of very wealthy parents, her father a harried playwright and her mother an eccentric, self-absorbed actress. Despite their opulent lifestyle, the family is broke. Because her parents are too busy for the teen, she keeps getting kicked out of boarding school. The servants (featuring a scene-stealing Fanny Brice as the maid) are her surrogate parents. The young girl takes it upon herself to single-handedly get her parents out of debt, repair their broken marriage and unite her older sister with the handsome cook who is really a talented singer. In this classless society, the cook can end up with the boss's daughter. Judy is more talented, level-headed and emotionally mature than the rest of her family. She does not need a caretaker because she is a caretaker. In the 1920s, neglected teens would become delinquent, but in the thirties, these same neglected teens would flourish. There is a clear dichotomy between the need for guidance and surveillance and the need for autonomy expressed by the screen teens of the Depression.

Listen Darling (1938) found Judy in the matchmaking mode, a theme common in many films about youth in the 1930s. Perhaps this trend can be read as a desire to create functional nuclear families in a time of rapid dislocation. Garland plays Pinky, the daughter of a widow, Dottie (Mary Astor), who is about to lose everything because her late husband was an impractical dreamer who failed to keep insurance. She is about to marry a rich banker because it is the only way she can see to support her family. Pinky and her friend Buzz kidnap Dottie in the family trailer and decide to find her a more suitable husband. Only marriage will provide the family with economic stability. They find her another impractical dreamer (but at least he's a lawyer). Interestingly, Pinky calls her mother "Dottie," signifying not a lack of respect but her mother's inability to be a responsible adult. She's more like a pal, more a sister than a mother. Early in the film Dottie laments her inability to take care of her family herself in an emergency. She tells Pinky of the importance of economic independence and the necessity of having a career so that she will be able to take care of herself, advice that Dottie has been unable to follow. Pinky can not only take care of herself, she can guide and nurture her mother as well, again reasserting the theme of a kind of role reversal between parents and children.

By far the most representative Garland films were the ones she made with Mickey Rooney. They were first paired in 1938, when Garland appeared in an Andy Hardy film, *Love Finds Andy Hardy*, often considered the best of the series. So successful was the collaboration, they were teamed in 1939 for Busby Berkeley's *Babes in Arms*, the quintessential "Hey, kids, let's put on a show!" film. This film can be credited with starting a new musical formula, the youth musical. The actual line said by Rooney is really, "Are you kids willing to stick together and pull us out of a hole? I'm going to write a show for us and we'll put it on right in Seaport. We'll get every kid in this town on our side." He thus affirms the importance of collective action and the reality of a youth coalition taking arms against the Depression.

They play the children of unemployed vaudevillians, Patsy and Mickey, who decide to produce a musical to help rescue their parents from debt. The scene of youths marching confidently down the streets of the town with lighted torches, gathering more and more children as they sing the theme song is strangely reminiscent of two other contemporary images: both the vigilante mob intent on destroying the monster in *Frankenstein* (1932), and Hitler's youth in Leni Riefenstahl's *Triumph of the*

Will (1934). The marching youths also underscore the importance of coalition, poised to combat the remains of economic instability and the growing winds of war. The triumphant song's final lyrics are sung on a school playground. In rendering their parents impotent, the Depression has also empowered these children. The dissonance is apparent: As they "play" on the trappings of childhood, they have clearly left childhood behind.

This film is perhaps one of the best examples of the children-as-savior trope. Patsy's and Mickey's youthful optimism is in sharp contrast to their parents' pessimism and discouragement. As May has found, many films of the 1930s featured goals centered on collective action. He also has found that in the 1930s, the old middle-class professions of upward mobility were increasingly replaced by entertainment-related occupation as an avenue of success. The show becomes a metaphor for using talent and ingenuity to solve problems. In the finale, Garland and Rooney appear as Eleanor and Franklin Roosevelt singing a stirring rendition of "God's Country." The president and first lady are benevolent authority figures transformed into entertainers.[34] "It's bigger than just the show," says Mickey with dawning clarity, "Say, it's everybody in the country." Youth represents optimism for an uncertain future.

On the heels of *Babes in Arms* came *Strike Up the Band*, also directed by Busby Berkeley. Rooney organizes a swing band at his high school and then spurs the other kids to ambition and ultimately success when they win a national contest sponsored by Paul Whiteman. Garland plays the loyal helpmate Mary, who is essentially a reprisal of her Betsy Booth persona in the Hardy series. Mary has a crush on Jimmy, but to him she's just "pal." She is his biggest fan and cheerleader, helping smooth over all obstacles to his dream. The self-absorbed Jimmy is oblivious to the desires of anyone but himself. Again the needs of the individual must be subsumed to the good of the many. Jimmy gives up a job with another orchestra when his mother convinces him that he is letting the other guys and Mary down. There is strength in unity. This theme is repeated in *Babes on Broadway* (1941), in which youth is enlisted in the American effort to win the war.

Garland and Rooney would make two more musicals together, *Babes on Broadway* and *Girl Crazy* (1943), which would repeat the formula established in their earlier musicals. In both Garland's and Durbin's musicals, songs are used differently: They can be a number in a "show," or they might simply further the narrative by commenting on a fictional development. Yet as the work of Jane Feuer shows, the musical number, which often appears spontaneous, becomes a powerful metaphor for the entire film industry. The importance of musical numbers for Feuer lies in the way that they appear to represent a form of folk art, while these numbers are, in fact, carefully orchestrated products of capitalism. As Susan Hayward points out, the movie musical is "extremely self-referential; it spends most of its time justifying its existence." The goal is to provide the spectator with utopian possibilities, while the entertainment itself becomes the utopia. "So again, self-referentiality is at work." One of the characteristics of this utopian sensibility according to Richard Dyer is the importance of community, everyone works in harmony for the well-being of the group.[35]

Certainly, the musicals of Durbin and Garland celebrate community and posit a utopian ordering of society. Though their films must be contexualized within the Depression, ironically, the Depression is often effaced by the narratives as never existing or about to end. Musical numbers appear seamless, part and parcel of the "magical" abilities of their stars. "Amateur" productions have high-rent production values that also serve to deny the reality of economic hardship. In the "God's Country" finale of *Babes in Arms*, for instance, Mickey and Judy as Eleanor and Franklin sing, "We've got no Duce, we've got no fuhrer, but we've got Garbo and Norma Shearer," thus affirming both the legitimacy and superiority of American cultural and governmental institutions. The potential not only of youth, but of the United States to transcend the national crisis is reinforced. All serve to affirm the superiority of both capitalism and the American way of life. Moreover, their films have as their basic premise, as did Shirley Temple's films, the transformative powers of love and optimism.[36]

THE GIRLS OF CARVEL

Certainly the most idealized portraits of family life in the thirties could be found in the Andy Hardy series. Even though the films centered on the needs and concerns of an adolescent boy, there were a host of ancillary female characters who provided a running commentary on female adolescence. In fact, the series is credited with launching the careers of Judy Garland, Lana Turner, Donna Reed, and Esther Williams.

Carvel, Idaho, home of the Hardys, became the prototype of the All-American town. The series began in 1937 with the low-budget film *A Family Affair*, based on an obscure 1928 play. Lionel Barrymore and Spring Byington were cast as the parents, Cecilia Parker and Julie Hayden as the older sisters, Sara Hayden as the spinster Aunt Millie, and Mickey Rooney as the girl crazy Andy Hardy. Although it began as a "B" picture, the film was an enormous success. The wholesomeness of the series further appealed to MGM studio head, Louis B. Mayer. He ordered a sequel—and then a series. There were sixteen Hardy films in all.

In the second film, *You're Only Young Once* (1938), Louis Stone and Fay Holden took over as Judge and Mrs. Hardy, roles they would continue for the duration of the series. The older sister played by Julie Hayden was dropped, but Cecilia Parker, Sara Hayden and Mickey Rooney would all reprise their roles. The *New York Times* was ecstatic in its praise of this fictional family:

The average American family (if, indeed, there is such a thing) has been so frequently libeled by the average film, it is a surprising experience and an occasion for relief to come upon a fictional group which can reasonably be accepted as such . . . and in which the individual members react like human beings instead of third rate vaudevillians.[37]

The family configuration was rather odd, however. In many ways Judge Hardy was a man with two wives. There was Mrs. Hardy, of course, but it was often difficult to discern what this intelligent man saw in his simpering, childlike and emotional wife. He called her "mother," but his attitude was usually patronizing and paternal. When the Judge needed adult conversation or guidance, he always turned to his sister-in-law, Aunt Milly, who could actually focus on what he was saying. Aunt Milly was a rock, but in *The Hardys Ride High* (1939), she finally complains to the Judge, "I'm an old maid, a schoolteacher, I want to do and see things before I get old!" He tries to soothe her, "You're my right hand," but she retorts, "No woman wants to be a man's right hand." Except for this burst of rebellion, Aunt Milly remained solid and competent throughout the series, and the judge had the best of both worlds, yet there remains a lingering suspicion that he married the wrong woman.

You're Only Young Once introduced Ann Rutherford as the recurring character of Polly Benedict. Polly is only supposed to be fifteen, but she acts like an affected grown-up. She is very prissy and demanding. She addresses Andy as "Mr. Hardy" and shakes her head and stomps her feet a lot. Polly disdains sex and often gets fed up with Andy's adolescent fumblings. She actually repeats the line to Andy in several films, "Don't you think of anything else besides grabbing people in dark corners?" Because of her disdainful attitude toward kissing, Polly is continually positioned as the nice girl. Andy often strays, but he always comes back to Polly. What's ironic about the character of Polly is that she was rarely an integral part of the plots of the Hardy films. Instead her leaving town or generally being unavailable served as a way for Andy to become "involved" with another girl. That "other" girl was always in direct opposition to Polly.

Such is the case in *You're Only Young Once*. The Hardy family is vacationing on Catalina, where Andy meets a precocious older woman (she's sixteen), Jerry Lane (Eleanor Lynn). Jerry is very sophisticated, a "poor little rich girl," whose mother has been divorced four times. Parental neglect causes Jerry to want "to have been everywhere and done everything by the time I'm eighteen." Here is a teen who is not rendered more competent because of parental dysfunction. She is well on her way to delinquency when she meets our hero, as Jerry smokes, drinks and encourages kissing, as opposed to the virtuous Polly. Judge Hardy warns Andy,

"This girl isn't good. . . . I suppose she's a product of the bad features of the age we live in, but that doesn't keep her from being rotten proof. She'd poison whatever she came into contact with mentally, morally, and spiritually." This is an uncharacteristically harsh and judgmental condemnation for Judge Hardy, who would usually blame the parents and not the children for abhorrent behavior. Jerry arranges a seductive evening with Andy and plies him with liquor, but Andy resists, admitting he prefers football. He returns to Polly, whom he would rather have to beg for a kiss than be given one free. This film would begin a tendency in their series to moralize subtly and not so subtly against certain kinds of female behavior.

The third Hardy film, *Love Finds Andy Hardy* (1938), introduced two new ingenues, Lana Turner and Judy Garland. Garland is delightful as Betsy Booth, the sweet, innocent twelve-year-old who idolizes Andy. He ignores her after their first meeting, and she mournfully laments, "I'll never be able to get a man, much less hold him. No glamour, no glamour at all." Betsy has a bad case of puppy love, and she functions as a surrogate mother, providing nurturing support and smoothing things out for the ungrateful Andy. Garland affirms qualities of traditional femininity to a much greater extent than does Durbin. She is vulnerable, nurturing and selfless.

Andy has eyes for Cynthia Potter (Turner) while the unsuspecting Polly is off on vacation. Cynthia is another miniature adult, a pouty flirt, again a little too "easy" by Carvel standards. Betsy is actually the only girl with whom Andy can be himself, but Andy wants "to have a sensational girl on my arm." Cynthia expects to be amused by Andy. She is vapid and silly, and has Andy wrapped around her finger. She will not go swimming because her hair might get wet. She will not play tennis as it might give her "muscles." One thing she does like to do is "neck." In the obligatory man-to-man talk between Andy and the Judge, Andy complains,

Sometimes I don't understand these modern girls. Polly, for instance. Sometimes she won't let you kiss her at all, but that Cynthia, she'll let you kiss her whenever you want. She doesn't want to swim, play tennis, all she wants to do is kiss you. I'm a nervous wreck! . . . Why is it when you want to kiss a girl and she won't let you, you want to kiss her all the time?

The implicit double standard is clear. Although Polly is a prissy bore, Andy respects her for playing hard to get. The constant affirmation of traditional gender roles and values might indicate that such values were increasingly passé with 1930s teens. In the film's conclusion, Polly unexpectedly comes back early from vacation and Andy finds himself with two dates for the dance. Miss Fix-it, Betsy, soothes it over and selflessly gets him and Polly back together.

In *Judge Hardy and Son* (1939), the family faces a crisis as Mrs. Hardy struggles with pneumonia. This does not preclude Andy from having girl problems, as he becomes mixed up with a giggly flirt who likes to talk in rhymes, and a Southern belle whom he convinces that a girl must have brains to be popular (which is clearly a shock to her). Andy must also contend with the hapless Polly, who is taking cooking lessons because Andy's parents have told her that a good wife is one who "cooks well." In this film's man-to-man, Judge Hardy advises the despairing Andy that men need "to mold and guide" women into becoming the perfect helpmate. He confides, "Your mother was a giggler too."

Garland and Rooney were reunited in *Andy Hardy Meets a Debutante* (1940). There Andy has a crush on Daphne Fowler, "Deb of the Year." He brags about knowing her; thus making Polly jealous enough that she calls his bluff by publishing the details of his "romance" in the school paper. Coincidentally, the Hardy family is about to leave for New York, and Andy must get proof of his relationship with Daphne.

Garland again is charming as the fifteen-year-old, awkward, flustered girl. Throughout the film the Hardys affirm the virtues of the "nice, old fashioned girl." Mrs Hardy says of Betsy, "You see Andrew, even in New York, a nice girl grows up thinking more about being a housewife than doing the rumble [*sic*]." Once more Betsy has a bad case of puppy love, and Andy is totally absorbed in his own problems. Again, Betsy makes herself indispensable as his faithful helpmate and ultimately solves his problem when she introduces him to Daphne, who happens to be her friend. By the end of the film, Andy takes his parents' advice to heart when he declares, "I want a nice, old fashioned girl—a girl who will look up to a man." He finally begins to appreciate Betsy and gives her her first screen kiss, as she plaintively tells Andy, "No boy has ever kissed me before."

What of Andy's forgotten sister, Marion? She is the problem child, which is not surprising, as Andy got most of the attention. In fact, in *Judge Hardy and Son* (1939), she admits to being jealous of Andy, because "it's more thrilling to be a boy than a girl." Andy is clearly the center of the Hardy universe. Marion and Andy are contentious siblings, constantly fighting or teasing one another. She is rarely in good humor. Poor Marion simply wants to get married, but she is only allowed a number of temporary relationships, usually to the wrong man. At one point she proclaims, "I'm never going to marry, I'll be a settlement worker!" Marion falls for a lifeguard in *You're Only Young Once* (1938), and in *Judge Hardy's Children* (1938), she becomes the pawn of a crooked lobbyist, who uses her to blackmail the judge. Her judgment is no better in *Andy Hardy's Double Life* (1942), where her boyfriend has lost his license for three months because he has a drinking problem and a penchant for driving under the influence.

Although Marion is afforded two differing paradigms of womanhood in the figures of her mother and Aunt Milly, she is unlike either of them.

Her incompetence in running a household is underscored in *Love Finds Andy Hardy*, when she gets to be in charge of the house. Marion is officious and bossy, she can't even make coffee and manages to alienate the housekeeper. Marion is just as incompetent in the work force. In *Andy Hardy Gets Spring Fever* (1939), Marion tells her father that she wants to earn her own living. Judge Hardy, articulating conventional sentiment of the Depression, counters that he would "hate to see you taking a paycheck away from a man," so he hires her himself as a personal secretary. Marion, however, isn't quite up to the task. Instead, she appears sentenced to a life of helping her mother in the kitchen and living on an allowance from her father.

Although the teens often look and behave like miniature adults replete with honorifics, formals, coats, ties, pumps and so on, they do depict a youth culture of sorts. Carvel High is the center of the social universe, where Polly and her friends in the "Junior League" function as the social arbiters and future clubwomen. It is a gendered universe to be sure, as the boys' lives revolve around cars, sports and figuring out how to pay for the social events created by the Junior League. The series also comments on the ways in which teens, particularly boys, have integrated technology into their lives, using telephones, ham radios, automobiles, radios and telegrams effortlessly. Mr. and Mrs. Hardy, on the other hand, seem baffled and uncomfortable with these inventions. For the most part, the representations of female adolescence are fairly ambivalent. In Hardy films of the late 1930s, girls are usually silly, vain, manipulative, dumb and either too easy or too frigid. There is little wonder that they drive Andy crazy.

Interestingly, representations of girls of the Hardy series in the early 1940s are much more competent. Even Polly Benedict appears to get the upper hand in *Andy Hardy's Double Life* (1942), as she and Esther Williams team up to teach the flirtatious Andy a lesson. The two girls are no longer in competition for Andy's affections—they are friends united against him. In *Andy Hardy's Blonde Trouble* (1944), the trouble turns on twin co-eds who swindle money from the naive Andy. In this film he also falls in love for the first time in the series with a young woman of sense and integrity, played by Bonita Granville. Unfortunately for Andy, she is in love with someone else. Her maturity stands in sharp contrast to Andy's recklessness, vanity, naiveté and immaturity. The girls of Carvel had finally grown up.

GIRLS AS FANS

Although Hollywood's vision of female adolescence was often based on what adults wanted to see, girls were still able to draw their own meanings from these representations. By the 1930s, fans were clearly able to respond critically to what was being presented on screen. Film historian Jeanine Basinger underscores this perspective:

Even as children, we knew how much of what we were seeing was untrue, wishful, escapist. What were we—idiots? I am always astonished at how much writing about old movies assumes that the audience believed everything in them. Of course we didn't. We entered into the joyful conspiracy of movie going. We chose what we temporarily wanted to pretend was true, and when real experience didn't provide a yardstick, we cautiously wondered and questioned. We grew to understand the great secret of Hollywood film: its ambivalence, its knowing pretense. You were a fool to believe any of it, but you were a fool if you didn't.[38]

Girls as fans learned to express their opinions and to assert both their preferences and their dislikes. One fan, writing in a 1937 edition of *Photoplay*, publically thanked Universal for "giving a bored movie public the thrilling fourteen year old Deanna Durbin. After such a long trend of Shirley Temple and Jane Withers, Deanna, with her striking beauty, her gifted singing, and her outstanding acting ability and personality, proves a refreshing treat."[39] This fan was clearly affirming the arrival of a distinct adolescent persona.

Adolescent girls were also a vocal force in letting juvenile magazines know what they wanted. *The American Girl's* monthly column "A Penny for Your Thoughts" featured reader mail. Through this forum, adolescents began to ask for features on movies. Although the magazine was slow to take up the topic of films and film personalities, by 1933 there were articles every few months on almost every aspect of filmmaking, from film profiles, to film histories, to behind the scene looks at film production. Instead of simply offering gossipy pieces, the articles were enlightening and informative looks at various aspects of filmmaking. By 1938 *The American Girl* added another monthly column, "What's On Screen," that rated the top film releases in that month for girls. By the early 1940s, the health and beauty columns often focused on the eating habits of adolescent female stars like Deanna Durbin, Bonita Granville, Ann Rutherford, Judy Garland or Gloria Jean, their favorite recipes or their favorite fashions.[40]

There were even some creative endeavors inherent in fandom. *Photoplay* began a monthly sketching competition, and hundreds of fans, many of them adolescent girls, sent in sketches of their favorite stars. Contests that tested fans' knowledge of trivia or features that asked for essays on various topics (such as "Why I Read Silver Screen," or "Your Opinion of Joan Crawford") were common as well. Most fan magazines had monthly columns in which fans could express their opinions for cash. Letters from teenage girls in the 1930s highlighted the importance of films in their lives. Typical was the following:

I am a high school student and I wish to tell you why I like pictures. Every time examination week comes around I make it a point to go to the show every single night. It makes me forget about the low grades I received, that is if I received any, which I generally do. [Films] make me dream pleasant dreams instead of dreaming the professor is chasing you with an examination paper marked zero.

Some letters illustrated the ways in which films contributed to the assimilation process. One Chinese American girl lauded films for teaching her father to speak English. "Until he heard the perfect speech of some of the screen actors, his English was much the same as that of any Chinese who came to this country . . . but now his pronunciation is almost without accent, and I am very proud of him."[41]

Fans often wrote poetry celebrating their idols, as was the case of a fan who "sent Janet Gaynor a booklet of 40 of her poems, ten poems to Shirley Temple . . . and to President Roosevelt for his first inaugural." These were not merely private writing, however, as fan-generated poetry had outlets in publications, not only of specific fan clubs, but in fan magazines as well. The poem "Our Gift," written by a girl fan, was published in *Deanna's Diary*. Extolling Durbin's many virtues, the poem began, "God took two stars from the skies. Fans lovingly crafted both private and public tributes to their favorite luminaries.[42]

Fan loyalty often lasted a lifetime. Jackie Stacey's analysis of the relationship between female stars and their fans illustrates the staying value of fandom. Although she interviewed her subjects some thirty to forty years after the stars' heyday, Stacy found that fans were still able to derive a great deal of pleasure from remembering how they saw their favorite stars when they were adolescent girls involved in fan activities. Such fan loyalty and staying power is further illustrated by fan letters written to Hedda Hopper about Judy Garland in the late 1940s and early 1950s. Hopper had been reporting on Garland's increasing professional difficulties. Women who had been teens in the 1930s quickly came to Garland's defense: "I am a great fan of Miss Judy Garland, and I think it's a damn rotten shame the way you are treating Miss Garland." Another wrote, "I am one of the millions who love Judy Garland. God sends a voice like that into the world to touch the heartstrings of human beings." After Hopper reported on Garland's removal from the film *Royal Wedding,* one fan wrote, " I think Judy Garland fans want her and no substitute. . . . Can't her boss understand she is nervous, and put up with a few things?"[43]

Fans not only wanted information about their favorite stars, they created it as well. They lovingly collected memorabilia, crafted scrapbooks, wrote letters, and composed poetry to celebrate their favorites. These creations were often a critical part of adolescent identity formation in the 1930s.

One consequence of the Depression on film teens was the ways in which they were forced to be more autonomous than their 1920s counterparts. Teenage girls were compelled to solve their own problems without parental support or guidance. Yet they seemed, for the most part, none the worse for the wear. Instead they were represented as magical, competent creatures, endowed with unique talents and sensibilities. Andy and Marion Hardy were almost alone in having a wise, all-knowing parent where benevolent authority was situated firmly within the family patriarch. Had Mrs. Hardy been a single parent, however, Andy and Marion would have been forced into the savior mode very quickly. Judge Hardy had the capacity to solve not only his family's problems but those of his community. He was not self-righteous, and, unlike other screen parents, he was capable of giving other people advice that he, himself, could follow. By the end of the 1930s, it appeared that fathers were getting a little respect again. But that wouldn't last long.

It seems appropriate that the decade would end with Judy Garland's characterization of Dorothy in *The Wizard of Oz* (1939). Dorothy is the ultimate child-as-savior, and it was a role originally envisioned for Shirley Temple, who was actually closer to the true age of the character. Temple was not available, and Louis B. Mayer capitulated to producer Arthur Freed's choice of Garland. Garland was essentially a seventeen-year-old adolescent playing the part of a child. Once again, Garland captured the essence of the adolescent dilemma: getting the adults around her to take her seriously. Once in Oz, they do. She also mirrored the role that female adolescents played in Depression films. Dorothy's leading her ragged band to confront "The Great Wizard of Oz" becomes a powerful metaphor for the 1930s. The film revealed both the darker side of childhood and the brash optimism of youth. In many ways, these themes of fear and hope were a perfect way to end the decade.

NOTES

1. Robert S. Lynd and Helen Merrell Lynd, *Middletown in Transition* (New York: Harcourt, Brace and World, 1937), 140–141, 170, 278.

2. Paula Fass, *The Damned and the Beautiful: American Youth in the 1920s* (New York: Oxford, 1977), 211. Lynd and Lynd, 171. See also Grace Palladino, *Teenagers: An American History* (New York: Basic Books, 1996), 9–15 for a discussion of the disparity between middle-class youth and other groups in high schools of the 1930s.

3. Palladino, 3–16, 40; George Sanchez, *Becoming Mexican American: Ethnicity, Culture and Identity in Chicano Los Angeles, 1900–1945* (New York: Oxford, 1995), 257; Lynd and Lynd, 452.

4. Vicki Ruiz, "Star Struck: Acculturation, Adolescence and Mexican American Women 1920–1950," in *Small Worlds: Children and Adolescents in*

America 1850–1950, eds. Paula Petrik and Elliott West (Lawrence, KS: University of Kansas Press, 1994), 69, 71, 73, 80.

5. Lynd and Lynd, 170–171. John D'Emilio and Estelle Freedman, *Intimate Matters: A History of Sexuality in America* (New York: Harper and Row, 1988), 258.

6. Palladino, 9–10, 21–22.

7. Ruth Wheeler, *Janet Hardy in Hollywood* (Chicago: Goldsmith Publishers, 1935) and *Jane, Stewardess of the Airlines* (Chicago: Goldsmith Publishers, 1934); Clair Blank, *The Beverly Gray Mystery Series* (New York: Grosset and Dunlap, 1934–1941); Margaret Sutton, *Judy Bolton Mysteries* (New York: Grosset and Dunlap, 1932–1950). For a history of the genre, see Bobbie Ann Mason, *The Girl Sleuth: A Feminist Guide* (New York: The Feminist Press, 1975). Karen Plunkett-Powell offers a comprehensive overview of the Nancy Drew series in *The Nancy Drew Scrapbook* (New York: St. Martin's Press, 1993), as do Carole Kismaric and Marvin Heiferman in *The Mysterious Case of Nancy Drew and the Hardy Boys* (New York: Fireside, 1998). See also Kathryn Heisenfelt, *Deanna Durbin and the Adventure of Blue Valley* (Racine: Whitman Publishing, 1940), *Deanna Durbin and the Feather of Flame* (Racine: Whitman Publishing, 1941), *Bonita Granville and the Mystery of Star Island* (Racine: Whitman Publishing, 1942), and Roy Snell, *Jane Withers and the Phantom Violin* (Racine: Whitman Publishing, 1934).

8. Lynd and Lynd, 262.

9. Marion Purcell, "Those Fifteen Year Olds," *Scribners* 44 (August 1933): 111–114. Helen Maynard, "Private School Was Our Answer," *Parents* 14 (May 1939): 38.

10. Palladino, 45. Ezra Bowen, ed., *This Fabulous Century: 1930–1940* (New York: Time-Life Books, 1972), 228–238.

11. Grace Palladino, 55, and Marjorie Rosen, *Popcorn Venus* (New York: Avon Books, 1973), 194–197, tend to conflate the image. David Considine, *The Cinema of Adolescence* (Jefferson, NC: McFarland, 1985), 13–33.

12. See Lary May,"Making the American Consensus: The Narrative of Conversion and Subversion in World War II Films," in *The War in American Culture: Society and Consciousness during World War II,* eds., Lewis Ehrenberg and Susan E. Hirsch (Chicago: University of Chicago Press, 1996), 71–104.

13. Rosen, 196. Dick Moore, *Twinkle Little Star but Don't Have Sex or Take the Car: Child Stars and Hollywood* (New York: Harper and Row, 1984), ix.

14. Richard Griffith and Arthur Mayer, *The Movies* (New York: Simon and Schuster, 1970), 296–297.

15. Lewis Jacobs, *The Rise of the American Film* (New York: Columbia University Press, 1948), 20.

16. Kathy Merlock Jackson, *Images of Children in American Film* (Metuchen, NJ: Scarecrow Press, 1986), 56. Arthur Knight, *The Liveliest Art* (New York: Macmillan, 1957); Andrew Bergman, *We're in the Money: Depression America and Its Films* (New York: Harper Colophon Books, 1972). Richard Griffith, *The Talkies* (New York: Dover Publications, 1971), 224.

17. Jackie Stacey, *Star Gazing: Hollywood Cinema and Female Spectatorship* (London: Routledge, 1994), 90–104.

18. Stacey, 106, 91.

19. For a discussion of the studio system, see Leo Rosten, *Hollywood: The Movie Colony, The Movie Makers* (New York: Harcourt Brace, 1941); Hortense Powdermaker, *Hollywood: The Dream Factory* (Boston: Little Brown & Co., 1950); Norman Zierold, *The Moguls* (New York: Avon Books, 1969); Philip French, *The Movie Moguls* (London: Weidenfeld and Nicolson, 1969); Alexander Walker, *Stardom: The Hollywood Phenomenon* (London: Michael Joseph Ltd., 1970), 240; Edgar Morin, *The Stars* (New York, Grove Press, 1960), 134.

20. Hedda Hopper, *The Whole Truth and Nothing But* (New York: Pyramid Books, 1963), 101.

21. Jackson, 65.

22. Rosen, 194.

23. "Boos and Bouquets," *Photoplay* (January 1936): 9.

24. "Girl's School," *Variety,* 27 September 1938, 6.

25. Anthony Slide, "A Tribute to Deanna Durbin," Academy of Motion Picture Arts and Sciences Program, 9 December 1978.

26. Her filmography includes: *Three Smart Girls* (1937), *100 Men and a Girl* (1937), *Mad about Music* (1938), *That Certain Age* (1938), *Three Smart Girls Grow Up* (1939), *First Love* (1939), *It's a Date* (1939), *Spring Parade* (1940), *Nice Girl?* (1941), *It Started with Eve* (1941), *The Amazing Mrs. Halliday* (1942), *Hers to Hold* (1943), *His Butler's Sister* (1943), *Christmas Holiday* (1944), *Can't Help Singing* (1945), *Lady on a Train* (1945), *Because of Him* (1946), *I'll Be Yours* (1946), *Something in the Wind* (1947), *Up in Central Park* (1948) and *For the Love of Mary* (1948).

27. For biographical sketches of Durbin, see Norman Zierold, *The Child Stars* (New York: Coward McCann, 1965); Gene Ringgold, "Deanna Durbin," *Screen Facts* 5 (1963): 3–22; "Notes on a Songbird," undated and unsourced, clipping files of the Academy of Motion Picture Arts and Sciences (AMPAS).

28. Kyle Crichton, "Nice and Young," *Colliers* 101 (21 May 1938): 19.

29. L. May, 72–79. I would like to acknowledge Mike Willard for pointing out this connection to me.

30. See Charles Eckert, "Shirley Temple and the House of Rockefeller," *Jump Cut* 2 (July/August 1974): 17–20. Eckert positions Temple's early films within the competing political argument over Depression relief programs. Temple's films emphasize the healing power of love, but it is a love precipitated by need. "Shirley turns like a lodestone toward the flintiest characters in her films—the wizened wealthy, the defensive unloved, figures of cold authority. . . . She assaults, penetrates and opens them, making it possible for them to give of themselves" (19). *100 Men's* Mr. Frost is not capable of redemption through love, whereas the industrialist in Durbin's film It Started with Eve is.

31. May, 72.

32. "End of the Rainbow," *Time,* 4 July 1969: 64; Judy Garland Clipping File, Academy of Motion Picture Arts and Sciences.

33. "End of the Rainbow," 19. For an account of her life, see Christopher Finch, *Rainbow: The Stormy Life of Judy Garland* (New York: Ballantine Books, 1975); Anne Edwards, *Judy Garland: A Biography* (New York: Pocket Books, 1975). For accounts of gay worship, see Richard Dyer, *Heavenly Bodies: Film Stars and Society* (New York: St. Martin's Press, 1987), and Janet Stai-

ger, *Interpreting Films: Studies in the Historical Reception of American Cinema* (Princeton, NJ: Princeton University Press, 1992).

34. L. May, 81; The term comes from Andrew Berman, *We're in the Money: Depression America and Its Films* (New York: Harper Colophon, 1972), 119.

35. Jane Feuer, *The Hollywood Musical* (London: Macmillan, 1982); Susan Hayward, *Key Concepts in Cinema Studies* (London: Routledge, 1996), 241; Richard Dyer, "Entertainment and Utopia," *Movie* 24 (1977), 3.

36. See Eckert, 201.

37. "You're Only Young Once," *New York Times*, 3 January 1938, 16. After seeing the first Hardy film, Louis B. Mayer reportedly said to the writers, "Don't make them any better."

38. Jeanine Basinger, *A Woman's View: How Hollywood Spoke to Women 1930–1960* (New York: Alfred A. Knopf, 1993), 4–5.

39. "Boos and Bouquets," *Photoplay*, May 1937, 110.

40. See "A Penny for Your Thoughts," *The American Girl* (October 1934): 40; (February 1934): 42. Helen G. Doss, "A Spring Wardrobe for You," *The American Girl* (March 1941): 11; Helen G. Doss, "Making the Most of Your Looks," *The American Girl* (April 1941): 18; Helen G. Doss, "Salads for the Stars," *The American Girl* (July 1943): 15; Helen G. Doss, "Favorite Vegetable Recipes of the Teen Age Stars," *The American Girl* (June 1943): 14.

41. Martin Levin, ed., *Hollywood and the Great Fan Magazines* (New York: Castle Books, 1970), 91, 119, 93.

42. See *Deanna's Diary* (1941), 29; Doris Diggle, "Our Gift," *Deanna's Diary* (1940), 10.

43. Stacey, 176–223; Hedda Hopper Collection, Academy of Motion Picture Arts and Sciences, "Judy Garland File #2."

4

The Bachelor and the Bobby-Soxer

A common technique among filmmakers during World War II was the use of authoritative overhead narrators and other cues that guided the audience to "think correctly" about the action. To further the action, directors often moved the camera inside the frame "to display like a microscope the real truth occurring beneath surface events." Although this technique was most often saved for war dramas, it was sometimes used in comedies as well. Such was the case with the 1944 film *Janie*. The narrator introduces us first to Hortonville, "an average American city, a homey little town, like yours or mine, calm, quiet, where nothing much seems to happen." The microscopic camera then zooms in on the alien species, "Everybody's sweetheart, Janie," and her haunts, "her school, the drugstore, where she buys her malts, magazines and breaks a heart on the average of twice a week . . . the beauty parlor, where she gets her permanent and caused two riots, and this is her home, one of Hortonville's finest." Although the aim of this camera technique in war dramas was "to infuse the environment with symbols of unity and authority," particularly religious and patriotic symbolism, Janie, the adolescent girl, actually works as a destabilizing image in this context. This young girl it seems has come from another planet to wreak havoc with the lives of her elders, particularly her dad. Compared to Janie, the war seems at worst a temporary inconvenience.[1]

The depiction of adolescent girls in the 1940s focused on the emergence of teens as a separate subculture with their own language, mannerisms, concerns, style and milieu. Certainly, this trend had to do with the increased market strength of teenagers because of the war. Just as the flapper in the 1920s, the marker of generational change in the 1940s was a teenage girl, the bobby-soxer. Although much of bobby-soxer culture had its origins in the 1930s, the lifestyle did not find its way to the screen until the early 1940s. The impact of war was negligible on these screen bobby-soxers, who seemed more concerned with what to wear or how to date soldiers than contributing to the war effort. In most cases, the war simply served as a backdrop for the antics of juvenile heroines.

The fear of female adolescent sexuality that had emerged in the 1920s reappeared in the1940s, but this time the dominant vehicle of films depicting this fear was the comedy, not the delinquent films. Even nostalgic representations of teenage girls in another time simply repackaged the bobby-soxer, as in *Adventure in Baltimore* (1948) and *Margie* (1946). Screen mothers were depicted as mediators, forced to translate their daughters' behaviors to uncomprehending, hapless fathers. Yet screen teens were almost blissfully naive, even though fathers might suspect the worst. Movies continued to depict very formal patterns of dating and courtship marked by evening clothes, corsages, high school dances and chaste good night kisses. The bobby-soxer was silly and self-absorbed, seemingly unaware of the national crisis. Although she stands in sharp contrast to the patriotic, able and competent woman increasingly being portrayed in "women's films" of the period, there was a subversiveness about this teen symbol. The screen bobby-soxer seemed intent not only on making her father miserable but on carving out her own distinct cultural niche.[2] This chapter explores the historical conditions of female adolescence in the 1940s as well as the cultural trope of the bobby-soxer. It ends with a discussion of what this representation meant to girls themselves.

MATERIAL CONDITIONS OF ADOLESCENCE

During World War II, adolescents remained one of the few segments of the population left virtually intact. Adult males were drafted, and adult women were absorbed into the work force. Teenage boys were drafted, too, and many underage boys signed up as well. Teenagers, especially girls, began to have an increased market viability. Before the 1940s, the film industry had catered primarily to female, adult audiences. This trend began to change in the 1940s as filmmakers recognized the market power of teens. Many adolescents began to take part-time jobs, and some seemed to profit from the war. In 1943, the head of the U.S. Children's Bureau stated that the increase of adolescent workers was nearly as great as the increase of women thirty-five and over. From 1940 to 1943, the percentage of adolescents in the labor force rose 300 percent. From slightly less than one million in 1940, there were three million adolescents between the ages of fourteen and seventeen employed by 1943. Adolescent girls were in demand as babysitters for women in the war industries. By 1948 the *Saturday Evening Post* would report that babysitting had become "a craft dominated by a militant minority of high school girls extracting at least $750 million a year."[3]

One contemporary observer noted:

Most of the teenagers work at odd jobs after school hours in war factories, soda fountains, department stores, etc., and hundreds of thousands of them have left school entirely in order to work full time. This means that . . . they now have more money to spend than they had before; and they can indulge themselves by seeing more movies, flocking to dance halls to hear expensive, "name" bands, and collecting records for private jive sessions.[4]

Adolescents thus emerged as a rich monetary source for advertisers and merchandisers. By 1941, this new market audience had been dubbed "teenagers . . . a commercial cross between authentic high school students and adult projections of what they should be: fun-loving, wholesome, high school conformists whose main goal in life was to be part of the crowd." Manufacturers of junior fashions and cosmetics geared especially to adolescent girls flourished, and by 1946, record companies were selling ten times as many records as they had in 1936.[5]

The most identifiable icon of this new teen market was an adolescent girl, a bobby-soxer. One contemporary observer described the bobby-soxer:

Her hair is stringy, her saddle oxfords are dirty, her Sloppy Joe sweater and blue jeans are almost a uniform. She wears too much lipstick, she speaks a language which few adults can hope to interpret, and the crooning of The Voice [Frank Sinatra] or the jumpy rhythms of her favorite dance band can send her into ecstacy which only the initiated may share. The jive jittery miss is one of the most discussed personalities of modern America. Thousands of words have been written criticizing her zany antics, *The March of Time* has devoted an issue to her, department stores have installed whole departments to woo her vagrant taste in clothes, movies and radio scripts have been built around her , magazines have been published to curry her favor, and sociologists have acquired lines and gray hair conducting investigations to try to discover the reasons for her curious behavior.[6]

The popular press was full of articles that perpetuated the image of the carefree adolescent girl living in an insular world. An article in *Life* on the eve of World War II rhapsodized about the "jolly world of the sub-deb" in suburban Detroit:

They run in noisy, cohesive gangs. They love open houses where there are plenty of records, cigarets, and "cokes." They never stay home on vacation nights. Their taste in male companionship runs less to steadfast devotion than to multiplicity of dates and quick turnover. The world at large means nothing to any of them;

the microcosm of their gang is everything . . . They speak a curious lingo of their own, adore chocolate milkshakes, and swing music, and wear moccasins everywhere.[7]

The term "subdeb" itself is worthy of note. The class distinctions are clear, subdebs are a preliminary to the role of the debutante, a girl making her formal entrance into society, but subdebs were not upper-class girls before their formal debuts. Though the word connotes privilege, it also has more than solely gender implications because the purpose of the debut is to make a good match. In 1941, *Life* defined subdeb as "any socially uninitiated, but acceptable maiden of fifteen to eighteen, who gallivants around town with the right young people. She may or may not have expectations of a debut, generally though she has joined a specific junior assembly or club at the approach of adolescence." In suburban Detroit there were two major social sororities, and the editors noted, "Subdebs are made or broken at the age of twelve. . . . Many a mother whose daughter has reached thirteen without making either [sorority] abandons all hope for her child's future."[8] The social pressure faced by adolescent girls is chilling and a stark reminder that baby boomers were certainly not the first to put an inordinate amount of pressure on their children.

The war seemingly did little to change the world of the subdeb. In 1944, *Ladies Home Journal* profiled their own subdeb, Robin Roberts of Nyack, New York. Robin was a yearbook editor; a basketball, baseball, hockey and tennis star; and a budding thespian. Although the editors painted an idyllic picture of middle-class life, it also found some disturbing trends. About half the girls polled between the ages of sixteen and eighteen smoked. In fact, Robin had been smoking since she was fifteen and was even thrown out of summer camp because she was caught. Moreover, the majority of girls had been drinking before the legal age. "Robin herself came home at least three times the past year with liquor on her breath and explained it by telling her mother 'she shared a glass of beer with one of the boys.' " When she was grounded for staying out all night, Robin sneaked out anyway to attend the Senior Prom. A typical date might consist of, "an evening get together at someone's home; a group ferry ride across the Hudson . . . ; an early movie; or as a special big date, a drive to a wayside inn . . . for "pizza pie," a succulent delicacy described by Robin as a "wonderfully drooly concoction." The evening might end with a drive through the wooded section of South Mountain." Her "uniform" consisted of jeans rolled to the knee and an old oversized shirt, although she owned "eighteen sweaters, nine plaid skirts, only four dresses," and eschewed all makeup but lipstick. Robin hated cooking (home economics was her worst subject), and she was hoping to marry a man who could cook. The article ends with a discussion of Robin's college plans, which included "a large Midwestern University, where she would like to study for the stage, to write short stories, or to be a foreign correspondent, depending on what she has been doing and thinking ten minutes before." Robin's concluding comments seem exemplary of the general attitude of media bobby-soxers toward the war, "If it weren't for the war and maybe a little intolerance, I don't think there would be anything wrong with the world!"[9]

Life echoed these sentiments in a 1944 photo essay, when it reported that "some 6,000,000 U.S. teenage girls live in a world all their own—a lovely, enthusiastic, funny and blissful society almost untouched by war." This issue devoted nine pages to girls ages fifteen to seventeen in Webster Grove, Missouri. Rolled down bobby socks were "in," as was wearing men's clothing, shetland wool sweaters, identification bracelets. Also "in" were Friday night "hen" parties, listening to records at Lemke's Record Store and doing homework with the radio "full blast." Tight sweaters were "strictly taboo," as was trying to act "sophisticated," which was reported as being the highest offense among teens ("A 'Sandwich Girl,' who puts herself in the midst of a crowd of boys, is considered a real crumb.") The only concession that these bobby-soxers made to the war was making their beds and doing more housework than they used to "when maids were easy to get."[10]

Many teens themselves, however, were offended by the carefree image perpetuated by the media. *Scholastic* magazine got so many letters from teens outraged at the *Life* article that they ran letters in two issues. One teen wrote, "Certainly, *my* life is far from the ecstasy of carefree existence which *Life* magazine would have me believe." Another girl responded:

Yes, it is a world all our own—a world of uncertainty, a world that has taken brothers, neighbors, and friends . . . some not to come back. Would you call that "lovely and gay?" "Enthusiastic?" Yes, we wanted to do our part in the war effort and we did as much as we were permitted. We accepted responsibility. Just ask our families and employers. "Funny and blissful?" It was funny to be at that age and have to knuckle down to overtime work. But hardly blissful. We teenagers have learned about war through experience. Our dreams, our plans, our hearts cannot help but be battle scarred.

Some teens were cynical. "No other generation has responded to the responsibility thrust upon our shoulders by our parents' war. We were left to grow up by ourselves and use our own resources." Another girl asserted, "For hours we discuss minority group problems, politics and the various aspects of peace and war." Finally, several teens questioned the representations of youth in general. Typical was this letter: "Magazine editors select the most fantastic pictures available and build a good story around them. Wouldn't actual pictures make a better story?"[11]

Grace Palladino has called the *pachucos* and *pachquitas,* the sons and daughters of some Mexican immigrants in Los Angeles, "the would be bobby-soxers of a less prosperous community." These young men and women developed their own distinctive style of dress, hair, and even their own dialect, called Calo. They appeared suspended between two cultures. Although *pachquitas* were called "little tornados of sexual stimuli," because of their suggestive dress and mannerisms, many girls went out of their way to affirm their allegiance to traditional values and to make it clear that they were still "nice girls." As one *pachquita* explained, "Mexican girls are full of fun, they laugh and joke with boys, but there is nothing bad between them. . . . We ride around and sing and laugh. . . . So we get some beer and have a lot of fun dancing and talking and singing and stuff. Americans do that too."[12]

Even in the internment camps, Japanese American youth seemingly embraced the values of the parent culture. Jeanne Wakatsuki Houston describes the high school yearbook in Manzanar:

In its pages, you see school kids with arm loads of books wearing cardigan sweaters and walking past rows of tar-papered shacks. You see chubby girl yell leaders, pompons flying as they leap with glee. You read about the school play—Growing Pains—the story of a typical American home. Seniors' pictures have the names of the high schools they would have graduated from.

After the war, Houston talks about her best friend in junior high, Radine, a white girl. They went to school in a diverse working-class neighborhood that included Asians, Blacks, Mexicans and migrants from the South. In high school, however, Houston's and Radine's paths diverged as Radine was asked to join sororities and became a "song girl," a group that excluded ethnic teens. Houston became the first Asian American majorette at her high school, but only after the band teacher got special board approval. Houston describes what she terms "a double impulse," the urge to disappear and the desire to be acceptable, which crystallized over her feelings about Radine:

What demoralized me was watching Radine's success. We had shared everything, including all the values I'd learned from the world I wanted into, not only standards of achievement, but ideas about how a girl should look and dress and talk and act, and ideas of male beauty—which is why so many of the boys I liked were Caucasian. . . . What I wanted was the kind of acceptance that seemed to come so easily to Radine. . . . She [represents] something I can never be, some possibility in my life that can never be fulfilled.[13]

Alice Barr Grayson, the pen name for Jean Grossman, a child psychologist who wrote an advice column for *Calling All Girls,* received many letters from adolescent girls decrying their "otherness." One Chinese American girl wrote complaining about racism directed toward her.

She was constantly called a "dirty Jap" by adults in her neighborhood. She stifled her desire to "tell them off" because"it would be rude of me to do so." A sixteen-year-old African American girl wrote of another form of racism. Although her white classmates were "very kind," she questioned their motives, fearing "they are doing this to keep friendly bases [sic] with me, so I can continue helping them with algebra and physics or whether they really want to be friends with me." Race wasn't the only basis of discrimination; as one girl wrote, "I am Jewish and very proud of it, but I'm left out of everything. I know things like this are not right, but I don't see much I can do about it." Another girl complained that she did not fit in with her "hepcat" friends, preferring classical music instead. She gave a party for her classmates and no one attended. She asked Grayson, "Do you think I ought to like jive instead?"[14] The process of identity formation was rife with peril for many adolescent girls not only as they tried to embrace norms of traditional femininity established by the parent culture but also as they struggled to conform to their peers.

Letters from all over the country underscored the need of adolescents to look and act like their peers. They worried about their looks, their clothes, their bodies. "Every girl my age wears lipstick and I want to too!" wrote one fifteen-year-old. Another protested, "My mother thinks I shouldn't even know a boy, but you know it's natural for a girl to have a boyfriend." Girls also grappled with their need for independence and autonomy. "I am twelve and I am still treated like a baby." One girl complained, "My parents are too strick [sic] with me!" As one reviewer noted:

Many of the girls who wrote these letters are the girls in bobby socks and sweaters, calling themselves "hepcats," swooning over Frank Sinatra, smearing themselves with lipstick and nail polish, and driving their mothers frantic.

The letters of Grayson's readers, however, revealed insecurity and uncertainty as these adolescents searched for their own identities and tried to get guidance.[15]

Many teenage girls wanted advice on sex. Adolescents often began dating when they were thirteen or fourteen, and going steady was increasingly accepted. Girls complained of the discrepancy between "what we're told to do," and "what the crowd really does." Adolescent social life was increasingly away from adult supervision. "Blanket parties," where adolescents brought blankets, portable radios and beer to remote rural areas, were a common leisure activity. Although many teens had more freedom than ever before, they were also admonished not to use that freedom.[16]

Although hardly representing a universal reality for teenage girls, bobby-soxers were significant because they were a potent signifier of generational and economic change in the 1940s, a new market voice and a highly targeted group. The signifier of this change was adolescent girls, formerly a powerless group. They now had social visibility and economic power, and they commanded the attention of adults. This trend would continue, and by the 1950s, youth culture would be firmly entrenched.

FILM REPRESENTATIONS OF ADOLESCENCE

By the 1940s, screen adolescents were usually represented as a distinct cultural group. They dressed alike and talked alike—all in opposition to their elders. There was a clear line of demarcation between adolescents and adults. Certainly, the increased market strength of teens made Hollywood sit up and take notice. The population of fourteen to seventeen year olds had increased in 1940s, 80 percent of the teen population was in high school. This distinct market segment had specific consumption preferences. As Grace Palladino notes, "It took almost no effort at all to persuade high school students to see themselves as a class apart, as 'teenagers,' according to popular standards, with their own age related tastes, styles and social concerns."[17] Teens began to see Hollywood's version of their needs and concerns projected back to them in two different ways. Either adolescent girls were represented as symbols of domesticity and bulwarks of the homefront, or they were portrayed as delinquents or bobby-soxers who, while subverting traditional notions of domesticity, always did so with the ultimate goal of marriage.

Since You Went Away (1944) was one of the most important films to document life on the homefront and is a good example of the ways in which girls were used as symbols of domesticity. Its opening title declares that "this is the story of that unconquerable fortress, the American home." At its center are the waiting women, a mother and her two adolescent daughters. With the husband gone to war, family finances are tight. The youngest daughter, Brig (Shirley Temple), suggests that they bring in a boarder. Jane, the older sister (Jennifer Jones), calls the idea "Communist," until she realizes that the boarder might be a young male. Then she decides the idea might be "patriotic." For all their financial worries, the Hilton's home is a model of upper-middle-class refinement and luxury, complete with the faithful black maid, Vedelia (Hattie McDaniel). She is so loyal that she continues to work for the Hiltons despite a pay cut and the promise of higher salaries in the war industries.

The impotence of adolescent girls in the face of the crisis is clearly delineated. Girls were allowed a symbolic role at best, to keep the home fires burning. Their frustration at not being able to do more for the war effort because of their age and gender is illustrated through both the characters of Brig and Jane. Temple, who has not yet adopted her bobby-soxer persona, gives an enduring portrayal of an honest, intelligent and spirited young teen. Jane is no bobby-soxer either. She is a dreamy romantic, suffering all the pangs of first love. Jane is also too young to be a WAC or a WAVE, or a nurse, and finally convinces her mother to let her work as a nurse's aide before going off to college. Jane matures through the film into a lovely young woman, primarily through her relationship with a young soldier, Bill. The film follows their doomed wartime romance to its conclusion as Bill is killed at Salerno. Unlike many of these screen counterparts, the war has a clear impact on these adolescents. The film depicts their transformation into young women of strength, courage and hope, and it is a glowing testament to the contribution of women to the homefront.

Yet their greatest contribution is clearly to maintain the home. Tim Hilton's study is left exactly as he left it, the imprint of his body remains in his easy chair. The film dramatizes what Lary May terms "patriotic domesticity," and offers a wealth of domestic detail. For instance, although these women are part of the work force, there is a clear expectation that what they are doing is only temporary. They will happily be displaced when the war is over. The two daughters, shaped by the exigencies of the war, will also be better wives for it. Early in the film, Jane is a careless teen. Vedalia scolds her, "If you don't learn to pick up your clothes you'll never have a husband." When Jane becomes interested in Bill, she suddenly becomes interested in her homemaking skills, is neat and efficient and even asks her mother to give her cooking lessons.[18]

Women have tremendous powers of healing as well. Jane helps Bill find his self-esteem and die a hero's death through her adoration, and she heals a shell-shocked sailor into re-enlisting. It would seem that adolescent girls are still capable of magic.

The theme is underscored in Jane Powell's first feature film, *Song of the Open Road* (1944). Powell plays a young film singing star. Tired of her fame, she steals away from the cameras to join a group of real teens who bicycle from youth hostel to youth hostel picking fruits and vegetables and doing other farm chores to help in the war effort. With the "Hey, kids, let's put on a show!" theme reprised, Jane must use her stardom to come to the aid of a rancher. In this film, youth is enlisted in America's fight to win the war.

Teenage girls could remind Americans of the values for which they were fighting by evoking a portrait of a vanished America far from the realities of the war. In *Meet Me in St. Louis* (1944), Judy Garland as Esther Smith signifies a simpler time. Her character underscores the notion that with faith and endurance, the world will be right again. Yet, while this film clearly celebrates the bourgeois family at the turn of the century, it also reveals not only the darker side of family life but also the darker forces of childhood. The Smith family idyllic home life in St. Louis on the eve of the World's Fair is shattered by the father's announcement of his transfer to New York. Mr. Smith is a kind of benevolent dictator, bumbling and autocratic. He is easily manipulated by his all-knowing wife and children and generally kept out of the loop on the activities of his family. Esther is much like Brig and Jane in *Since You Went Away* in her feelings of being powerless to control her life. Not only is she impotent to do anything about the impending move, Esther also lacks the ability to control the affections of the "boy next door." Yet she struggles to be the dutiful daughter subverting her feelings of anger and frustration to the needs of the family.

Five-year-old Tootie, played by Margaret O'Brien, however, is given outlet for her anger. She is fearful, morbid and fascinated with violence. She pretends that her dolls have fatal illnesses and then plans their elaborate funerals and burials. One scene chillingly re-enacts the terrors of childhood, as Tootie and her sister prepare for Halloween. It is a night of scary looking children in masks and grotesque costumes, talking of murdering and torturing their neighbors. In order to show her bravery, Tootie volunteers to throw flour at the face of the most feared neighbor, an act that signifies killing him. Her success earns her the approbation of the other children gathered around a huge bonfire as they declare her "the horriblest of us all." Christmas Eve, the night before the move to New York, Esther tries to comfort Tootie with the song "Have Yourself a Merry Little Christmas," the cheerful lyrics in sharp contrast to the melancholy melody of the song. Tootie then graphically acts out her anger toward her father as she runs outside and smashes the snow people family that her family had lovingly created earlier in the day. As Mr. Smith watches from his window, he has an epiphany about the importance of putting home and family above his career, and he decides the family will stay in St. Louis. The film's ending at the 1904 World's Fair reaffirms the commitment to community and traditional values.

The American Girl offered a review of *Meet Me in St. Louis* for its readers. Although they generally liked the film, Tootie was too dark a character for the reviewer. "Unfortunately Margaret's intensity in portraying childish fears and anger gets out of hand, and creates an uncomfortable sense of hysteria." In many ways, Tootie is the most realistic character in her projection of fear and sadness, feelings probably shared by many children in wartime.[19]

The dislocation caused by the war served as a catalyst for the exploration of delinquency once again by filmmakers. Hollywood addressed this problem in two 1944 films, *Youth Runs Wild* and *Are These Our Parents? Youth Runs Wild* was "inspired" by a *Look* magazine story, "Are These Our Children?," an exposé of the problems of unsupervised wartime youth. Charles W. Koerner, vice-president in charge of production for RKO, was so excited by the story, he immediately called the editor and pledged "his cooperation in translating the American youth problem and its solution into what will undoubtedly be one of the year's most important motion pictures." Koerner imported Ruth Clifton, the founder of the Moline, Illinois Plan for Youth Guidance to act as technical advisor for the film.[20]

The resultant film diverges from the article on which it is based. The film opens with a montage of headlines about delinquency and youth superimposed over newsreel-like shots of adolescents getting into trouble. The shot then focuses on a sign, "Drive Slowly, We Love Our Children," as a speeding car careens wildly around the corner and knocks the sign over. This less-than-subtle visual hint suggests that children's welfare is really of little concern to the citizens of this defense town. The muddled plot centers on two sixteen-year-old teenagers, Frankie and Sara, whose parents are war workers. Sara's parents have a penchant for drinking and card playing in their leisure time, forcing Sara to parent her younger siblings. Sara is a sweet, responsible girl, nothing like her neglectful, hard drinking parents. Frankie falls in with the wrong crowd in his desire to earn some money; Sara is thrown out of her house after failing to come home on time. She is forced to get a job at "Rocky's Nightclub," and as a distraught Frankie puts it, "You know what that means."

Frankie's brother-in-law, Dan, a wounded soldier functioning as the narrator and conscience of the film, offers Sara a room and a "real job," but she has become hardened. "It's too late, I've grown up, I'm not a kid anymore." Yet underneath she is still a nice girl. She tries to break up with Frankie because she is afraid that she is not good enough for him anymore. Then Frankie gets into trouble and is sent before the juvenile court, where a wise judge offers his analysis of the problem: "It's not their fault. Kids may be guilty of crime, but its rarely their own fault. Neglectful parents, modern life, and the breaking up of the home. They've got so many reasons for trouble."

Frankie is sent to a youth forestry camp, and Sara quits her job at the roadhouse to help Frankie's sister run a day-care center for the children of war workers. Although Sara is now involved in useful work, she complains to Dan that she still feels as if she does not belong.

The frustration of young women and their inability to actively contribute to the war effort is again evident. Dan chides Sara for growing up too fast and launches into a polemic about the need to "help youth help itself by encouraging juvenile citizens instead of delinquents." The music swells and he continues, "The point is there's a girl like you in Moline, Illinois, named Ruth Clifton. A year ago Moline was having a problem getting worse every day. Ruth had an idea for a recreation center." Documentary footage reveals images of the youth of Moline involved in wholesome activities as Clifton narrates. Then Dan concludes, "Because after all, girls and boys are what we're fighting for." Youth must be enlisted in the American effort to win the war.

However, as Palladino points out, youth were "supposed to find satisfaction in superficial tasks that mimicked adult reality." Moreover, although the war certainly opened up new opportunities for teens, especially young men in the service and in defense jobs, the National Youth Administration began phasing out training programs for girls younger than eighteen. Although older teens did find work in clerical positions and factory jobs, younger adolescents really were at loose ends.[21]

Dan's speech inspires Sara. "Good-bye Dan," she says. "Where are you going?" he asks. "I've got places to go, people to see," she replies resolutely as she marches off in this ambiguous conclusion. Although this film blames parental neglect for the problems of their children and offers a half-hearted excuse because the parents of Frankie and Sara are war workers, it does not convince us that these parents would be any more responsible even if they were not working in defense plants. Nonetheless, the film is unique in its depiction of the effects of the war on youth and its plea for institutionalized leisure activities. In many towns, the funding for recreational facilities had been cut by local authorities in favor of funding for servicemen.

A cheaply made and poorly acted "B" film about female delinquency that recycled themes from the 1920s, *Are These Our Parents?* featured Noel Neill (later to gain fame as television's Lois Lane) as a spoiled, neglected teen. She is constantly getting into trouble by frequenting roadhouses, getting drunk and generally acting sophisticated in a desperate attempt to get her society mother's attention. At one point she cries to her mother, "Why don't you spank me, at least I'd know that you love me." She is accidentally implicated in the murder of a nightclub owner, but the film places the blame squarely on her mother for failing to be a better parent. As the opening credits warn, "The Gods visit the sins of the parents upon the children." The war might be counted as one of those sins. There is a sense that another front included a battle for the souls of American youth.

There was increased public attention on the issue of sexual delinquency and the war. A 1942 *Life* article described delinquent girls as those who leave home "to play harlot." The editors blamed the war for a 20 percent increase in delinquency among teenage girls. "When fathers go to war and mothers go to work, children seek companionship and amusement in pool rooms, poorly policed parks, and areas where crime breeds freely. War's sanction of violence and hatred make children feel it's smart to be immoral." Thus the juvenile justice system continued to enforce a rigid standard of sexual behavior for girls that was not applied to boys.[22]

Sexually promiscuous girls were known by a number of euphemisms such as "amateur girls," "Khaki-wackies," "victory girls," and "good-time Charlottes." One moralist complained, "The old time prostitute in a house or a formal prostitute in the street is sinking into second place. The new type is the young girl in her late teens and early twenties . . . who is determined to have one fling or better." In 1944 *Newsweek* announced that the "gravest home front tragedy of the war was the moral break-down among American girls." They reported that in New York City, the numbers of "victory girls or the bobby sox brigade" had swelled to such alarming proportions that police were forced to impose a curfew for girls under sixteen in Times Square:

Detectives had little trouble spotting the froussy victory girls who hung around the dance halls, bars, restrooms and bus terminals, side streets and rooming houses. But pinning delinquency on them was another matter. Some bobby-soxers—many are as young as thirteen—flashed social security cards and claimed they had war jobs. Others had fled cops by showing marriage licenses. In many cases the girls had married servicemen they barely knew.

One teenage girl told the *Newsweek* reporter, "I've only gone with three or four men a week since I've been here and I didn't take any money from any of them." The National Probation Association reported that the increase in delinquency for girls since the war began was 23 percent as compared with a 5 percent increase for boys.[23] On screen, however, this fear of female adolescent sexuality was subverted by making it a running gag in the comin-of-age comedies about bobby-soxers that permeated the 1940s, other than a social problem as it was in the 1920s.

A CULTURAL TROPE

If the apogee of representations of female adolescence in film during the war was *Since You Went Away,* then the nadir was *Janie* (1944). Brig and Jane Hilton's sacrifice and selflessness stand in sharp contrast to the frivolous Janie Conway. For Janie, the war simply serves as a backdrop for her dating life. She stands, however, as perhaps the most representative trope of adolescence in the 1940s, the bobby-soxer. A subversive force to her frustrated father, who is unequipped to deal with her, the bobby-soxer, his alien daughter, is a young woman so coddled, so protected, that the war hardly makes a dent in her existence. The father-daughter tension that permeates *Janie* and other bobby-soxer films may be attributed to what William Tuttle calls "the erosion of male authority" during the war years. Due to the physical absence of men, mothers were left to represent security and continuity.[24] The middle-class families of this and later bobby-soxer films are virtually interchangeable: the hapless father; the patient, facilitator mother; the maid; and the bratty younger or older sibling—all set against a backdrop of chintz and respectability. The dominant vehicle of these adolescent stories was comedy. Although there were real concerns about adolescents, filmmakers decided that it was better to laugh at the foibles of girls than to dramatize them. In doing so, they trivialized them as well.

Janie turns on adolescent fads and fashions. Although their slang is already unintelligible to their elders, Janie and her friends even invent their own language so that their parents won't understand. Her father is played by Edward Arnold, who has gone from playing heartless but competent industrialists in the 1930s to unfortunate fathers in the 1940s. He seems impotent to deal with his adolescent daughter, choosing instead to wring his hands and complain about the "horrible music" of Janie and her "platterbug friends." As David Considine points out:

To her hapless father, Janie appears as a foreigner. While his wife does her best to cope with any situation, he can only denounce, "the way the children of today dance and the records they play." Unable to really communicate, he looks upon his daughter as an alien; she speaks differently, acts differently, and seems to live in a world with customs and codes totally unknown to him. This, Hollywood claimed, was the typical American home.[25]

The bobby-soxer was an important cultural icon and the dominant trope of privileged, white, teenage life. As with the flapper of the 1920s, adolescent girls represented generational change in the 1940s. As Palladino comments, "Her carefree, upper class style set an alternate new standard for teenagers nationally, who envied their freedom, their casual approach to the future, their cars, their free spending ways, their fun and good times."[26]

The film *Janie* lampoons the public discourse on bobby-soxers as carefree beings who "lived in a jolly world of their own." *Life* magazine was a critical component of this construct, and in *Janie* a *Life* photographer is on hand when Janie and her friends hold a "Blanket Party" at the beach, thus satirizing a staple of the magazine, "Life goes to a party." *Life* chronicled the haunts, habitats, and customs of teens in an effort to explain these strange creatures to their readership. Janie, getting kissed by her boyfriend Scooper, ends up the unwitting and unwilling cover girl.

Janie offers a distinctively adolescent permutation of "patriotic domesticity." Thus flirting and looking good becomes a "patriotic act," another way to keep up morale. These messages were clearly perpetuated by numerous ad campaigns, such as Modess and Tangee Lipstick ("Yours to Serve"), during the war. After the military police are forced to break up a wild party full of soldiers at Janie's house, she offers a tearful plea to the commander, "Don't be too hard on them. It'll be something for them to look back on." The film ends with the departure of the army and the arrival of the marines as the overhead narrator intones, "And leaving the marines to Janie, we say goodbye to calm Hortonville, where nothing ever happens." There is a fine line between sexual delinquency and Janie, but she does not cross it. It's a delicate balancing act at best.

Janie also illustrates the fad-driven nature of adolescent girls' culture. Adherence to fads is both a marker of rebellion and the need to conform. This conformity means social protection and emotional reassurance among girls who share similar economic and emotional needs. Once again, as with the flappers of the 1920s, female adolescents have become signifiers of capitalist consumer culture. As Mica Nava points out, there are many contradictions inherent in consumerism. On the one hand their roles as consumers offered girls an area of authority and expertise and a sense of entitlement, on the other, capitalism has shaped gender roles, indoctrinated in girls a desire for commodities and exploited their labor. As Nava reports, "The buying of commodities and images can be understood both as a source of power and pleasure for women (it has indeed given them a sense of identity, purpose and creativity) and simultaneously as an instrument which secures their subordination."[27]

The ambivalence of film teens to this war probably reflected to some degree the ambivalence of teens in real life. On the one hand, many teens resented the war with its deprivations and shortages, the real sense of loss, and the need to abandon the protection of childhood. On the other hand, many teens, particularly girls, resented not being able to contribute more to the war effort. Even though teens raised millions in war bond drives, built scale models for the Navy, collected salvage, recycled and grew victory gardens, many believed that they could be doing more.[28]

By 1945, Shirley Temple was increasingly becoming one of the most ubiquitous bobby-soxers on screen. In 1942, she made *Miss Annie Rooney,* in which she gets her first screen kiss. She has begun to take on the accouterments of adolescence, with her jive talk sprinkled between quotes from Shakespeare. Her concession to the war was in the context of fashion as she remarks, "It's so difficult to get a proper gown what with the war and all." In 1943 she played the self-centered younger niece of Ginger Rogers in *I'll Be Seeing You*. When her mother chides her for her low neckline, Temple responds, "For goodness sakes mother, it's a morale builder." It is also a film that allowed Temple to stretch her emotional repertoire. Conjuring up the bratty Bonita Granville of the 1930s, Temple breaks up her aunt's romance by revealing that her aunt is an ex-convict to her serviceman boyfriend. The film climaxes with her hysterical confession to Rogers of her betrayal. There are malevolent forces under the surface of this bobby-soxer after all, but this was only temporary, as the glibness would return in her next screen role.

In the film *Kiss and Tell* (1945), based on the stage play by F. Hugh Herbert, the war hardly makes a dent in the lifestyle of fifteen-year-old Corliss Archer, and the soldiers stationed in her home town only add to her father's frustration level. Her patriotism is demonstrated by her kissing twenty-two servicemen at a charity bazaar. The film turns on Corliss's efforts to conceal not only her best friend Mildred's secret marriage to her brother, but Mildred's pregnancy as well. When the local gossip sees Corliss leaving the obstetrician's office with Mildred, rumors spread all over town that Corliss is pregnant and a soldier with whom she has been flirting is the father. Corliss is immediately suspect because of her flirtatious behavior and because she is outspoken and flip. Local gossips are mean spirited and judgmental, and small towns are sharply stratified into the old and the young. As in *Janie*, there appears real anxiety over the increased opportunity for social fraternization with soldiers, free of adult supervision. Although this anxiety is covert, encoded in comedic formulas, it is clear that adults were concerned with the morals of their girls.

One of the most endearing portrayals of adolescence was the 1945 film *Junior Miss*, based on the book by Sally Bensen and the radio character played by Temple. Thirteen-year-old Judy Graves (Peggy Ann Garner) is poised between childhood and womanhood, a melodramatic highly imaginative, meddlesome adolescent. Judy's family consists of her pretty, self- absorbed, bossy sister (Mona Freeman), her understanding mother and her harried father. It is fairly representative of adolescent girls' film families of the 1940s, which were firmly entrenched in the middle class. Judy has a best friend Fuffy, who lives in the apartment downstairs. Fuffy is overweight, perpetually hungry, bossy, sarcastic and loyal. She is a juvenile version of Eve Arden, the quintessential sidekick, offering trenchant commentary on the foibles of adults. She lampoons the silly clichés of grown-ups who remark on growth, "What do they expect us to do, get smaller?"

Both Fuffy and Judy are slaves to conformity and sport the standard bobby-soxer garb, bulky sweaters, pleated skirts, bobby socks, saddle shoes. Judy constantly compares life to her favorite movie plots. Her father says of her behavior, "No, it's not a fever, it's a double feature. Tonight she's Stella Dallas," reflecting just how important films continued to be in the dream lives of teens.

Mistaken intentions again abound in this film. When Judy sees her father talking intimately with his boss's daughter Ellen, she immediately concludes that they are having an affair, "Like Myrna Loy in that movie that she played a secretary." In order to foil their "romance," Judy engineers a meeting between Ellen and her uncle, who promptly fall in love and elope, thereby jeopardizing her father's job. Judy saves the day in the end, however, as her date for her first formal turns out to be the son of the client her father's law firm has been trying to sign. The themes of the 1930s and the 1940s are conflated, adolescent as matchmaker/good fairy versus adolescent as subversive/threat.

As in other films about bobby-soxers, the film questions the efficacy of communications between girls and their fathers, who constantly ascribe different meaning to each others' actions. Either the fathers suspect their daughters of illicit behavior or vice versa. Whereas fathers are perplexed, confused and worried, mothers are patient and understanding and serve as mediators between husbands and daughters. They are charged with translating the moods, concerns and habits of their off-spring to their spouses, underscoring how connected women are to the psychic life of their families and how much men are not.

A poignant scene establishes the essential dilemma of adolescence. It is Christmas morning and Judy has just received a coat from the children's department that no longer fits ("Oh dear," sighs her mother, "perhaps we should begin to shop in the Junior Miss Department.") and her first pair of high heels. Judy has also received a doll from her father's well-intentioned boss. She is insulted that someone would think she was young enough to still play with dolls. Yet, when she is alone under the Christmas tree, wearing the tight coat and her new heels over her bobby socks, Judy lovingly sits and cradles the doll, signifying not only how close to childhood she still is, but the ambivalence of adolescence itself.

Both the film's title and Mrs. Graves's reference to the Junior Miss Department point to another important aspect of this trope of adolescence—style. Fashion merchandisers soon realized that "teen identity could be packaged and sold in department stores." However, at the exact time that merchandisers were creating specialty markets for girls, many bobby-soxers were rejecting retail standards in favor of their own costumes. Barbara Hudson sees the clothing styles and choices of adolescent girls as a result of their conflicted social status. As Lisa Lewis points out, girls often challenge the discourse of femininity by adopting male styles. "In a sense girls make themselves into access signs . . . in an attempt to strike symbolic resonances that will facilitate an impression of control and subjectivity."[29]

There was a certain subversiveness in the style of the middle-class bobby-soxer. Her look was uniformly described as "sloppy." Her uniform of choice was oversized, long-tailed men's shirts, bulky sweaters, men's pajamas, rolled jeans or boys' slacks. This clothing did not have to be bought, it could simply be borrowed from fathers or brothers. There were even reports of girls being arrested for wearing loose shorts, and boys often jeered at girls for their dangling shirttails. *Life* underscored the appeal of the clothing to teenage girls:

[Girls] defend this costume on the grounds of its great comfort and practicality. . . . Mothers don't mind. . . . But teachers, fathers and boyfriends find it shockingly sloppy. This makes the custom exciting as well as comfortable, and keeps the girls firmly united against all protests.[30]

Although these style practices may seem superficial and far from the politics of resistance, the subversive elements are hardly surprising in light of the origins of bobby-sox culture in the jive culture of the 1930s. The jazz musicians' culture was often mired in drugs, alcohol and wild abandon. By the 1940s, swing culture had been homogenized and gentrified for teen consumption. The term jitterbug not only stood for a dance craze but was interchangeably used to refer to female fans of swing. As Angela McRobbie points out, "Dance is where girls are always found in subculture. It was their only entitlement." Certainly, this style was a form of cultural production and served as a way to publicize the subculture and create opportunities for cultural authority.[31]

Grace Palladino plays down the subversive nature of the bobby-soxer culture, choosing instead to focus on the continuity with the past. "Their wholesome image and respectful style spread the reassuring word that teenagers and adults shared the same basic values, even if they danced to wildly different beats." The trailer for *Janie* echoed this sentiment. "Janie is the girl her mother was." Yet, although filmic representations stressed that the fear was overblown or exaggerated, there were also clear indications that values had changed. The uncertainty fostered by both the Depression and World War II had an impact on the world of the bobby-soxer in both reel and real life.

There is a great deal of continuity between bobby-soxer portrayals both during the war years and after. This is reflected by the postwar film *The Bachelor and the Bobby-Soxer* (1947). Though by this time married and desperately trying to get away from this kind of role, Shirley Temple once again found herself playing a flighty teen. Temple is Susan, a privileged seventeen-year-old in love with love, who finds it in the unfortunate character of Cary Grant. Grant was an expert at playing the harried type, as he had in *Arsenic and Old Lace* and *Mr. Blandings Builds His Dream House*. Grant is forced to submit to this unwanted adoration by Susan's sister Margaret, who also happens to be a judge, in lieu of being caught with Susan in a compromising position. Margaret is an ambitious, capable career woman in a loveless, sexless relationship. Her psychiatrist uncle comments on his niece, whom he terms "a mountain of ice," to Grant, "She appears to be a very dominant woman, but her dominance is merely a retreat, a manifestation of the Oedipus complex." Grant awakens not only Susan's sexuality, but her sister's as well. Though Margaret's power is seen as a pose, Susan's power over this adult is real.

Susan speaks in unintelligible slang, is highly imaginative and also mercurial. She changes constantly, flitting from fad to fad, goal to goal, "depending on who lectured at school that week." Grant satirizes the cultural milieu of the bobby-soxer, by taking on the mannerisms, dress and slang of a "hepcat" in order to diminish Susan's affections. This seventeen-year-old has the capacity to wreak havoc on grown men, who seem powerless in her presence.

It would appear from many films about female adolescents that teenage girls were the bane of adult males' existence. If they were not the love objects, then they might have the misfortune to be the parents of these alien creatures. Such was the case in the 1948 film *Mickey*, starring Lois Butler. *Mickey* centered around the transformation of a tomboy into a young girl in love. Without feminine guidance, Mickey has not adopted the norms of femininity. When she finally falls in love, Mickey must struggle "to get Hank to see her as a girl," and to convince him that she now likes "that kind of mush."

By the late 1940s, film fathers became increasingly anxious about the real or imagined loss of their daughter's virginity. In *Mickey,* through a series of misunderstandings, the heroine finds her reputation ruined when she is mistakenly seen going into a bar. She is then socially ostracized by the rest of the townsfolk for something she did not even do. This rebounds on her father, who loses his job with the hospital for her supposed indiscretion, because small-town America is populated by self-righteous, judgmental and prudish citizens. Local gossips nearly ruin the lives of other film families as in *Youth Runs Wild, Adventure in Baltimore* and *Kiss and Tell*. In *Mickey,* however, the daughter both saves her father from the clutches of a scheming widow and makes an impassioned speech on his behalf at the school recital.

Although sexual norms among American teens clearly became even more permissive in the 1940s, there is no evidence that their screen counterparts were following suit. Screen teens seem almost blissfully ignorant of the finer points of sex, even though the adults suspect the worst. Instead, movies continue to depict very formal patterns of dating and courtship, marked by evening clothes, corsages, high school dances and chaste good night kisses. This preoccupation with the virtue of teenage girls represents a real fear about changing sexual values.

In *Father Was a Fullback* (1949), Fred MacMurray plays another hapless father concerned with his daughter's reputation. He is the coach of a losing football team at a large state university. To make his life worse, his oldest daughter Connie is shunned by boys because as she puts it, "I'm the lowest classification a girl could fall in. I'm chintzy." Betty Lynn offers a hilarious portrait as the distraught Connie, who suffers all the pains of adolescent angst and causes their cynical housekeeper to refer to her as "Ophelia." Connie laments, "I think like Madame Pompadour, feel like Lana Turner, and look like Connie Cooper."

Her bungling father decides to invent an imaginary boyfriend to bolster Connie's self-esteem. The scheme backfires when Connie learns of her dad's plan. "Her psyche will be scarred for the rest of her life," his ever-patient wife (Maureen O'Hara) explains to McMurray, but she also reassures him, "It's just adolescence dear, she'll live through it." It is not at all clear, however, that her father will. "Next time dear, couldn't we have a nice, quiet cocker spaniel?" he moans as he desperately tries to understand his daughter.

Convinced that she will be an old maid, Connie decides to be a writer. She begins research for an article she plans to write for a confession

magazine, "I Was a Fifteen Year Old Mother," by sending away for literature on childbirth. When her father comes across the literature, of
course he believes that she is pregnant, which is odd as her biggest problem up to this time has been getting a date. Connie is more successful as
a writer than a femme fatale, when she finally gets one of her articles
published, "I Was a Child Bubble Dancer" ("When my parents are asleep,
I sneak down to the Gaiety Theater . . . "). Although her father almost
loses his job because of her story (not because of his losing record), her
new found notoriety as an author finally brings her the popularity she
desires. But in the "adolescent as savior" mode, Connie saves her father's
job when the top quarterback in the state decides to come to the university to be near Connie. Just as her father is breathing a sigh of relief in
the film's conclusion at the successful navigation of his daughter's awkward age, he realizes that his youngest daughter is about to enter adolescence herself.

The plots of 1940s adolescent films were almost interchangeable. The
New York Times review of *A Date with Judy* (1948), commented on this
trend, "Hollywood has developed an extensive and rigid set of conventions for its unceasing stream of comedies of adolescence, and Judy ad-
heres carefully to all of them." The film contains all the formulaic
elements: the meddlesome teen (Jane Powell), the harried father (Wallace Beery), the comic "vamp" (Carmen Miranda), and the mistaken belief that her father is having an affair with Miss Rosita. As in *Janie,* the
film uses the microscopic camera shot and the voice-over narration to introduce the audience to "that typical American city, Santa Barbara," and
all of Judy's haunts including "Pop Scully's Soda Fountain." This is Louis
B. Mayer's 1940s version of Carvel, Idaho.

In many ways, *A Date with Judy* can be read in terms of postwar af-
fluence and consumption. Although Judy continually compares her lifestyle with that of the wealthy Pringles, it is clear that Judy is the one to
be envied. Her father owns a cannery, and she lives in a charming home
complete with white picket fence and "Nightingale," the black maid. It is
a home filled with consumer goods. Judy's world revolves around the radio, the record player, her "boogie-woogie" records and her clothes. Her
parents will celebrate their twentieth wedding anniversary with a catered party and entertainment by the band leader Xavier Cugat. Judy
and her "wacky" family also predate the typical situation-comedy family
of the 1950s, which turned on simple misunderstandings.

Some girls were not allowed to become bobby-soxers. Elizabeth Taylor's last adolescent role was in *Cynthia* (1947), in which she plays the
overprotected teen of the title. Her parents, who have given up their own
youthful ambitions because of the birth of a sickly daughter, are forced
to settle in a small town in Illinois. They project all their fears and dis-
satisfactions to their daughter, who at fifteen has become a virtual

invalid. Her father (George Murphy) had once planned on becoming a doctor. Instead, he is a manager of a hardware store and does not even make enough money to own his own home. His wife finally confronts his overprotection, "There's a sickness here, worse than Cynthia. You, Larry, you're sick, sick with fear. Every day of your life you're afraid of saying or doing anything, because you've haven't the courage to demand what's coming to you." It is Cynthia who finally teaches her father to confront his fears as she confronts hers, going to a school dance without getting sick. The father is emasculated, the daughter must lead him. By the film's end, her father has stood up to his boss, and Cynthia has turned into a full-blown bobby-soxer with all the accoutrements of her screen sisters. Her father will no longer have to worry about her health, but her virtue.

An unusual feature of films about adolescent girls in the 1940s was the nostalgia for the past, yet the teens who populate the nostalgic films do not appear very different than their bobby-soxer counterparts. *Our Hearts Were Young and Gay* (1944) featured Dianna Lynn and Gail Russell as two flappers on the Grand Tour of Europe. *Margie* (1946) was another film that featured Jeanne Crain as the mother of a bobby-soxer daughter, who shares her own memories of her awkward adolescence in the 1920s.

Adventure in Baltimore (1949) featured a bobby-soxer at the turn of the century, Dinah Sheldon (Shirley Temple). The voice-over narration at the beginning of the film draws this parallel. "What could be more symbolic of America than the modern American schoolgirl, intelligent, restrained, dignified," as the shot cuts to Temple as a bobby-soxer listening to loud music and talking on the phone. The narrator clears his throat and continues, "Let's go back to the girl of 1925," over a shot of Temple as a flapper with a graffiti-filled raincoat doing the Charleston. The narrator goes back to the girl of 1905, "demure, sedate, obedient," as the shot reveals Dinah doing china painting. It soon becomes clear that she is a bobby-soxer in disguise as she tells her horrified art teacher that she would rather paint the human form. She is promptly expelled for her liberal ideas about art and women's rights.

Certainly, Dinah is a handful for her patient minister-father, and her exploits almost cause him to lose his nomination for the bishopric. Yet paternal power and dignity are restored in *Adventure in Baltimore*. Many of Dinah's liberal ideas have come from her wise father, who refuses to give in to local gossips. He encourages her to stand up for her ideals and to hold on to her ambition of being an artist. After a long hiatus, it would appear that father finally knows best again.

THE YOUNGEST PROFESSION

By the 1940s, moviegoing had become institutionalized as an important ritual of adolescence. Sociologist A. B. Hollingshead called moviegoing "the most popular recreation participated in by the students," with 91 percent of teens attending the movies regularly. Carol Traynor Williams remembers the psychic importance of going to the movies: "First I went to the movies as a child attached to my parents . . . later as a dating teenager, one who in every generation is part of a social rite rather than an audience."[32]

Juvenile girls' magazines continued to feature articles and profiles of adolescent stars. *Calling All Girls* debuted in 1942, featuring monthly profiles of favorite girl movie and radio stars. *Seventeen* followed suit in 1944 by offering monthly movie columns.[33]

The concerns and activities of female adolescent fans and representations of female adolescents would intersect in a 1943 MGM film, *The Youngest Profession*. The film centered on a new breed of fan, the teenage autograph hunter. Virginia Weidler played Joan, the president of a fan club, "The Guiding Stars Limited," of a New York City high school. Club members held weekly meetings during which they would write letters to their favorite stars and read their replies, share autographs, and circulate information on stars who might be in the city. They also haunted railroad stations and fancy hotels in the hopes of landing autographs. In the process, they manage to meet Greer Garson, Walter Pidgeon, Robert Taylor and William Powell, more than most fans would meet in a lifetime. The film also offered a subplot that would repackage every cliché of bobby-soxer films. As in *Junior Miss* and *A Date with Judy*, Joan mistakenly believes that her harried attorney father (Edward Arnold) is having an affair with his secretary. She takes it upon herself to break up the "romance," thus wreaking havoc in the lives of all the adults around her. Screen writers must have imagined that a film focusing solely on the club activities of girl fan would not have been able to sustain an entire film.

What is most significant about this film is the way in which it comments not only on the critical nature of fandom but on the cultural authority of adolescent girls. Joan exhorts her members, "It is our duty to keep stars informed of how fans feel." The film's writers drew on real fan mail to show that while some fans were complementary, many were critical of everything from screenplays, to hair styles to costumes, to dialogue. Adolescent fans could be very vocal, and there were many venues through which they could express their feelings. Reel life echoed real life, in that the "Guiding Stars Limited" could be a fickle group, effortlessly transferring their loyalties from one star to another.

The critical nature of female adolescent fans is further underscored by a letter written to Hedda Hopper by a thirteen-year-old girl in the 1940s, regarding the divorce of Shirley Temple from John Agar:

She may have been tops as a child star, but how she grew up. . . . I don't blame John for getting drunk after living with Shirley and her fame. The reporters say she's spoiled, but if you ask me, I think she's well aware of her own importance. Just remember, Hedda, the younger generation would rather have Rita [Hayworth]. She is the most talented, the height of Hollywood [*sic*], and the best that is Hollywood. For our money, give us Rita!

Another fan echoed the sentiments, "This is one letter you are receiving that is not in favor of Little Miss Brat." Other fans rushed to her defense. A twelve-year-old girl wrote, "I think Shirley is wonderful, with a Capital 'W.' People seem to hold it against Shirley Temple that she grew up! Well for goodness sake, it's not her fault!"[34]

Kelly Schrum detailed the active role that teenage girls played in the creation of *Seventeen* magazine. *Seventeen* actively solicited reader response, and it is clear that teenage girls were not passively accepting all of its prescriptive advice.[35] The same can be said of girls and the film representations of adolescence offered to them. By the 1940s adolescent girls had become savvy consumers of the moving image. They had become conversant with most every aspect of filmmaking and the star system, and they clearly felt comfortable displaying their cultural knowledge. They did not accept uncritically the images presented to them of screen teens. In many ways, *The Youngest Profession* plays to two sides. It lampoons not only fans, but representations of girls in film. It is a very self-referential film, full of inside jokes and caricatures. At one point, Joan tells her father that she "wants to have a man-to-man, like in the Hardy pictures," satirizing the trope of the kindly, wise father and the errant (almost always male) teen. The line between life and a movie plot is blurred, as every situation in Joan's life seems to mirror one she has seen in a film. The texts of popular culture are sacred to these screen teens, who "swear on a stack of *Photoplays.*" Movie magazines have replaced the Bible as the source of moral and cultural authority.

From the magical creatures of the 1930s, the female screen teens of the 1940s were increasingly represented as a comedic stereotype. No longer were they capable girls solving other peoples's problem, they were now the problem themselves. The bobby-soxer was a destabilizing trope, represented as an alien species, wreaking havoc on her elders, especially her father who seems all but powerless in the face of her cultural practices. The comedic genre did not disguise the real anxiety over female adolescent sexuality that re-emerged in the 1940s. Such tensions could seemingly be released in a "safe" manner through the vehicle of comedy. Yet girls themselves seemed able to discriminate between film representations and react to them as critical consumers.

NOTES

1. Lary May, "Making the American Consensus," in *The War in American Culture*, eds. Lewis Ehrenberg and Susan Hirsch (Chicago: University of Chicago Press, 1996), 75.

2. For a discussion of "women's films," see Andrea Walsh, *Women's Film and Female Experience 1945–1950* (New York: Praeger, 1984).

3. James Gilbert, *A Cycle of Outrage: America's Reaction to the Juvenile Delinquent in the Fifties* (New York: Oxford University Press, 1986), 19. Cited by Marjorie Rosen, *Popcorn Venus* (New York: Avon, 1973), 251.

4. Mary H. Hinant, "Paging Miss Bobby Sox," *Library Journal* 70 (15 September 1945): 803.

5. Grace Palladino, *Teenagers: An American History* (New York: Basic Books, 1996), 52; Rosen, 252.

6. Hinant, 803.

7. "Subdebs Live in a Jolly World of Their Own," *Life* 10 (27 January 1941): 77–79.

8. Ibid., 77.

9. Maureen Daly, "Meet a Sub-Deb," *Ladies Home Journal* 61 (December 1944): 137–140.

10. "Teen-Age Girls—They Live in a Jolly World of Their Own," *Life* 17 (11 December 1944): 91–99. In 1965, teens in Webster Grove were revisited in the documentary film, *Sixteen in Webster Grove*.

11. Gay Head, "Jam Session," *Scholastic* 47 (22 October 1944): 42 and (29 October 1944): 30.

12. Palladino, 56–57. See Mauricio Mazon, *The Zoot-Suit Riots: The Psychology of Symbolic Annihilation* (Austin: University of Texas Press, 1984), 2–4; and Beatrice Winston Griffith, *American Me* (Westport, CT: Greenwood Press, 1973), 55–59, 76–77.

13. Jeanne Wakatsuki Houston, *Farewell to Manzanar* (Boston: Houghton Mifflin, 1973), 87, 138,147–148.

14. Alice Barr Grayson, *Do You Know Your Daughter?* (New York: Appleton-Century Co., 1945), 262, 265, 267, 53.

15. Catherine Mackenzie, " Teen Age Daughters," *New York Times Magazine*, 14 January 1945, 29.

16. Maureen Daly, ed. *Profile of Youth* (Philadelphia: Lippincott, 1949), 147, 151.

17. Palladino, 51, 53.

18. L. May, 91.

19. "What's On the Screen," *The American Girl*, January 1945, 28.

20. "Are These Our Children?" *Look* 7 (21 September 1943): 21–27. "Are These Our Children: *Look*'s Widely Praised Article Will Become a Movie," *Look* 7 (5 October 1943): 21–23. See also Richard B. Jewell, with Vernon Harben, *The RKO Story* (London: Arlington, 1982), 195.

21. Palladino, 63, 60.

22. "Juvenile Delinquency," *Life* 13 (26 October 1942): 58.

23. Estelle Freedman and John D'Emilio, *Intimate Matters: A History of Sexuality in America* (New York: Harper and Row Publishers, 1988), 261. "Combating the Victory Girl," *Newsweek* 23 (6 March 1944): 88.

24. William Tuttle, *Daddy's Gone to War: The Second World War in the Lives of American Children* (New York: Oxford, 1993), 30, 89.

25. Considine, 37.

26. Palladino, 54.

27. Mica Nava, *Changing Cultures: Feminism, Youth and Consumerism* (London: Sage, 1992).

28. Palladino, 72–73.

29. Palladino, 54; Barbara Hudson, "Femininity and Adolescence," in *Gender and Generation*, ed. Angela McRobbie and Mica Nava (London: Macmillan, 1984), 31–53; Lisa Lewis, *Gender Politics and MTV* (Philadelphia: Temple University Press, 1990), 166.

30. See "America's Kid Sister," *Colliers* 116 (27 October 1945) : 17; "Teen-Age Girls—They Live in a Jolly World of Their Own," *Life* 17 (11 December 1944): 93.

31. Palladino, 57; Angela McRobbie,"Shut Up and Dance: Youth Culture and Changing Modes of Femininity," in *Postmodernism and Popular Culture* (New York and London: Routledge, 1994), 169.

32. A. B. Hollingshead, *Elmstown Youth: The Impact of Social Classes on Adolescence* (New York: John Wiley and Sons, 1949), 301; Carol Traynor Williams, *The Dream Besides Me: The Movies and the Children of the Forties* (Rutherford, NJ: Farleigh Dickinson University Press, 1980), 13.

33. See Kelly Schrum, "Teena Means Business: Teenage Girls' Culture and *Seventeen* Magazine" in *Delinquents and Debutantes: 20th Century American Girls Culture*, ed. Sherrie Inness (New York: New York University Press, 1998), 134–163.

34. Hedda Hopper Collection. Academy of Motion Picture Arts and Sciences. Shirley Temple File #1.

35. Schrum, 149–152.

5

The Female Movie Fan

The opening scene of the 1943 film *The Youngest Profession* offered a behind-the-scene look at MGM's fan mail department. A young mail-room worker dumps a load of fan mail on Lana Turner's desk, "Here's some more trouble, Miss Turner." "Oh, it's never trouble," she replies, "when the fan mail stops, then it's trouble." Never mind that producer Joseph L. Mankiewicz had once referred to teenage autograph hunters as "those little beasts that run around in packs like coyotes." In *The Youngest Profession*, stars are depicted as being grateful for their support. Turner is shown happily autographing her pictures and personally answering her mail. She writes to the "Guiding Stars Limited" Fan Club:

You young people who collect autographs are the mainstay of our industry. It is your enthusiasm and loyalty that makes the motion picture player a star. Remember, we members of the acting profession are ever grateful to you autograph collectors, who might be called the youngest profession.

In many ways, this film paid tribute to its most devoted audience.

Exploring the link between the adolescent female spectators in the audience and fandom is essential, not only in analyzing a representation's appeal but in exploring the cultural agency of girls. In the period before World War II, joining fan clubs was not one way that girls interacted with film personalities, and also a way they organized their social lives. Fan activity has too often either been dismissed as unimportant, or stigmatized as fanatic, thereby effacing a useful venue for social historians. Any serious study of fan activity must be gendered, as adolescent females comprise the majority. Focusing on girls as fans offers a window into the historical spectator, as well as the ways in which spectators produce meaning through cultural products.

Throughout this book, I have looked at fan-generated texts in relation to film representations of female adolescence. In this chapter, I look at how fan club membership constituted a specific form of cultural expression by focusing on the fans and the texts created by the Deanna Durbin Devotees. The Devotees were one of the largest and best organized of fan clubs in the 1930s and 1940s. I discuss how fans used the discourse of fandom to make sense of the Depression and World War II. These fans also created cultural products through which teens could explore dimensions of female identity that went beyond normative definitions of gender.

THE HISTORICAL SPECTATOR

One of the most contentious debates among feminist film theorists has been how to conceptualize the female spectator. It seems to me that this should be the concern of historians as well. Laura Mulvey began this debate in 1975 in her essay "Visual Pleasure and Narrative Cinema." Drawing on Freudian psychoanalytic theory and Lacanian structuralism, Mulvey argues that in classical Hollywood cinema, the female object is positioned to be voyeuristically consumed by the male spectator. Women exist in film to be looked at; thus, spectatorship is essentially a male prerogative. In the 1980s, using Mulvey's work as a springboard, theoreticians began to conceptualize the female spectator. Most theoretical paradigms offer a model of a passive, fixed, female spectator who is controlled by the text.[1] The debate persists, but there is still no real agreement as to what actually constitutes the female spectator. Mary Ann Doane distinguishes between this ambiguous, psychologically constructed spectator and the "real" spectator when she argues, "I have never thought of the female spectator as synonymous with the woman sitting in front of the screen, munching her popcorn. . . . The female spectator is a concept, not a person." Yet it seems to me that historians must be primarily concerned not with concepts but with precisely the women sitting in darkened Bijous, munching their popcorn. As Jackie Stacey argues:

Devoid of sociality and historicity, the spectator has often been seen to be a subject position produced by the visual and narrative conventions of a film text, and assumed to respond to it in particular ways due to the universal workings of the female psyche. The women in the cinema audience have been virtually absent from consideration within much feminist, film theory, and the model of female spectatorship has been criticized for its ahistoricism and lack of details to contextual specificities.[2]

One way to conceptualize the historical spectator is through a study of fan behavior. Belonging to fan clubs was a way adolescent girls organized their social lives in the 1930s and 1940s. Fan membership also constituted a specific form of cultural expression. The Deanna Durbin Devotees and the journal that her fans created become useful sites to examine the historical discourse of fandom. I am particularly interested in the social aspects of fandom—girls' relationships not only to the star but to each other. Fan clubs comprise communities of spectators joined together by a particular pleasure in consumption, a pleasure that extends beyond the moviegoing context.

Jeff Bishop and Paul Hoggett argue that hobby groups constitute distinct subcultures organized around leisure activities. They note that "collective leisure offers opportunities . . . to reassert values not related to passive consumerism, but to production for one's own use and enjoyment." They refer to this as "mutual aid." The same can be said of fandom and spectatorship. Spectatorship has most often been conceptualized in terms of consumption. Looking at fans might also allow us to think of spectatorship in terms of production, and the ways in which fans negotiate the two. Spectators produce not only meanings but cultural texts and practices outside the moviegoing context as well. Moreover, the concept of "mutual aid" becomes even more significant when considered in relation to the dominant ideology of gender, which constructs female identity as the object of male pleasure. The Deanna Durbin Devotees used fandom to construct alternative gender identities that went against the dominant cultural perception of fandom, even Durbin's own perception of fans, and the dominant cultural perception of femininity for young girls.[3]

Joli Jensen notes what she calls "the stigma of fandom," the tendency to construct fandom as pathological and deviant. Fans are often seen as cultural dupes, totally lacking in critical faculties and easily manipulated. Fan activity is most often associated with marginal groups, those for whom identity formation and conflict are most intense, particularly adolescents. According to audience researchers, 75–90 percent of all fans in the 1930s and 1940s were younger than twenty-one, and approximately 80 percent of fans were female. It is probably reasonable to assume that the pathology of fandom also constructed fans as female. The feminization of fandom further delegitimized and trivialized fan activity. Durbin herself negatively stigmatized not only her fans, but her adolescent persona as well. In a 1967 interview, Durbin said, "I never had any feeling or identity with the 'Deanna Durbin' born from my early pictures, and from a mixture of press agents, publicity, and fan worship. . . . The fact that even today with the world's terrifying problems, people are still interested in the synthetic old Durbin of the thirties only shows what escape from reality I must have meant."[4]

FANS AND FAN CLUBS

As Kathryn Fuller points out, the term "fan" originally dates from the discourse of sports. It referred to those who were enthusiasts of spectator sports in the nineteenth century and was rarely applied to women. The advent of "stars" created by the new medium of motion pictures changed the nature of fandom. Before 1909 there were no motion picture stars, because work in motion pictures was not consistent. Moreover, because of the stigma associated with film work, few actors were willing to be identified to the audiences. Yet by 1909, fans had been writing "Who?" letters to the major production companies to inquire after the names of the performers. They also began asking for photographs of their favorite stars, and even started sending in marriage proposals. The term "movie fan" was coined in about 1910 to refer to men and women who were regular patrons of the nickelodeons. There was a short period roughly between 1910 and 1920 that the gender identity of the movie fan was comprised of both males and females. Yet by the 1920s, popular cultural forms began to reinforce representations of the film fan as being female, thus marginalizing masculine interest particularly in the technical aspects of filmmaking.[5]

According to pioneer film historian Terry Ramsaye, in 1910, Carl Laemmle, then an independent producer, staged what is generally considered the first publicity stunt. In the process, he supposedly launched the first "movie star." In the early days of the film industry, film studios such as Biograph focused on story development without identifying actors to the public. In 1909 the executives of the leading pioneer film companies formed the Motion Picture Trust, a monopoly designed to reduce competition from independents. Some Trust companies made a deliberate effort to ensure their actors' anonymity in an effort to keep star salaries down. In Ramsaye's account, looking for a way to draw customers from the all-powerful Trust companies, Laemmle acquired one of the leading stars of Biograph, a Trust company, Florence Lawrence. On March 12, 1910, the citizens of St. Louis read in their newspapers that Lawrence (the first time her actual name was used in print) had been killed in a street car accident. Immediately after the article appeared, Laemmle took out an advertisement declaring that the story was just a rumor spread by the Trust to destroy his business. Miss Lawrence, he declared, was not only alive but would be appearing in films for his new company. On a personal appearance tour shortly thereafter, Lawrence was mobbed by admirers who "demonstrated their affection by tearing the button's off [her] coat, the trimmings from her hat, the hat from her head." Thus the movie fan was officially born. Most contemporary film historians, however, consider the Ramsaye story apocryphal, as Lawrence had been employed by Laemmle a full six months before his publicity stunt. Moreover, in the same month, another actress, Florence Turner, known as the Vitagraph Girl, was called a "motion picture star" in print after making a personal appearance tour in Brooklyn. After the Lawrence episode the once despised "Who?" letters had to be taken seriously.[6]

Even after Laemmle's publicity stunt, some Trust producers continued to resist publicizing their stars. Independents were not as hesitant and ultimately caused a defection of some major players from the larger studios to the independents. By 1911 the Trust studios began to capitulate to demand as they started to issue film posters bearing the names of their actors.

Fandom was facilitated by the creation of fan magazines. J. Stuart Blackton of Vitagraph began the first fan magazine, *Motion Picture Magazine,* in 1911 to publicize Vitagraph films and players. At first the magazine was only distributed to Vitagraph exhibitors, but the demand for the magazine was so great that it was soon sold on newsstands. Blackton understood that fans wanted to be more directly engaged in all aspects of filmmaking, from writing film scenarios, to discussing film plots and stars, to breaking into movies themselves. Kathryn Fuller credits Blackton with what she calls the "gendered construction of the movie fan," as he began to target the female urban readers and to represent the movie audience as dominated by women through the discourse of his magazine.[7]

Other companies followed with their own publications. Such publications created star personas through anecdotes, legends and myths. In 1914 James R. Quirk became the editor of *Photoplay,* which encouraged artistry and quality in film by critically reviewing films. By the mid-1920s, Quirk also made his readers conversant in the language of the film industry by offering monthly features that included insider secrets and read more like a trade journal than a fan magazine. Nevertheless, Quirk continued to underscore the feminine character of the movie fan.[8]

At first, studio administrators were hostile to fan demands as fans were generally considered a nuisance. Fan mail was regarded as a costly burden by studios because of the costs involved in hiring clerical support and in answering and sending back photos. Although occasionally ambitious actors such as Joan Crawford answered their fan mail on their own, they were the exception. Yet by the late 1920s, fans began banding together to further the careers of particular stars. Fan club organizers were not allowed within the studio gates in the 1920s. However, by the early 1930s, the situation began to change as studios realized that fans constituted useful pressure groups on local theater owners through which to sell their films via block bookings. Fan clubs offered a free form of publicity, and fan clubs and fan mail were used to evaluate the popularity of stars by the studios.

By the 1940s all the major studios had fan mail departments. For example, in 1942, MGM employed about forty people in their fan club department answering fan mail requesting photographs. Usually studio workers or personal secretaries simply forged a star's signature on a photo. One studio handler said that "not one of the so-called autographed pictures of [her client], cherished throughout the county, has been signed by him and in two years, he has signed only one letter to a fan." A star's secretary writing in the "Boos and Bouquets" section of *Photoplay* complained about fan letters that asked for favors or jobs. "Don't pry into their private lives, don't ask for their home addresses, and don't tell them your problems," she admonished.[9]

Film fans could have enormous influence on a star's career. In 1924, *Movie Weekly* sponsored a contest for its readers to come up with a new name for starlet, Lucille Le Seur. The winning name was "Joan Arden," but that name turned out to belong to another bit player. The second choice was "Joan Crawford," submitted by a handicapped women in Albany who used the $500 in prize money to get medical treatment. In 1925, *Photoplay* asked fans to decide what kinds of roles they wanted to see thirty-two-year-old Mary Pickford play. Twenty thousand fan replies clearly called for Pickford to continue to play children. *Photoplay* gave a prize to a woman who asked Pickford not to abandon "the illusion that you are a little girl, in spite of the fact we know you are a grown-up." Pickford had become such a symbol of youth to her fans that perhaps her maturing screen roles reminded them of their own mortality.[10]

Fan clubs could be very political groups. As film historian Richard Griffith writes, "The more obsessed of these votaries formed fan clubs designed, among other things, to convince their idol's employers that she had greater and more puissant legions than the box office said she did, and the furtherance of fan club activities became a life work for more than one lonely soul." Griffith estimates that there were five million Americans who were rabid fans in the 1930s. Often, the stars themselves gave their clubs financial support to publish newsletters. In the 1930s, Irene Dunne told her fan club president that she could no longer afford to support the activities of the club. The disgruntled president wrote an angry letter to *Photoplay* complaining of Dunne's behavior, and threatening to throw her support to Ann Harding or Ginger Rogers, or some newcomer who might be more "grateful."[11]

They also functioned as powerful lobbyists. Sociologist, Margaret Thorp, said of fans in the 1930s, "Fan clubs are useful not only to the established, but to the aspiring actor. The enthusiasts . . . bombard the powers in Hollywood with letters expressing admiration for their idols and entreating that she may be seen more and more often in better roles." Thorp further characterized fandom as being "almost a profession."[12]

Fan clubs operated at an international, national and local level. For example, the Joan Crawford Fan Club—one of the oldest, organized in 1931—had a national president who collected dues and chartered local branches. Marion Dommer, the national president, wielded a great deal of influence. The advertisements for Crawford's film *Mannequin* carried a quote and a picture of Dommer endorsing the film. Dommer wrote to prospective fans in the 1930s:

Miss Crawford takes a keen interest in all of our activities. Not only does she send personally autographed pictures to all of our new members, but she writes a long letter to the members for each edition of our club publication; and she also answers all your questions about her in "Joan's Question Box," a regular feature of the magazine.

The journal published by the Crawford Fan Club, "The Crawford News," had a regular editorial staff comprised of club members and put out six issues a year.[13]

There were also national consortiums of fan clubs such as the Fan Club Federation, The International Fan Club League, and the Fan Club Friendship Federation. These organizations would often converge in Hollywood for yearly conventions. Many fans took their avocation very seriously, indeed. One such group was the Deanna Durbin Devotees.

THE DEANNA DURBIN DEVOTEES

In 1941, Hedwig Federowicz of Rhode Island wrote to *Deanna's Diary*, the official magazine of the Deanna Durbin fan club:

Like millions of girls I have grown to love Deanna more than just a child star . . . but now as a grown actress . . . I have attended operas, balls, visited an emperor, worn beautiful clothes . . . not in reality, but by living through each and every Durbin picture.[14]

Durbin's fans found comfort and meaning in her screen characterizations. Her films presented them an opportunity to make sense of the Depression, World War II, and more often, their own identities as young women regardless of the normative definitions of gender that prescribed a narrow range of legitimate female behavior.

Durbin's career spanned the Depression and World War II. Her screen characterizations not only register the conflicts of both periods, but they also begin to explain her appeal both to adolescent girls who would join her fan clubs and to their parents as well. For young girls, her portrayals of independent young women in the Depression may have communicated an expanded and empowered definition of teenage femininity. For adults, her portrayal of family devotion and filial piety during the war may have assuaged fears of juvenile delinquency and simultaneously promoted consensus for the war effort.

The Deanna Durbin Devotees—which originated in 1937 after Universal had released only one of her feature films, *Three Smart Girls*—became one of the largest international fan clubs, with over 300 chapters around the world. There are still active chapters of Durbin's fan club today, particularly in Great Britain, where they are known as the Deanna Durbin Society. The original Deanna Durbin Fan Club was founded in 1937 by four teenaged girls, Marguerite Slaney, May Blockwell, Ann Inman, and Marian Jentz. Shortly after it was founded, the fan club had enough support to publish *Deanna's Journal*, a mimeographed newsletter that featured biographical notes, editorial comments by its founders and profiles of Durbin's family members. In 1938, a *Life* magazine feature on Durbin generated a number of enthusiastic fan letters. One of the letter writers, Jay Gordon, became somewhat of a celebrity himself when he wrote to the editors, "Thanks a million for the liveliest picture ever printed in *Life*—that full page photograph of Deanna Durbin. I'm framing it and redecorating my room around that picture." Gordon received hundreds of letters and decided to form his own fan club, the Deanna Durbin Devotees, which eventually merged with the original club. The club under the auspices of the four teenage girls was essentially a small undertaking. Gordon was an ambitious young man and he quickly transformed the organization to his own ends. *Deanna's Journal* became *Deanna's Diary*, under the editorship of Nelson Blair, the new club's vice president. Durbin herself became the honorary president of the Devotees. Because of the entrepreneurial promotion skills of Gordon, the Devotees soon enjoyed their own feature article in *Life* in a profile that detailed club activities.[15]

The branch meeting highlighted in the 1938 issue of *Life* was also organized by a young adult male. The host was a twenty-five-year-old fingerprint expert for the FBI, and the meeting was attended by about thirty high school students, mostly female. *Life* noted that this branch met "irregularly," and, given the membership, it was probably more of an occasion for a photo shot than a usual occurrence. At this meeting, Devotees shared scrapbooks and drawings of Durbin, wrote her poetry and fan letters and sang songs from her films. They even had a contest to see which Devotee most resembled Durbin. It is difficult to know just how "typical" this branch club was. This meeting was organized by a young, adult man, and was comprised primarily of young, adolescent girls, much like the *Diary* itself, where young men set the parameters and girls defined the content. The club mirrored traditional gender hierarchies, in that men were the administrators and women the rank-and-file. Although there were boys and men who were Devotees, most Devotee fan clubs were organized by and made up of adolescent girls.[16]

Universal Studios was very supportive of the undertaking. It funded the publication of the fan club's journal and a small stipend for Gordon and other club officers. The studio also gave club officers and reporters unlimited access to Durbin and often allowed them on the set to watch her work. One of the Devotee's most important contacts at Universal was Kathleen Ehlen, who was the head of the Fan Mail Department. She gave the club assistance in securing possible names for membership, fan letters, photographs, and other publicity material. Ehlen estimated that Durbin generated about 3,000 letters a week.[17]

In 1942 both Gordon and Blair went into in the army. Blair's wife Eunice, whom he met through the club, and Pat Schoonmaker, the wife of a club advisor, became co-directors of the club and editors of the *Diary*. Their tenure was short-lived, however, as the *Diary* ceased publication in 1943. The *Universal Outlook*, published by James Stannage, was the British counterpart of the *Diary*. For two years, American Devotees would receive at least one issue of the *Outlook* each year with their membership. The *Outlook*'s existence was quite short, from 1940 to 1941, when Stannage ceased publishing the journal to join the Royal Air Force.

Although largely forgotten in the United States today, Deanna Durbin was one of the major box office stars from the late 1930s to late 1940s.[18] She is unique in that she was one of the few stars to bridge the gap successfully between adolescence and young adulthood on screen. Moreover, adoration of Deanna generated a huge number of fan-driven texts. She is also significant, because, unlike other adult film stars with huge fan followings, Durbin was the same age as many of her fans. She was not only a role model but a cohort. The age factor is important in examining her appeal, and the role fandom played in identity formation.

Before examining the meanings that adolescent fans created around Durbin, it is important to understand that her characterizations spoke to the specific material conditions of the 1930s and 1940s. Durbin's film portrayals complicate ideas about female spectators advanced by feminist film critics. Durbin's appeal cannot be explained by theories of spectatorship that conceptualize the female spectator as ahistorical and passive. In fact, Durbin's appeal was probably so great precisely because her screen characterizations were often bold, assertive, autonomous, young women in control of the circumstances and active participants in civic life. These might have translated into an agency that corresponded to fan activities.

THE HISTORICAL CONDITIONS OF FANDOM

Fan activity remained an affordable, easily accessible diversion during the Depression and the war. Being a member of an organized fan

club allowed teens a space to create texts for personal consumption outside the official, market economy, and thus outside the realm of the
dominant ideology regarding gender. The Deanna Durbin Devotees
found a sphere of cultural production in which they could explore dimensions of female identity that went beyond parental and mass media
definitions of femininity. We can begin to flesh out the historical spectator through teenage consumer behavior because consumers are engaged
in identity formation through consumption. Consumption itself can be a
political act, and as much a process of identity formation and meaning
making as is production.[19] Fan club activity was one way girls struc-
tured their leisure activities and, in this sense, can be read as constitut-
ing a specific subculture.

Deanna Durbin was a powerful symbol of youthful optimism during
the Depression and the war. She sang at Franklin Roosevelt's birthday
ball in 1941. Universal, besieged by soldiers' requests, sent photos and
Durbin records to military installations all over the world, and her
photo was the most requested from the British armed forces. Her popularity earned her the rank of honorary colonel in the U.S. Air Force. Winston Churchill numbered among her fans, as did Benito Mussolini, who
even sent her a fan letter. Anne Frank had a picture of Durbin on the
wall of her room in her hiding place in Amsterdam. To underscore her
enormous international appeal, Soviet archivists report that at the
siege of Leningrad, inhabitants of the city found comfort watching Durbin in *Spring Parade* and that her fans in the U.S.S.R. numbered in the
"hundreds of millions."[20]

There is clear evidence that her fans read her in relation to the war effort. The following poem, written by Gladys Brooks, a Devotee, is representative of the kind of mail she received during the war:

> **D**ear songbird of the silver screen
> **E**asiest the fairest I have ever seen
> **A**ngels have not sweeter voice
> **N**or nightingales when they rejoice
> **N**o larks can trill a higher note
> **A**s through the summer sky they float
> **D**ear songbird do not cease to sing
> **U**ntil the end of everything
> **R**emain in song for evermore
> **B**ecause when to the top you soar
> **I** can forget, and for an hour
> **N**o thoughts of war my spirit sour.[21]

The large majority of letters published in the *Diary* in 1942 and 1943
were from soldiers stationed all over the world. One British soldier
wrote:

You epitomize everything that is missing from my present existence: sincerity, tenderness, music, and laughter. After a day [of driving a tank through the mud]—it is just a little piece of Heaven to be able to visit the garrison cinema, see you and feel the sweetness and peace which surrounds you.

Four soldiers in Syria wrote,

We have an old battered gramophone here in camp, and a few of your records, and when we play them at night . . . the noise of the camp is hushed as the boys all stop to listen to your wonderful voice. And many a heart is stirring and many eyes are dimmed with tears as they think of their former homes when they listened to your voice in happier surroundings.

A U.S. soldier stationed in the South Seas wrote about a makeshift viewing of *It's a Date* against a tropical sky: "The vision seemed to blend with your beautiful 'Ave Maria.' We are fighting a war and we believe it is for the preservation of all that is represented in that picture."[22] Female fans learned about war conditions from soldiers who extolled Durbin for representing an ideal of youth that coincided with the aims of the war effort.

The Durbin trope was appropriated as a tangible symbol of U.S.-British cooperation. The *Outlook* contained a photo of Durbin walking confidently toward the camera with the caption, "Miss Anglo-American 1941, Clear eyed, intelligent, lovely to look upon, Miss Anglo-American, 1941, faces her destiny unafraid. . . . She and her generation see through the dark clouds of the present to the broad uplands that are beyond." The Durbin persona represented both a longing for the past and an optimism for the future for fans in both the United States and Great Britain.

There was a possessiveness about Durbin's fans that took on national significance. What Jackie Stacey has called "the battle over national identity," the rivalry over British and American cinema, played itself out in the pages of the *Diary* and the *Universal Outlook*. There was a real debate on what country truly "owned" Durbin. James Stannage, editor of the *Outlook*, in an article written for the *Diary* summed up the feelings of his members:

Much resentment has been caused among Devotees here by the report that Deanna's next picture is to be called "The American Girl." We think that such a title would be most inappropriate, not only because Deanna's appeal is essentially international, but we believe that Deanna Durbin, born in Canada of English parentage, is more typically a British, than a typically American girl, although she combines the best qualities of them both. In fact, Deanna is Anglo-American, a living example of the bonds which unite our two great nations, a unity, which, we hope, will prevail forever.

Jay Gordon, in his "Editor's Note" to Stannage's letter, diplomatically replied:

May I say that typical American and typical British girls are alike in this one re-spect: THEY BOTH WANT TO BE LIKE DEANNA! Also it may prove materially benefi-cial to Britain if "The American Girl" achieves its purpose—to stimulate American patriotism in a time of national crisis.[23]

The film was eventually released as *Nice Girl*. Concerns about the Brit-ish and Canadian box office were surely a factor in the decision.

The desire to appropriate Durbin's national identity continues to play out most notably in the pages of *Universal Outlook*. Miss Georgia Win-terborn expressed what Stannage described as the "thoughts of us all" when she wrote, "We Britishers love Deanna all the more because she speaks so much like ourselves, and sings songs which are loved so much by us all." Implicit in Winterborn's statement is the notion that only the British could appreciate Durbin's refinement and talent. This reflects a hierarchy of tastes among Devotees themselves. Not only do they as a group believe they are more cultured than other fans, but British fans believed they were superior to American fans. The war was experienced more keenly by these fans as well.

By 1943, American fans were more clearly affected by the war, and lo-cal clubs began to "do their part" for the war effort. The "Warbler Chap-ter" of the Devotees, headquartered at the "Good Eats Cafe" in Layton, Utah, might have represented a typical club in the 1940s. The group of eight met three times a month, with each of its members taking a turn at hosting a meeting. Most meetings were given over to the war effort. All members were writing to men in the armed forces, and they often in-vited soldiers into their homes on the night of meetings. In many ways they appeared to be more a USO than a fan club. Their admiration for Durbin was occasion for socializing and companionship.[24]

THE CULTURAL ECONOMY OF THE DEVOTEE SUBCULTURE

Durbin herself seemingly had little identification with her fans. Her disdainful attitude can be seen in an interview:

My fans sat in the dark, anonymous and obscure, while I was projected larger than life on the screen. Fans took home an image of me and studio and press agents filled in the personal details. They invented most of them, and before I could resist . . . this worldwide picture of me came back stronger than my real person and very often conflicted with it . . . I was a typical thirteen year old American girl. The characters I was forced into had nothing in common with my-self—or with other youth of my generation for that matter.[25]

Although much of what fans were responding to in the Durbin persona was totally artificial, according to Durbin, who disavows her own characterizations, fans were still able to derive enormous pleasure from the representations. Perhaps this illustrates that fans were able to create alternative meanings, and thus alternative identities, from Durbin's screen characterizations. *Deanna's Diary,* in attempting to pinpoint Durbin's appeal, gave voice to the adolescent fans themselves when it noted, "Deanna Durbin owes much of her popularity to the fact that she always has portrayed on screen girls who do the things most girls dream of doing." What she rarely did on screen was to defer to the adults or other figures of authority. Instead she was often brash, impudent, impertinent, sarcastic and independent, hardly the qualities touted for female adolescents in prescriptive literature that targeted youth and offered guidelines for teenage feminine behavior.[26] Fans might have transposed Durbin's agency on screen to their own fan activities.

Using Pierre Bourdieu's model of culture as an economy, John Fiske describes what he calls the "shadow cultural economy" of fan culture. That is, fans create a culture with its own system of production and distribution that lies outside official culture yet appropriates certain values and characteristics of that culture. Fiske isolates three major characteristics of fandom: discrimination and distinction, productivity and participation, and capital accumulation.[27] I would like to look specifically at the cultural economy of the Devotee subculture.

One form of productivity noted by Fiske is textual productivity, fan-produced texts that circulate among and help to define the fan community. These texts are created outside the official market economy for consumption among the fan community. Unlike products produced by the official culture, these texts are not produced for profit and thus often lack technical merit or a certain sophistication. The *Diary,* however, was fairly glossy for a fan publication. It usually had a studio photo on the cover and a number of publicity and fan-generated photos. A typical issue consisted of contributions from Jay Gordon and other club officers, Branch Club News, a personal letter from Durbin, a selection of fan letters sent to Durbin from all over the world, a Correspondence Club, fan poetry or prose and a profile of Durbin's latest film or a biographical note. The overwhelming majority of the content was fan-generated, allowing adolescents a forum to express their cultural tastes publicly.[28]

An important form of textual productivity among fans, not meant for public consumption, were the scrapbooks. Making a scrapbook was a very individualized activity and a creative aspect of fandom that has often been overlooked as a source of historical investigation. These are tangible artifacts that illustrate the participatory nature of fandom. Scrapbooks created opportunities for creative expression and the chance to develop a sense of achievement and pride in one's personal collection. Scrapbooks might contain photos clipped from newspaper or periodicals, film programs, and even a fan's own creative expression through poetry and drawings. Collections might be contained in store-bought scrapbooks, notebooks, a box, or they were sometimes made by pasting pictures onto a telephone book or magazine. Scrapbooks are also, as Lisa Lewis points out, a way for fans "to chronicle or represent their own histories," by including a program from a Durbin film the fan had attended, a letter or photo from Durbin, or a correspondence letter with another fan, all of which might reflect a particular sense of time and place for a collector. Scrapbooks became a venue through which fans could organize the cultural resources of fandom. Moreover, the pleasure of consumption could be repeated any time a fan worked on or looked at her scrapbook. Carol Traynor Williams talked about her own scrapbook:

I pasted pictures cut every month from a dozen or more movie magazines. I had thought the insanity grew from the competition between my scrapbook and Florence's, but I see now . . . that [it] was a bulwark holding off confusion, a retreat . . . to the symbols of childhood comfort.[29]

Many branch clubs of the Devotees required members to produce collections of memorabilia. As Fiske points out, the capital accumulation of fandom tends to be inclusive rather than exclusive. The goal is to collect as much as possible, and the objects are often those that lack value according to the standards of the official culture. One adolescent girl, Loraine McGrath, attained prominence among Devotees because she had the largest collection of "Durbiniana" in the world, with four scrapbooks full of clippings and an additional 1,500 photos of Durbin. The pleasure, histories, and personal memories associated with scrapbooks are a tangible artifact of identity formation, and the pride of creating a collection was an alternative arena of achievement. Instead of concentrating on their man-pleasing and -catching skills, girls could take pride not only in their unique creative endeavors but in displaying their expertise.[30]

Capital accumulation in the shadow economy of fandom was facilitated by the official market. Like Shirley Temple, Durbin became a marketing bonanza. The Durbin name was licensed to about a dozen manufacturers. There was a line of Durbin clothes and hats for pre-teens, based on the outfits that she wore in her films. There were also Durbin dolls, bags, songbooks, records and even a fictional series based on her character. Durbin did endorsements for soap, gum, shampoo and a variety of other products. She received 5 percent of the gross sales of all her merchandise.[31]

Devotees tried to draw distinctions between themselves and other spectators. Their mission statement underscores their desire for a more intimate connection with Durbin: "[The Devotees] was formed by a group of sincere admirers . . . in order to provide for Miss Durbin's followers the world over a closer contact than is possible through ordinary channels." Devotees also publicly proclaimed and signaled membership. They were given membership cards and official pins, and some branch chapters had jackets with a special insignia. Fans might also signal membership by appropriating Durbin's appearance. Female fans often adopted her hairstyle, mannerisms or attire. Many issues of the *Diary* featured the Durbin look-alikes. "There are a few girls on earth who not only pattern their conduct after Deanna's, but actually resemble her physically—one or two actually possessing singing voices of high quality." As Lisa Lewis points out, dressing like the star represents the acquired textual knowledge of fans, "Female culture based knowledge and textual knowledge join to create a field of authority that is both gender and fan specific."[32] It is in this area that female fans in the pages of the *Diary* come the closest to appropriating normative definitions of femininity. Yet the Deanna lookalikes strove for emulation of the star as an end in itself rather than as the way to attract a date.

The discourse of the *Diary* is much like the private writings of adolescent girls, full of superlatives—dramatic, flowery, romantic, sometimes full of anguish. One Devotee wrote, "The photos you sent me are lovely - every time I get one from you I just squeal with delight—honest! And isn't the new Diary simply grand?" The *Diary* stressed that as Devotees, they had access not only to her public persona but her private life as well, a special kind of insider's knowledge. For example, Devotees were well versed on the names of not only her dog and her immediate family but her maternal grandmother, her secretary, her manager, her directors and even the various studio administrators through the articles that were written by or about them in the *Diary*. Durbin fans in the *Diary* often position themselves as being more culturally refined and discriminating than the fans of other popular stars because of Durbin's association with "highbrow," instead of popular, music. In the case of the Devotees, there is a blurring of distinction between high and pop culture. Her fans often mention a preference for classical music and a vast knowledge of opera, with a proficiency for a musical instrument. The *Diary* turns on a celebration of talent and achievement, both Durbin's and the fans themselves.[33]

Many of the fan letters published in the *Diary* are very chatty, gossipy letters full of personal news, the kind of letters that are exchanged with a friend or confidant. Lisa Lewis posits that these letters "suggest a reciprocity between fan and textual persona, a pattern of identification, a relationship not unlike girls' friendships in which secrets and wishes are exchanged." Many of the letters are informational. For example, a fan in Paraguay wrote to tell Durbin the names of her films in Spanish, or a fan in Egypt wrote about the pyramids. Many letters simply recorded the uneventful occasions of daily life, such as the antics of a pet.

Sometimes, a fan wrote to give Durbin advice. One fan in New York suggested that she request a clause in her contract prohibiting placing her films on a double bill. There is a feeling of familiarity about her fan letters. Fans seemed to gravitate to Durbin because she represented a friend, a confidant, someone who would care. Such exchanges are also an example of the ways in which same sex relationships are formed and maintained.[34]

Bourdieu's metaphor of the cultural economy is characterized by struggle and competition between class factions whose interests are often in conflict. Yet I would argue that the cultural economy of fandom is marked by community and support. The values of the fan's cultural economy are radically different from those embedded within the formal economy. As Bishop and Hoggett argue, "They are the values of reciprocity and interdependence as opposed to self interest, collectivism as opposed to individualism, the importance of loyalty and a sense of 'identity' or 'belonging' as opposed to the principle of forming ties on the basis of calculation, monetary or otherwise."[35] In addition, the ways in which female fans constructed understandings of gender identity can also be considered communal. Club activities emphasized alternative conceptions of female behavior and female identity, such as talent, expertise, achievement, creativity and a knowledge of current events. Within the ideology of romantic love, women were encouraged to view other women as their competitors.

However, with Durbin fans there seems to be evidence of girl-girl solidarity, both in their identification with Durbin and in their friendships with each other. This solidarity was fostered by the Devotee Correspondence Club, which essentially functioned as a pen pal service. Each issue of the *Diary* featured about fifteen to twenty letters from correspondents looking for a fellow Durbin fan with whom to share their hobbies, interests, fill gaps in their Durbin collections or to learn about a specific geographical location. There was an ongoing exchange about music, movie stars, books, hobbies and sports. Moreover, during World War II, war news from soldiers and European fans was an integral part of the *Diary*.[36] Writing to other fans was a tangible way that adolescent girls constructed a community of spectators and created friendships with diverse people that they might not otherwise have had the opportunity to meet. Getting mail from all over the world probably heightened the pleasure of fandom, and collecting such letters became a part of the capital accumulation of fandom.

Bishop and Hoggett argue that leisure activities "consistently offer enthusiasts the opportunity to develop a sense of value and identity . . . through their creations and collections, or simply through their involvement in discussion and debate. Fan club activity constituted not only a space "to do" but also a space "to be."[37] In the uncertain days of the Depression and World War II, fandom was one way that adolescent girls could structure their leisure activities and create new forms of meaning, enjoyment and identity. Fandom also provided girls with alternative areas of expertise and legitimacy and their own cultural capital. The Devotees produced cultural texts outside of the market setting for personal consumption. Fan-produced texts, such as scrapbooks and *Deanna's Diary*, contained fan-produced meanings sometimes at odds with normative definitions of gender. Studying the Devotees allows us to think about spectatorship as a process both of production and consumption, and to look at the ways in which the two are negotiated. It also allows us to examine the ways in which spectatorship can occur outside of the moviegoing context. Being Devotees allowed girls a specific form of cultural expression that offered them a public forum for what normally has been private discourse. It also enabled them not only to attain a form of cultural authority but to acquire and construct knowledge in their own way. The Deanna Durbin Devotees allowed female adolescents autonomy, agency and a uniquely creative voice.

NOTES

1. Laura Mulvey, "Visual Pleasure and Narrative Cinema," *Screen* 16 (1975): 6–18. Mulvey revisited her argument in "Afterthoughts on 'Visual Pleasure and Narrative Cinema' inspired by *Duel in the Sun*," *Framework*, 6 (1981): 12–18. The special issue of *Camera Obscura* 20/21 (1989) summarized the debate on spectatorship. See also Jackie Stacey, *Stargazing: Hollywood Cinema and Female Spectatorship* (London: Routledge, 1994), 19–24 for an excellent critique of spectating positions.

2. Mary Ann Doane, untitled entry, *Camera Obscura* 20/21 (1989): 142–147, quoted by Stacey, 22–23. Stacey, 36. For a similar criticism of spectating positions, see Janet Staiger, *Interpreting Films: Studies in the Historical Reception of American Cinema* (Princeton, NJ: Princeton University Press, 1992) and Teresa de Lauretis, *Alice Doesn't: Feminism, Semiotics, Cinema* (London: Macmillan, 1984).

3. Jeff Bishop and Paul Hoggett, *Organizing around Enthusiasms: Mutual Aid in Leisure* (London: Comedia, 1986), 43–44.

4. Joli Jensen, "Fandom as Pathology," in *The Adoring Audience: Fan Culture and Popular Media*, ed. Lisa Lewis (New York: Routledge, 1992), 9–27. For a further discussion of some misconceptions about fans, see Lawrence Grossberg, "Is There a Fan in the House?: The Affective Sensibility of Fandom," in Lewis, 50–65. Edgar Morin, *The Stars* (New York: Grove Press, 1960), 102. Quoted by Anthony Slide, "A Tribute to Deanna Durbin," Academy of Motion Pictures Arts and Sciences Program, 9 December 1978. In my own private correspondence with Durbin, she cryptically wrote, "Don't believe everything you read," to this characterization of her fans. She is notoriously private and would not comment further, so I have no way of knowing if the quote used by Slide was erroneous.

5. Kathryn Fuller, *At the Picture Show: Small-Town Audiences and the Creation of the Movie Fan* (Washington, DC: Smithsonian Institution Press, 1996), 119–124. See also Eileen Bowser, *A History of American Cinema 1907–1915* (New York: Charles Scribner's Sons, 1990), 107–114.

6. Terry Ramsaye, *A Million and One Nights* (New York: Simon and Schuster, 1926), 523–531; Bowser, 113.

7. Fuller, 133–149.

8. Richard Griffith, *The Talkies: Articles and Illustrations from a Great Fan Magazine 1928–1940* (New York: Dover Publications, 1971), v–vii.

9. Marjorie Shuler, "Applause by Mail," *Christian Science Monitor* (November 1936): 6; "Rules for Writing to a Star," *Photoplay*, January 1939: 8.

10. Bob Thomas, *Joan Crawford* (New York: Bantam, 1978), 42; Robert Windeler, *Sweetheart: The Story of Mary Pickford* (New York: Praeger, 1974), 129.

11. Griffith, xvii.

12. Margaret Thorp, *America at the Movies* (New Haven: Yale University Press, 1939; reprint, New York: Arno, 1970), 39, 99.

13. Ibid., 100–101.

14. "Correspondence Club," *Deanna's Diary* 5 no. 1 (1941): 29. Thanks to Mary Rothschild and Barry Schenck for their comments on a draft of this article presented at the Maple Leaf and Eagle Conference in Helsinki, Finland, 1996. I would also like to acknowledge Michael Willard for getting me to think more about identity formation and fan behavior in the context of the Depression and World War II.

15. See Jay Gordon, "A History of Deanna's Diary," *Deanna's Diary* 4, no.1 (1940): 25. For Gordon's letter see, "Letters to the Editor," *Life* (4 April 1938): 6.

16. "Deanna's Fans Have a Devotee Club," *Life* (3 October 1938): 33–34.

17. For Universal's role, see Jay Gordon, "Editor's Last Word," *Deanna's Diary* 5, no.1 (1941): 31.

18. Although her appeal was and continues to be enormous among fans, Durbin has virtually been ignored by film scholars. Durbin is particularly useful to study because her career is so self-contained and finite. She literally walked away from films never to return. She is forever frozen in celluloid as a young woman.

19. Angela McRobbie and Jenny Garber, "Girls and Subcultures," in *Resistance through Rituals: Youth Subcultures in Post War Britain*, eds. Stuart Hall and Tony Jefferson (London: Hutchinson, 1976), 211–213.

20. Slide; "Dearest Deanna," *Time* (16 June 1941): 29.

21. Gladys Brook, "The Songbird," *Deanna's Diary* 6, no. 2 & 3 (1942): 8.

22. "Deanna's Own Fan Letters," *Deanna's Diary* 6, no. 2 & 3 (1942): 9.

23. Stacey, 53. James Stannage, "Hands Across the Sea," *Deanna's Diary* 4, no. 1 (1940): 12, and Jay Gordon, "Editor's Note."

24. Eunice Blair, "Branch Club News," *Deanna's Diary* 7, no. 1 (1943): 4.

25. Quoted by Norman Zierold, *The Child Stars* (New York: Coward McCann, 1965), 203. Ironically, Durbin seems to have mellowed with age. Today, she appears to remember both her past and her fans with a great deal of fondness as evidenced by a letter to the author.

26. "Durbin Doubles, " *Deanna's Diary* 5, no. 1 (1941): 28. For a discussion of prescriptive sources in the 1930s and 1940s, see Palladino, 20–33.

27. Pierre Bourdieu, *Distinction: A Social Critique of the Judgement of Taste* (Cambridge: Harvard University Press, 1984). John Fiske, "The Cultural Economy of Fandom," in *The Adoring Audience*, ed. Lisa Lewis (New York: Routledge, 1991), 30–48.

28. See Fiske, 42–43. For this study, I looked at issues of *Deanna's Diary*, the official journal of the Devotees, between 1937 and 1943, as well as fan letters published in popular periodicals, and fan-created artifacts, such as scrapbooks, poetry, drawings and other personal memorabilia created by fans themselves.

29. Lisa Lewis, *Gender Politics and MTV* (Philadelphia: Temple University Press, 1990), 157. I have a child's scrapbook from the 1930s that was, in fact, created by pasting pictures onto a local telephone directory. I would also like to thank Kimberly Cooper of Twentieth Century Fox, for sharing her personal antique scrapbook collections, and Adele Droll and Val Finhert, for sharing their Durbin memorabilia. For a discussion of capital accumulation, see Fiske, 42–44. Carol Traynor Williams, *The Dream Besides Me* (Rutherford, NJ: Farleigh Dickinson University Press, 1980), 163.

30. See Fiske, 42–44. McGrath was profiled in *Life* magazine in October 1938.

31. See "Deanna Durbin," *Fortune* 20 (October 1939): 158, and "Notes on a Songbird," Unsourced document (ca. 1941). Clipping Files of the Academy of Motion Picture Arts and Sciences (AMPAS).

32. "Apologia," *Deanna's Diary* 5 no. 1 (1941): 1; "Durbin's Doubles," *Deanna's Diary* 5, no. 1 (1941): 28. Lewis, *MTV*, 168.

33. "Deanna's Own Letters," *Deanna's Diary* 4, no.1 (1940): 22. For examples of "insider's knowledge," see "Introducing Granny," *Deanna's Journal* 1 (1937): 5; "Informal Chat with a Proud Mother," *Deanna's Diary* 5, no.1 (1941): 28; Nelson Blair, "Meeting Members," *Deanna's Diary* 4, no. 1 (1940): 13. For discussions of musical proficiency see "Correspondence Club," *Deanna's Diary* 5, no. 1 (1941): 29, and Jay Gordon, "Editor's Last Word," *Deanna's Diary* 5, no. 1 (1941): 31.

34. Lewis, *MTV*, 169. See Eunice Blair, "Branch Club News" and "Correspondence Club," *Deanna's Diary* 7, no. 1 (1943).

35. Bishop and Hoggett, 2.

36. For Correspondence Club see "DDD Correspondence Club," *Deanna's Diary* 5, no.1 (1941): 29, or Eunice Blair, "Correspondence Club," *Deanna's Diary* 6, no. 2 & 3 (1942): 10. For examples of the ways in which the *Diary* was informed by the war, see James R. Stannage, "Hands Across the Sea," *Deanna's Diary* 4 no. 1 (1940): 11–12, and "Deanna's Own Fan Letters," *Deanna's Diary* 5, no. 2 & 3 (1941): 9.

37. Bishop and Hoggett, 53, 127.

6

Conclusion

In 1943, at a reception hosted by David O. Selznick to introduce his new publicist, two adolescent screen legends, Shirley Temple and Mary Pickford, met for the first time. Because this was the stuff of photo opportunities, Pickford skillfully steered Temple before the waiting camera of a photographer from *Life*. She then surprised Temple by announcing that Temple would soon star in a remake of her 1929 film, *Coquette*. Although nothing ever came of the project, that single picture is reported to be "the greatest single-day news photo coverage in movie history." Over four million copies of *Life* were sold, and the picture made its way to the front page of 1,200 newspapers. The photo was captioned, "World's Two Greatest Has Beens." This story underscores not only the vagaries of the viewing public but the transitional nature of the adolescent experience in film.[1]

EPILOGUE

At the end of World War II, despite large box office returns, Hollywood was plagued by strikes, increasing production costs and the problems of reopening foreign markets. Moreover, the House Committee on Un-American Activities resulted in an unofficial black list that meant the departure of many important talents. The decline of the studio system was hastened by the departure of talent, and also by the failure to develop performers comparable to those of the first generation. Perhaps, most importantly, television changed the studio system, forcing the studios to cut back on production costs. Soon there were more stars under contract than there were roles. The studio system was further weakened in 1949 when the Supreme Court ordered film companies to rid themselves of their theater chains within five years. The studio system was dead.[2]

Movie attendance dropped by almost 50 percent between 1946 and 1960. The industry tried a number of gimmicks to revive the sagging box-office, such as "3–D," technicolor and stereophonic sound, but nothing helped to revive the industry. Up to this time Hollywood producers had targeted the female audience because of their ability to dictate the choice of film to the rest of the family. By the early 1950s, however, the industry had lost some control over its audiences when it lost control over theaters by the 1948 Court decision. This now meant that local theaters had relatively more autonomy over the selection of their features. As a result, the audience became increasingly segmented, and industry forces began to cater to the lucrative teen market.[3]

Filmic tropes of teenage girls began to change as well. The carefree bobby-soxer evolved into the conflicted teen of the 1950s. Our collective memory of the 1950s is somewhat flawed, and I believe that what we think of as the 1950s is really the early 1960s. In fact, representations of happy, carefree teens was hardly a feature of the 1950s adolescent film, and in the 1950s, humor was strangely lacking in Hollywood's vision of screen teens. In the 1950s, Americans were no longer laughing at the antics of youth. Films about adolescent girls in the 1950s increasingly began to reflect a very liberal attitude about sex, attitudes that are in many ways more liberal than their early 1960s counterparts. Films like *A Summer Place* (1959), *Blue Denim* (1959) and *Peyton Place* (1957) subtly warned against the double standard and adult hypocrisy, and suggested that teenage sex was often inevitable.[4]

As Hollywood increasingly depended on the youth market, it began to cater to them through a cycle of delinquency films. Exploitation and sensationalism were used to attract a teen audience. James Gilbert argues that teenage culture, when magnified and reflected by mass media, was actually mistaken for an outbreak of juvenile delinquency, and the mass culture that had helped to spread youth culture appeared to be at fault. Although films like *Rebel without a Cause* (1955), *The Wild One* (1954) and *The Blackboard Jungle* (1955) won critical acclaim, the mainstay of the genre were the cheaply produced films of American International Pictures (AIP). AIP was responsible for almost all films made about teens in the 1950s. In 1954, three independent producers, Sam Arkoff, James Nicholson and Roger Corman, formed the studio to make inexpensive films that would cater specifically to teens. The formation of AIP occurred at a time when other studios producing low-budget, "B" films were shutting down. Nonetheless, the AIP producers reasoned that exhibitors still needed B-fare that was topical, sensational, geared to youth and, most importantly, cheap to make. During the 1950s, AIP released over twenty films dealing with delinquency alone. The average cost for their films was about $125,000, and they grossed about half a million to a million per film. The genre reached its apogee in the 1960s with the cycle of beach films.[5]

Depictions of teens in the 1950s made after the period have often distorted the representation. Teens of the 1950s have been the subjects of a type of revisionism, which has reinforced the reductionist view of the period. The image of lighthearted girls in poodle skirts, saddle shoes and pony tails has little resemblance either to the screen image of alienation or the reality of the insular, conformity-conscious generation. In many ways the troubled teens of the f1950s were a kind of dress rehearsal for the revolt of youth in the 1960s.[6]

In the 1960s, films began to offer what television could not—sex. Filmmakers started to go as far as the censors would allow. In the 1960s at least 70 percent of box office revenue continued to come from people between the ages of sixteen to twenty-nine, and studios continued to cater to the youth audience. In the early 1960s, they did so by repackaging concepts and ideas about youth that had been successful in the 1950s. Juvenile delinquency was repackaged in films like *Because They're Young* (1960) and *Kitten with a Whip* (1964). In many ways, the films about adolescents in the early 1960s look more like our idealized image of youth of the fifties. In films as well as life, the early 1960s continued to look like the 1950s: Change came only at the end of the decade.[7]

By the 1960s, films detailing juvenile delinquency lost their relevancy. As one film critic noted about the failure of *Hot Rods to Hell*, "By 1967 a film about drunken hot rodders terrorizing the highway had as much topicality as a Davy Crockett hat or a hula hoop." The press even abandoned the subject, and delinquents stopped being a marketable commodity.[8]

Something was needed to take the place of delinquents, and Hollywood found it on the beach instead of the dragstrip. Once again AIP was at the forefront of the new teen craze. William Asher, the director of AIP's first three beach films, commented on the shift, "Our audiences welcome good, clean sex. They are bored with juvenile delinquency." AIP capitalized on the increasing public fascination with the culture of Southern California. One film critic underscored the appeal of these films, which "featured a convoy of surfing buffs gamboling on the beach with tantalizing bikini-clad maidens who shake their collective chassis to the Watusi, lead them in giddy technicolor chases and entangle them in some of the most fantastic plots available."[9] The cycle began in 1963 with *Beach Party* and would continue through *Beach Blanket Bingo* (1964), *Bikini Beach* (1964), and *How to Stuff a Wild Bikini* (1965).

After the angst and teenage rebellion of the screen teens in the 1950s, Hollywood turned to more lighthearted, safer and predictable themes about females in the 1960s. There was a return of the "harried father guarding his daughter's virginity" films of the 1940s. The 1960s daughters were, in fact, much sexier than their bobby-soxer counterparts and thus more deserving of their father's concern in films like *Take Her She's Mine* (1963), *I'll Take Sweden* (1965) and *The Impossible Years* (1968). Other films about teenage sexuality gave conflicting messages about the permissible boundaries of sexual behavior. Whereas *Susan Slade* (1961) warned of the hazards of teen sex, *Splendor in the Grass* (1961) warned of the hazards of repressing sex.

Two very different satires on the American teen emerged during the decade. *Bye Bye Birdie* (1963) lambasted hero-worshiping teens and their culture, while *Wild in the Streets* (1968) explored the consequences of such adulation, and the downside of youth culture. Several factors contributed to the evolution of the teen film genre in the 1960s. By the late 1960s, a generation of students had become politicized and inspired by Civil Rights activism, the Vietnam War and the student movement. These social protest movements constituted a strong indictment of the American middle class and their values. But for the most part, these anti-establishment attitudes did not filter down to high school youths. If the minority of adolescents in the fifties were juvenile delinquents, so too were the minority of teens in the 1960s hippies or student activists.

By the early 1970s, even the "king" of teenpics, Samuel Arkoff, was floundering.

Our pictures in the sixties mirrored the teenagers as they went from high spirited to rebellious. . . . Kent State was the turning point. It was no longer fun and games to call policemen pigs. You could get shot. The big body of teenagers turned off into nothingness by 1970. . . . There's no way to sell the young today that's as clear cut as in the past. I don't think our audience is the same audience anymore for two different pictures. Each picture must be attractive to some segment of youth. . . . But you can't buckshot anymore. You must aim dead center at what you consider your audience for a specific picture and hope what you will have will also attract a peripheral audience. Falling between the two stools is not my idea of comfort.[10]

Although the biggest audience for films well into the 1980s continued to be teenagers, Arkoff was not the only producer finding it increasingly difficult to track the tastes of adolescents. Filmmakers resorted to a time-honored formula for success—sex. The 1970s saw a large number of films that focused on sexual activity among teens as in *The Last Picture Show* (1971), *Pretty Baby* (1976), *The Little Girl Who Lived Down the Lane* (1977) and *Manhattan* (1979). Moreover, the ways in which adolescent boys and girls were relating also began to change in the

the first of many such evenings made possible because Mrs. Canfield knew Sally and trusted her implicitly—and blindly." Mrs. Canfield tends to have a blind spot as far as her husband is concerned as well.

Soon Sally is a full-blown flapper. She frequents an illegal roadhouse where she meets an older, worldlier man, Don Hughes. Sally has sex with Don almost immediately, and as the title proclaims, "And so Sally has passed another milestone on the Road to Ruin [sleeping with more than one man] from which intelligent guidance could have saved her."

A few nights later, Sally and Eve get into a strip poker game at Don's apartment. The close-up lingers sensuously on Sally face flushed with excitement and desire. The audience is positioned voyeuristically, as we see the scene through the eyes of a passerby standing outside an open door. Within a short time they are all in their underwear, but before it turns into a full-blown orgy, they are apprehended by the police. Sally and Eve are taken to Juvenile Hall, where they are told they will be examined by a doctor. When a tearful Sally asks why, she is told, "It is the rule of the Police Juvenile Bureau that all girls brought in under suspicion of delinquency be examined by our physician." The scene of Juvenile Hall fades, and the title announces that Eve has "tested positive" [for venereal disease] and will be "detained for treatment."[33]

Sally is taken home to her mother by the social worker, who presumably must tell Mrs. Canfield about the condition of Sally's hymen. Instead of being upset at Sally, Mrs. Canfield's anger is directed to the messenger. The lovely, refined social worker is the voice of moral authority as she tells Mrs. Canfield,

You are like ninety percent of the mothers with whom we deal in our work. We are not condemning your daughter, only asking your cooperation to prevent mistakes like this from being repeated. . . . It is the duty of parents to protect their children by intelligent instruction and advice on the subject of sex.[34]

Instead of disciplining Sally, Mrs. Canfield promises not to tell her father. Not only has Mrs. Canfield been too trusting, she has not warned Sally to control her sexual desire until marriage. The social worker's words go unheeded. Sally continues down the road to ruin. Shortly after her arrest, she discovers that she is pregnant, and the title moralizes "Those who transgress the moral laws must pay the bitter price." When she tells Don she is "in trouble," he refuses to marry her and arranges a back-alley abortion with a seedy doctor.

Although she is very ill after the abortion, Sally consents to going to a party given by Don's boss. What Sally does not know is that Don's boss runs a house of prostitution. She is immediately ushered into a back bedroom, where her would-be client turns out to be her father. Sally loses consciousness when confronted with the fact.

take that message to heart as they were all being detained as sexual delinquents.[36]

Films of the 1920s had become quite suggestive as a result of competition among film companies. In addition, a number of scandals had rocked the film industry. In an effort to appease pro-censorship forces, film magnates formed a trade association, the Motion Picture Producers and Distributer's Association (MPPDA), and hired Will Hays in 1922 as its first president. The purpose of this new organization was the regulation of the morals of the film industry and films themselves. Hays, a Presbyterian elder, had once been chair of the Republican National Committee and had served briefly as Warren Harding's postmaster general.[37]

Will Hays initiated a number of reforms, among them the insertion of morality clauses in performer's contracts, which permitted cancellation if actors were accused of immorality. In 1927 he appointed Jason Joy, formerly of the War Department, to read screenplays and to advise producers of potential problems with local censorship groups. He synthesized rules from censorship boards throughout the country and introduced "The Don'ts and Be Carefuls," in an attempt at self-regulation. Producers were advised to avoid nudity, profanity, sex perversions, white slavery, venereal disease, abortion, and sex hygiene. Two years later, both *Port of Missing Girls* and *Road to Ruin* would blatantly ignore such proscriptions. They seemed to do so under the pretext of realism, and as contemporary chronicler Frederick Lewis Allen noted, the Hays Office made "moral endings obligatory" and "sexy pictures were smeared over with platitudes." Ironically, the same can be said of the actual vice reports of delinquents themselves. Girls' lives were scrutinized, and juvenile reports could be very titillating and even pornographic. Female delinquency became fetishized both on screen and off.[38]

Films about adolescents in the early Depression continue to echo themes made popular in the 1920s. An exemplary film, *High School Girl* (1933) could have easily been made in the 1920s, so similar was it in its theme of the breakdown in communication and the need for surveillance between girls and their clubwoman mothers. The film looks very much like the exposés of the 1920s, such as *Port of Missing Girls* and *Road to Ruin*. Although *High School Girl* again focuses on the result of parental neglect on an adolescent girl, it goes even further than earlier films and becomes a blatant polemic for sex education not only in the home but in the school as well.

Beth Andrews (Cecilia Parker, who would gain fame later in the decade as the sister of the screen's most famous teen, Andy Hardy) is a lonely, confused teenager with little or no guidance from her busy parents. Her mother, not surprisingly a middle-class clubwoman, self-righteously preaches about the evils of leaving children alone, while she neglects her own daughter for her voluntary activities. The first shot of about Teen Movies," in *King of the B's: Working within the Hollywood System,* eds. Todd McCarthy and Charles Flynn (New York: E. P. Dutton, 1975), and J. Hoberman, "Don't Knock the Schlock," *Village Voice,* 2 July 1979, 60.

6. For a discussion of the idealization of the fifties see Stephanie Coontz, *The Way We Never Were: American Families and the Nostalgia Trap* (New York: Basic Books, 1992). Television teens of the 1950s in shows like *Bachelor Father, Leave It to Beaver,* and *Dobie Gillis* conform more to the idealized images of the 1950s than do screen teens.

7. Larry Cohen, "The New Audience: From Andy Hardy to Arlo Guthrie," *Saturday Review* 27 (December 1969): 9. What we think of as the 1960s (hippies, youthful activism, and protest movements) is not reflected until later in the decade.

8. Gilbert, 213; McGee and Robertson, 56.

9. Cited by Staeling, 236. Martin Abramson, "Surf-Sand-and-Sex Films," *New York World Telegram,* 8 February 1966, 8.

10. Quoted by Aljean Harmetz, "The Dime Store Way to Make Movies and Money," *New York Times Magazine,* 4 August 1974, 12.

11. Considine, 276.

12. See Gilbert, 127–142.

Filmography

*Adventure in Baltimore.*1948. Screenplay by Lionel Houser; from a story by Lesser Samuels and Christopher Isherwood. Directed by Richard Wallace. Produced by Richard Berger for RKO.

Andy Hardy Gets Spring Fever. 1939. Screenplay by Kay Van Riper; based on the characters created by Aurania Rouverol. Directed by William S. Van Dyke. Produced by J. J. Cohn for MGM.

Andy Hardy Meets a Debutante. 1940. Screenplay by Annalee Whitmore; based on the characters created by Aurania Rouverol. Directed by George B. Seitz. Produced by J. J. Cohn for MGM.

Andy Hardy's Blonde Trouble. 1944. Screenplay by Harry Ruskin, William Ludwig and Agnes Christine Johnson; based on the characters created by Aurania Rouverol. Directed by George B. Seitz. Produced by J. J. Cohn for MGM.

Andy Hardy's Double Life. 1942. Screenplay by Agnes Christine Johnson; based on the characters created by Aurania Rouverol. Directed by George B. Seitz. Produced by J. J. Cohn for MGM.

Andy Hardy's Private Secretary. 1940. Screenplay by Agnes Christine Johnson; based on the characters created by Aurania Rouverol. Directed by George B. Seitz. Produced by J. J. Cohn for MGM.

Angel of Crooked Street. 1922. Screenplay by C. Graham Baker; based on a story by Harry Dittmar. Directed by David Smith. Produced by Albert Smith for Vitagraph.

Anne of Green Gables. 1934. Screenplay by Sam Mintz; based on the book by L. M. Montgomery. Directed by George Nicholls. Produced by Kenneth McGowen for RKO.

Are Parents People? 1925. Screenplay by Francis Agnew; based on a story by Alice Duer Miller. Directed by Malcolm St. Clair. Produced by Jesse Lasky for Paramount.

Are These Our Parents? 1944. Screenplay by Michael Jacoby; based on a story by Hilary Lynn. Directed by William Nigh. Produced by Jeffrey Bernerd for Monogram.

Assassin of Youth. 1937. Screenplay by Elmer Clifton; based on a story by Leo J. McCarthy. Directed by Elmer Clifton. Produced by Leo McCarthy.

As the World Rolls On. 1921. Screenplay by W. A. Andlauer. Directed and produced by W. A. Andlauer for Andlauer Productions.

Babes in Arms. 1939. Screenplay by Jack McGowan and Kay Van Riper; based on the original book by Richard Rogers and Lorenz Hart. Directed by Busby Berkeley. Produced by Arthur Freed for MGM.

Babes on Broadway. 1941. Screenplay by Fred Finklehoffe and Elaine Ryan. Directed by Busby Berkeley. Produced by Arthur Freed for MGM.

The Bachelor and the Bobby-Soxer. 1947. Screenplay by Sidney Sheldon. Directed by Irving Reis. Produced by Dore Schary for RKO.

Beloved Brat. 1938. Screenplay by Lawrence Kimble; based on a story by Jean Negulesco. Directed and produced by Arthur Lubin for Warner Brothers.

The Birth of a Nation. 1915. Adaptation by D. W. Griffith; based on the novel *The Clansmen* by Thomas Dixon. Directed and produced by D. W. Griffith.

Broadway Melody of 1938. 1938. Screenplay by Jack McGowan. Directed by Roy Del Ruth. Produced by Jack Cummings for MGM.

Broken Blossoms. 1919. Screenplay by D. W. Griffith; based on a story by Thomas Burke. Directed and produced by D. W. Griffith for United Artists.

Campus Flirt. 1926. Screenplay by Louise Long and Lloyd Carrigan. Directed by Clarence Badger. Produced by Adolph Zukor for Paramount.

Chatterbox. 1936. Screenplay by Sam Mintz; based on the play by David Carb. Directed by George Nicholls. Produced by Robert Siske for RKO.

The Courtship of Andy Hardy. 1942. Screenplay by Agnes Christine Johnson; based on the characters created by Aurania Rouverol. Directed by George B. Seitz. Produced by J. J. Cohn for MGM.

Cynthia. 1947. Screenplay by Harold Buchman and Charles Kaufman; based on a play by Vina Delmar. Directed by Robert Leonard. Produced by Edwin Knopf for MGM.

Daddy Long Legs. 1919. Screenplay by Agnes Johnson. Directed by Mickey Neilan. Produced by Mary Pickford for First National.

A Date with Judy. 1948. Screenplay by Dorothy Cooper and Dorothy Kingsley; based on the characters created by Aileen Leslie. Directed by Richard Thorpe. Produced by Joe Pasternak for MGM.

Delightfully Dangerous. 1947. Screenplay by Walter DeLeon and Arthur Phillips; based on a story by Irving Phillips, Edward Verdier and Frank Tashlin. Directed by Arthur Lubin. Produced by Charles E. Rogers for United Artists.

Delinquent Parents. 1938. Screenplay by Nick Barnes and Robert St. Clair. Directed by Nick Ginde. Produced by Melville Shyer for Progressive Pictures.

Ella Cinders. 1926. Screenplay by Frank Griffith and Mervyn LeRoy. Directed by Afred E. Green. Produced by John McCormick for First National.

Everybody Sing. 1937. Screenplay by Florence Ryerson and Edgar Allan Woolf. Directed by Edwin Marin. Produced by Harry Rapf for MGM

Every Sunday. 1936. Written and directed by Felix Feist. Produced by Mauri Grashin for MGM.

A Family Affair. 1937. Screenplay by Kay Van Riper; based on the play by Aurania Rouverol. Directed by George B. Seitz. Produced by Lucien Hubbard and Samuel Marx for MGM.

Father Was a Fullback. 1949. Screenplay by Aileen Leslie, Casey Robinson, Mary Loos and Richard Sale; suggested by a play by Clifford Goldsmith. Directed by John H. Stahl. Produced by Fred Kohlmar for Twentieth Century Fox.

Finishing School. 1934. Written by David Hempstead. Directed by Wanda Tuchock and George Nicholls Jr. for RKO.

Girl Crazy. 1943. Screenplay by Fred Finklehoffe; based on the play by Florence Ziegfeld. Directed by Busby Berkeley and Norman Taurog. Produced by Arthur Freed for MGM.

Girls' Dormitory. 1936. Screenplay by Jean Markey; based on a play by Ladislaus Fodor. Directed by Irving Cummings. Produced by Raymond Griffith for Twentieth Century Fox.

Girls on Probation. 1938. Screenplay by Crane Wilbur. Directed by William McCann. Produced by Bryan Foy for Warner Brothers.

Girls' School. 1938. Screenplay by Tess Slesinger, based on a story by Tess Slesinger. Directed by John Brahm. Produced by Samuel Marx for Columbia.

Girls Under 21. 1940. Screenplay by Jay Dratler and Fanya Ross. Directed by Max Nosseck. Produced by Ralph Cohn for Columbia.

The Godless Girl. 1928. Screenplay by Jeanne MacPherson. Directed and produced by Cecil B. DeMille for Pathe.

Handcuffs and Kisses. 1921. Screenplay by Lewis Allen Browne; from a story by Thomas Edgelow. Directed by George Archibald. Produced by Lewis J. Selznick for Selznick Pictures.

The Hardys Ride High. 1939. Screenplay by Kay Van Riper and Agnes Christine Johnson; based on the characters created by Aurania Rouverol. Directed by George B. Seitz. Produced by J. J. Cohn for MGM.

Harold Teen. 1928. Screenplay by Thomas J. Geraghty; based on the comic strip by Carl Ed. Directed and produced by Mervyn Leroy for First National.

The Heart o' the Hills. 1919. Screenplay by John Fox; based on his story. Directed by Kenneth Harlan. Produced by Mary Pickford for First National.

High School Girl. 1933. Screenplay by Wallace Thurman. Directed by Crane Wilbur. Produced by Bryan Foy for State's Rights.

Hitler's Children. 1943. Screenplay by Emmet Lauery; based on the book by Gregor Ziemer. Directed by Edward Dmytryk. Produced by Edward A. Golden for RKO.

Holiday in Mexico. 1946. Screenplay by Isobel Lennart. Directed by George Sidney. Produced by Joe Pasternak for MGM.

House of Youth. 1924. Screenplay by C. Gardner Sullivan; from the book by Maud Radford Warren. Directed by Ralph Ince for Regal Pictures.

Hula. 1927. Screenplay by Ethel Doherty. Directed by Victor Fleming. Produced by Adolph Zukor and Jesse Lasky for Paramount.

I'll Be Seeing You. 1943. Screenplay by Charles Martin. Directed by William Dieterle. Produced by Dore Schary for United Artists.

Imitation of Life. 1934. Screenplay by William Hurlbut; based on the novel by Fannie Hurst. Directed by John Stahl. Produced by Carl Laemmle for Universal.

Inside the White Slave Traffic. 1913. Written, directed and produced by Samuel London for Universal.

I Remember Mama. 1948. Screenplay by DeWitt Bodeen; based on the play by John Van Druten from the novel by Kathryn Forbes. Directed and produced by George Stevens for RKO.

It. 1928. Screenplay by Hope Loring and Louis Lighton; adapted form the story by Elinor Glyn. Directed by Clarence Badger. Produced by Adolph Zukor and Jesse Lasky for Paramount.

It's a Date. 1939. Screenplay by Jane Hall, Fred Kohner. Directed by Henry Koster. Produced by Joe Pasternak for Universal.

It Started With Eve. 1941. Screenplay by Norman Krasna and Leo Townsend; based on a story by Hans Kraly. Directed by Henry Koster. Produced by Joe Pasternak for Universal.

Janie. 1944. Screenplay by Agnes Christine Johnson and Charles Hoffman; from the play by Josephine Bentham and Herschel Williams. Directed by Michael Curtiz. Produced by Alex Gottleib for Warner Brothers.

Judge Hardy and Son. 1939. Screenplay by Carey Wilson; based on the characters created by Aurania Rouverol. Directed by George B. Seitz. Produced by J. J. Cohn for MGM.

Judge Hardy's Children. 1938. Screenplay by George B. Seitz and Kay Van Riper; based on the characters created by Aurania Rouverol. Directed by George B. Seitz. Produced by J. J. Cohn for MGM.

Junior Miss. 1945. Screenplay by George Seaton; based on the book by Sally Benson. Directed by George Seaton. Produced by William Perling for Twentieth Century Fox.

Kathleen. 1941. Screenplay by Mary C. McCall; based on the story by Kay Van Riper. Directed by Harold S. Bucquet. Produced by George Haight for MGM.

Kiss and Tell. 1945. Screenplay by Hugh Herbert; based on a story by Hugh Herbert. Directed by Richard Wallace. Produced by Sol Siegal for Columbia.

Life Begins for Andy Hardy. 1941. Screenplay by Agnes Christine Johnson; based on the characters created by Aurania Rouverol. Directed by George B. Seitz. Produced by J. J Cohn for MGM.

Lilies of the Streets. 1925. Screenplay by Harry Chandlee; supervised by Mary Hamilton. Directed by Joseph Levering for Belban Productions.

Listen Darling. 1938. Screenplay by Anne Chapin and Elaine Ryan; based on the story by Katherine Brush. Directed by Edwin Marin. Produced by Jack Cummings for MGM.

Little Annie Rooney. 1925. Screenplay by Hope Loring and Louis Leighton; based on a story by Katherine Hennessey. Directed by William Beaudine. Produced by Mary Pickford for United Artists.

The Little Firebrand. 1927. Screenplay by Frederick Chapin. Directed by Charles Hutchinson. Produced by William Steiner for Hurricane Film Corporation.

Little Women. 1933. Screenplay by Sarah Mason and Victor Heerman; based on the novel by Louisa May Alcott. Directed by George Cukor. Produced by Kenneth McGowan for RKO.

Love Finds Andy Hardy. 1938. Screenplay by William Ludwig; based on the characters created by Aurania Rouverol. Directed by George B. Seitz. Produced by J. J. Cohn for MGM.

Lovey Mary. 1926. Screenplay by Agnes Christine Johnson and Charles Maigne; based on the book by Alice Hegan Rice. Directed and produced by King Baggot for MGM.

Mad about Music. 1938. Screenplay by Bruce Manning and Felix Jackson; based on a story by Marcella Burke and Frederick Kohner. Directed by Norman Taurog. Produced by Joe Pasternak for Universal.

Maid of Salem. 1936. Screenplay by Walter Ferris, Bradley King, Durwood Grinstead; based on a story by Bradley King. Directed and produced by Frank Lloyd for Paramount.

Make Way for a Lady. 1936. Screenplay by Gertrude Purcell; based on a novel by Elizabeth Jordan. Directed by David Burton. Produced by Zion Myers for RKO.

Margie. 1946. Screenplay by F. Hugh Herbert; based on the stories by Ruth McKenny and Richard Bransten. Directed by Henry King. Produced by Walter Morosco for Twentieth Century Fox.

Meet Me in St. Louis. 1944. Screenplay by Irving Brecher and Fred Finklehoffe; based on the book by Sally Benson. Directed by Vincente Minnelli. Produced by Arthur Freed for MGM.

Mickey. 1948. Screenplay by Muriel Roy Bolton and Agnes Christine Johnson; from the novel by Peggy Goodin. Directed by Ralph Murphy. Produced by Aubrey Schenck for Eagle Lion Films.

Miss Annie Rooney. 1942. Screenplay by George Bruce. Directed by Edwin L. Marin. Produced by Edward Small for United Artists.

M'liss. 1936. Screenplay by Dorothy Yost; based on a story by Bret Harte. Directed by George Nicholls. Produced by Robert Siske for RKO.

My Bill. 1938. Screenplay by Vincent Sherman and Robertson White; based on the play by Tom Barry. Directed by John Farrow. Produced by Bryan Foy for Warner Brothers.

Nancy Drew and the Hidden Staircase. 1939. Screenplay by Kenneth Gamet; based on the stories by Carolyn Keene. Directed by William Clemens. Produced by Bryan Foy for Warner Brothers.

Nancy Drew, Detective. 1938. Screenplay by Kenneth Gamet; based on the stories by Carolyn Keene. Directed by William Clemens. Produced by Bryan Foy for Warner Brothers.

Nancy Drew, Reporter. 1939. Screenplay by Kenneth Gamet; based on the stories by Carolyn Keene. Directed by William Clemens. Produced by Bryan Foy for Warner Brothers.

Nancy Drew, Trouble Shooter. 1939. Screenplay by Kenneth Gamet; based on the stories by Carolyn Keene. Directed by William Clemens. Produced by Bryan Foy for Warner Brothers.

National Velvet. 1944. Screenplay by Theodore Reeeves and Helen Deutsch; based on the novel by Enid Bagnold. Directed by Clarence Brown. Produced by Pandro Berman for MGM.

100 Men and a Girl. 1937. Screenplay by Bruce Manning, Charles Kenyon, M. Kraly and James Mulhauser. Directed by Henry Koster. Produced by Jack Chertok for Universal.

One Wild Week. 1921. Screenplay by Percy Heath; from a story by Frances Harmer. Directed by Maurice Campbell for Realart Productions.

Our Dancing Daughters. 1928. Screenplay by Josephine Lovett. Directed by Harry Beaumont. Produced by Hunt Stromberg for MGM.

Our Hearts Were Young and Gay. 1944. Screenplay by Sheridan Gibney; from the book by Cornelia Otis Skinner and Emily Kimbrough. Directed by Lewis Allen for Paramount.

Our Modern Maidens. 1929. Screenplay by Josephine Lovett. Directed and produced by Jack Conway for MGM.

Peter Pan. 1924. Screenplay by Herbert Brenon; based on the story by James Barrie. Directed and produced by Herbert Brenon for Paramount.

The Plastic Age. 1925. Screenplay by Eve Unsell and Frederica Sagor. Directed by Wesley Rugges. Produced by B. P. Schulberg for B. P. Schulberg Productions.

Pollyanna. 1920. Screenplay by Francis Marion; from the novel by Eleanor Porter. Directed by Paul Powell. Produced by Mary Pickford for United Artists.

Port of Missing Girls. 1928. Screenplay by Howard Estabrook. Directed by Irving Cummings for Brenda Pictures.

Prodigal Daughters. 1923. Screenplay by Monte Katterjohn; from the book by Joseph Hocking. Directed by Sam Wood. Produced by Adolf Zukor for Paramount.

Rags. 1915. Screenplay by James Kirkwood; from a story by Edith Barnard Delano. Directed by James Kirkwood. Produced by Adolph Zukor for Paramount.

Rebecca of Sunnybrook Farm. 1917. Screenplay by Francis Marion; from the play by Kate Douglas Wiggins. Directed by Marshall Neilan for Paramount.

Rebellious Daughters. 1938. Screenplay by John Krafft. Directed by Jean Yarbrough for Progressive Pictures.

Reckless Youth. 1922. Screenplay by Edward Montagne. Directed by Ralph Ince. Produced by Lewis J. Selznick for Selznick Pictures.

Road to Ruin. 1928. Screenplay by Willis Kent. Directed by Norton S. Parker. Produced by Cliff Broughton for True Life Photoplays.

Sheltered Daughters. 1921. Screenplay by Clara Beranger; based on a story by George Bronson. Directed by Edward Dillon for Realart Pictures.

Short Skirts. 1921. Screenplay by Doris Schroeder. Directed by Harry B. Harris. Produced by Carl Laemmle for University Film Manufacturing.

Since You Went Away. 1944. Screenplay by David O. Selznick; based on the book by Margaret Buell Wilder. Directed by John Cromwell. Produced by David O. Selznick for United Artists.

The Song of Bernadette. 1944. Screenplay by George Seaton; from the novel by Franz Wertel. Directed by Henry King. Produced by William Perling for Twentieth Century Fox.

Song of the Open Road. 1944. Screenplay by Albert Mannheimer; based on a story by Irving Philips and Edward Verdier. Directed by Sylvan Simon. Produced by Charles Rogers for United Artists.

Sparrows. 1926. Screenplay by C. Gardner Sullivan; based on the story by Winifred Dunn. Directed by William Beaudine. Produced by Mary Pickford for United Artists.

Stella Dallas. 1937. Screenplay by Sarah Y. Mason and Victor Heerman, based on the novel by Olive Higgins Prouty. Directed by King Vidor. Produced by Samuel Goldwyn and released by United Artists.

Strike Up the Band. 1940. Screenplay by John Monks, Jr. and Fred Finklehoffe; based on the play by Edgar Selwyn. Directed by Busby Berkeley. Produced by Arthur Freed for MGM.

Sweet Sixteen. 1928. Screenplay by Arthur Hoerl; from a story by Phyllis Duganne. Directed by Scott Pembroke. Produced by Trem Carr Productions.

That Hagen Girl. 1947. Screenplay by Charles Hoffman; based on the novel by Edith Roberts. Directed by Peter Godfrey. Produced by Alex Gottleib for Warner Brothers.

These Three. 1936. Screenplay by Lillian Hellman from her play, *The Children's Hour*. Directed by William Wyler. Produced by Samuel Goldwyn and released by United Artists.

They Won't Forget. 1937. Screenplay by Robert Rosson and Aben Kandel. Directed and produced by Mervyn LeRoy for Warner Brothers.

Three Daring Daughters. 1948. Screenplay by Albert Manheimer. Directed by Fred Wilcox. Produced by Joe Pasternak for MGM.

Three Smart Girls. 1936. Screenplay by Adele Commandini from her story and play. Directed by Henry Koster. Produced by Joe Pasternak for MGM.

Three Smart Girls Grow Up. 1939. Screenplay by Bruce Manning and Felix Jackson. Directed by Henry Koster. Produced by Joe Pasternak for Universal.

Traffic in Souls. 1913. Screenplay by Walter MacNamara and George Tucker. Directed by George Tucker for Imp.

A Tree Grows in Brooklyn. 1945. Screenplay by Tess Slesinger and Frank Davis; from the novel by Betty Smith. Directed by Elia Kazan. Produced by Fred Kohlmar for Paramount.

True Heart Susie. 1919. Screenplay by Marion Fremont. Directed and produced by D. W. Griffith for Paramount.

White Slaver. 1913. Written and directed by Theodore Kremer for Ascher and Adler Productions.

Who Cares? 1925. Screenplay by Doug Doty; based on a story by Cosmo Hamilton. Directed by David Kirkland for Select Picture Corporation.

Wild Boys of the Road. 1933. Screenplay by Earl Baldwin; based on a story by Daniel Ahearn. Directed by William Wellman. Produced by Robert Presnell for First National.

The Wild Party. 1923. Screenplay by Hugh Hoffman; based on a story by Marion Orth. Directed by Herbert Blache for Universal.

The Wizard of Oz. 1939. Screenplay by Noel Langley and Florence Ryerson; based on the book by L. Frank Baum. Directed by Victor Fleming. Produced by Mervyn LeRoy for MGM.

The Youngest Profession. 1943. Screenplay by George Oppenheimer, Charles Lederer and Leonard Spigelgass; from the book by Lillian Day. Directed by Edward Buzzell. Produced by B. F. Zeidman for MGM.

You're Only Young Once. 1938. Screenplay by Kay Van Riper; based on the play by Aurania Rouverol. Directed by George B. Seitz. Produced by J. J. Cohn for MGM.

Youth Runs Wild. 1944. Screenplay by John Fante; based on a story by Fante and Herbert Kline. Directed by Mark Robson. Produced by Val Lewton for RKO.

Selected Bibliography

Abbott, Mary Alice. "A Study of Motion Picture Preferences of Horace Mann High School." *Teachers College Record* 28 (April 1927): 830–832.

Abramson, Martin. "Surf-Sand-and-Sex Films." *New York World Telegram*, 8 February 1966, 8.

Adams, Elizabeth. "What the American Woman Thinks." *The Woman Citizen* 8 (26 December 1924): 16–17.

Addams, Jane. *A New Conscience and an Ancient Evil.* New York: Macmillan, 1912.

Alexander, Ruth. *The Girl Problem: Female Sexual Delinquency in New York.* Ithaca, NY: Cornell University Press, 1995.

Allen, Frederick Lewis. *Only Yesterday.* New York: Harper and Brothers, 1930.

———. *Since Yesterday.* New York: Harper and Row, 1940.

America's Kid Sister." *Colliers* 116 (27 October 1945): 17.

"Are These Our Children?" *Look* 7 (21 September 1943): 21–27.

"Are These Our Children: *Look*'s Widely Praised Article Will Become a Movie." *Look* 7 (5 October 1943): 21–23.

Austin, Bruce. *The Film Audience: An International Bibliography of Research.* Metuchen, NJ: The Scarecrow Press, 1983.

Austin, Joe, and Michael Willard, eds. *Generations of Youth: Youth Culture in History and 20th Century America.* New York: New York University Press, 1998.

Banning, Margaret Culkin. "What a Young Girl Must Know." *Harpers* 168 (December 1933): 51–53.

Barron, Milton. *The Juvenile Delinquent in Society.* New York: Alfred A. Knopf, 1959.

Basinger, Jeanine. *A Woman's View: How Hollywood Spoke to Women 1930–1960*. New York: Alfred A. Knopf, 1993.

Baxter, John. *Hollywood in the Sixties*. New York: A. S. Barnes, 1972.

Bergman, Andrew. *We're in the Money: Depression America and Its Films*. New York: Harper Colophon Books, 1972.

Bettelheim, Bruno. "The Problem of Generations." In *The Challenge of Youth*, ed. Erik Erikson, 64–92. New York: Basic Books, 1963.

Bishop, Jeff, and Paul Hoggett. *Organizing around Enthusiasms*: *Mutual Aid in Leisure*. London: Comedia, 1986.

Black, Shirley Temple. *Child Star: An Autobiography*. New York: Warner Books, 1988.

Blanchard, Phyllis, and Caroline Manasses. *New Girls for Old*. New York: The McCauley Company, 1930.

Bliven, Bruce. "Flapper Jane." *New Republic* (9 September 1925): 65–67.

Blumer, Herbert. *Movies and Conduct*. New York: Macmillan, 1933.

Blumer, Herbert, and Philip M. Hauser. *Movies, Delinquency and Crime*. New York: Macmillan, 1933; reprint, Arno Press, 1970.

Blumgarder, Helen. "The Problems of the High School Girl." *Journal of Home Economics* 25 (June 1933): 473–474.

Bourdieu, Pierre. *Distinction: A Social Critique of the Judgement of Taste*. Cambridge: Harvard University Press, 1984.

Bowen, Ezra, ed. *This Fabulous Century: 1930–1940*. New York: Time-Life Books, 1972.

Bowser, Eileen. *A History of American Cinema 1907–1915*. New York: Charles Scribner's Sons, 1990.

Brenzel, Barbara. *Daughters of the State: A Social Portrait of the First Reform School for Girls in North America 1856–1905*. Cambridge: M.I.T. Press, 1983.

Brienes, Wini. *Young, White and Miserable: Growing Up Female in the Fifties*. Boston: Beacon Press, 1992.

Brownlow, Kevin. *Behind the Mask of Innocence*. New York: Alfred A. Knopf, 1990.

———. *The Parade's Gone By*. New York: Ballantine Books, 1968.

Brumberg, Joan Jacobs. *The Body Project: An Intimate History of American Girls*. New York: Random House, 1997.

"Came the Movie Dawn." *Business Week* 2 (9 November 1935): 18.

Clapp, Emily. "When Your Daughter Approaches the Teens." *Parents* 8 (December 1933): 22–23.

Cohen, Larry. "The New Audience: From Andy Hardy to Arlo Guthrie." *Saturday Review* 27 (December 1969): 8–11.

Collins, Frederick. "Are the Boys Better Than the Girls?" *Colliers* 73 (9 February 1924): 16.

"Combating the Victory Girl." *Newsweek* 23 (6 March 1944): 88.

Connolly, Vera. "The Girls Who Run Away." *Good Housekeeping* 85 (July 1927): 40–41, 195–197.

Considine, David. *The Cinema of Adolescence*. Jefferson, NC: McFarland, 1985.

Coontz, Stephanie. *The Way We Never Were: American Families and the Nostalgia Trap*. New York: Basic Books, 1992.

Crane, Frank. "The Flapper." *Colliers* 74 (11 October 1924): 23.

Creel, Blanche Bates. "Job or Joy Ride: Is It Harder Work to Be a Mother Than a Daughter?" *Century* 115 (November 1927): 41–46.

———. "The Painted Age." *Colliers* 79 (2 April 1927): 18, 46.

Crichton, Kyle. "Nice and Young." *Colliers* 101 (21 May 1938): 19–20.

Croy, Homer. "Atheism Beckons to Our Youth." *World's Work* 54 (May 1927): 18–26.

———. "Atheism Rampant in Our Schools." *World's Work* 54 (June 1927): 140–147.

Dale, Edgar. *Children's Attendance at the Motion Pictures*. New York: Macmillan, 1935.

Daly, Maureen. "Meet a Sub-Deb." *Ladies Home Journal* 61 (December 1944): 137–140.

———, ed. *Profile of Youth*. Philadelphia: Lippincott, 1949.

"Deanna Durbin." *Fortune* 20 (October 1939): 158–159.

Deanna's Diary. 3–7 (1939–1943).

"Deanna's Fans Have a Devotee Club." *Life* (3 October 1938): 33–34.

"Dearest Deanna." *Time* (16 June 1941): 29.

de Lauretis, Teresa. *Alice Doesn't: Feminism, Semiotics, Cinema*. London: Macmillan, 1984.

Demos, John, and Virginia Demos. "Adolescence in Historical Perspective." In *The American Family in Social-Historical Perspective*, ed. Michael Gordon, 209–221. New York: St. Martin's Press, 1978.

Dimmitt, Richard Bertrand. *A Title Guide to the Talkies*. New York: The Scarecrow Press, 1963.

Doherty, Thomas. *Teenagers and Teenpics: The Juvenilization of American Film*. Boston: Unwin Hyman, 1988.

Dyer, Richard. "Entertainment and Utopia." *Movie* 24 (1977): 3.

———. *Heavenly Bodies: Film Stars and Society*. New York: St. Martin's Press, 1987.

———. *Stars*. London: British Film Institute Publishing, 1979.

Eckert, Charles. "Shirley Temple and the House of Rockefeller." *Jump Cut* 2 (July/August 1974): 17–20.

Edwards, Anne. *Judy Garland: A Biography*. New York: Pocket Books, 1975.

Fass, Paula. *The Damned and the Beautiful: American Youth in the 1920s*. New York: Oxford University Press, 1977.

Feuer, Jane. *The Hollywood Musical*. London: Macmillan, 1982.

Finch, Christopher. *Rainbow: The Stormy Life of Judy Garland*. New York: Ballantine Books, 1975.

Fisher, Willis. "Alcohol and the Adolescent." *Parent* 11 (March 1936): 22–23.

Fiske, John. "The Cultural Economy of Fandom." In *The Adoring Audience*, ed. Lisa Lewis, 30–48. New York: Routledge, 1991.

Forman, Henry. *Our Movie Made Children*. New York: Macmillan, 1933.

Freedman, Estelle. *Maternal Justice: Miriam Van Waters and the Female Reform Tradition*. Chicago: University Chicago Press, 1996.

Freedman, Estelle, and John D'Emilio. *Intimate Matters: A History of Sexuality in America*. New York: Harper and Row, 1988.

French, Philip. *The Movie Moguls*. London: Weidenfeld and Nicolson, 1969.

Fuller, Kathryn. *At the Picture Show: Small-Town Audiences and the Creation of the Movie Fan*. Washington, DC: Smithsonian Institution Press, 1996.

Gilbert, James. *A Cycle of Outrage: America's Reaction to the Juvenile Delinquent in the Fifties*. New York: Oxford University Press, 1986.

Gish, Lillian. *The Movies, Mr. Griffith and Me*. Englewood Cliffs, NJ: Prentice Hall, 1969.

Gledhill, Christine, ed. *Home Is Where the Heart Is: Studies in Melodrama and Women's Film*. London: British Film Institute Publishing, 1987.

Goldstein, Ruth M., and Edith Zorrow. *The Screen Image of Youth: Movies about Children and Adolescents*. Metuchen, NJ: The Scarecrow Press, 1980.

Gordon, Linda. *Heroes of Their Own Lives: the Politics and History of Family Violence*. New York: Penguin, 1988.

Grayson, Alice Barr. *Do You Know Your Daughter?* New York: Appleton-Century Co., 1945.

Greenwood, Cora Wilson. "When Boys and Girls Step Out." *Parents* 13 (December 1938): 19.

Griffith, Beatrice Winston. *American Me*. Westport, CT: Greenwood Press, 1973.

Griffith, Richard. *The Talkies: Articles and Illustrations from a Great Fan Magazine, 1928–1940*. New York: Dover Publications, 1971.

Griffith, Richard, and Arthur Mayer. *The Movies*. New York: Simon and Schuster, 1970.

Grossberg, Lawrence. "Is There a Fan in the House?: The Affective Sensibility of Fandom." In *The Adoring Audience: Fan Culture and Popular Media*, ed. Lisa Lewis, 50–65. New York: Routledge, 1992.

Hall, G. Stanley. *Adolescence: Its Psychology and Its Relation to Physiology, Anthropology, Sociology, Sex, Crime, Religion and Education*. 2 Vols. New York: D. Appleton and Company, 1904.

Hall, Leonard. "What about Clara Bow?" *Photoplay* (October 1930); 24–25.

Hall, Stuart, and Tony Jefferson, eds. *Resistance through Rituals: Youth Subcultures in Post War Britain*. London: Hutchinson, 1976.

Handel, Leo. *Hollywood Looks at its Audience*. Urbana: University of Illinois Press, 1950.

Hansel, Eva. "Why Children Run Away." *Parents* 11 (July 1936): 18.

Harmetz, Aljean. "The Dime-Store Way to Make Movies and Money." *New York Times Magazine*, 4 August 1974, 12, 32–34.

Harris, Cora. "The Synthetic Girl." *Ladies Home Journal* 45 (April 1928): 37.

Haskell, Molly. *From Reverence to Rape: The Treatment of Women in the Movies*. New York : Penguin, 1974.

Hawes, Joseph. "The Strange History of Female Adolescence in the United States." *The Journal of Psychohistory* 13 (Summer 1985): 51–63.

Hayward, Susan. *Key Concepts in Cinema Studies*. London: Routledge, 1996.

Head, Gay. "Jam Session." *Scholastic* 47 (22 October 1944): 42.

———. "Jam Session." *Scholastic* 47 (29 October 1944): 30.

Henderson, Robert. *D. W. Griffith: His Life, His Work*. New York: Oxford University Press, 1972.

Higashi, Sumiko. *Virgins, Vamps and Flappers: The American silent Movie Heroine*. Montreal: Eden Press, 1978.

Higham, Charles, and Joel Greenberg. *Hollywood in the Forties*. New York: A. S. Barnes, 1968.

Hinant, Mary. "Paging Miss Bobby Sox." *Library Journal* 70 (15 September 1945): 803–805.

Hoberman, J. "Don't Knock the Schlock." *Village Voice*, 2 July 1979, 9.

Hollingshead, A. B. *Elmstown Youth: The Impact of Social Classes on Adolescence*. New York: John Wiley and Sons, 1949.

Hopper, Hedda. *The Whole Truth and Nothing But*. New York: Pyramid Books, 1963.

Houston, Jeanne Wakatsuki. *Farewell to Manzanar*. Boston: Houghton Mifflin, 1973.

"How Wild Is Wild Youth?" *New Republic* 46 (5 May 1926): 318–319.

Inness, Sherrie, ed. *Delinquents and Debutantes: 20th Century American Girls Culture*. New York: New York University Press, 1998.

Jackson, Kathy Merlock. *Images of Children in American Film*. Metuchen, NJ: Scarecrow Press, 1986.

Jacobs, Lea. "Reformers and Spectators: The Film Education Movement in the Thirties." *Camera Obscura* 22 (January 1990): 29–49.

———. *The Wages of Sin: Censorship and the Fallen Woman Film 1928–1942*. Madison: University of Wisconsin Press, 1991.

Jacobs, Lewis. *The Rise of the American Film*. New York: Columbia University Press, 1948.

Jensen, Joli. "Fandom as Pathology." In *The Adoring Audience: Fan Culture and Popular Media,* ed. Lisa Lewis, 9–27. New York: Routledge, 1992.

Jewell, Richard B., with Vernon Harben. *The RKO Story*. London: Arlington, 1982.

Jowett, Garth. *Film: The Democratic Art*. Boston: Little Brown and Co., 1976.

Jowett, Garth, Ian C. Jarvie and Kathryn H. Fuller. *Children and the Movies: Media Influence and the Payne Fund Controversy*. New York: Cambridge University Press, 1996.

"Juvenile Delinquency." *Life* 13 (26 October 1942): 58–59.

Kaplan, Ann. *Women and Film: Both Sides of the Camera*. New York: Methuen, 1983.

Keniston, Kenneth. "Social Change and Youth in America." *Daedalus* (Winter 1962): 145–171.

Kett, Joseph. *Rites of Passage: Adolescence in America 1790 to the Present*. New York: Basic Books, 1977.

King, Irving. *The High School Age*. Indianapolis: Bobbs-Merrill, 1918.

Knight, Arthur. *The Liveliest Art*. New York: Macmillan, 1957.

Leff, Leonard, and Jerold Simmons. *The Dame in the Kimono: Hollywood, Censorship and the Production Code*. New York: Grove Weidenfeld, 1990.

Levin, Martin, ed. *Hollywood and the Great Fan Magazines*. New York: Castle Books, 1970.

Lewis, Lisa. *Gender Politics and MTV*. Philadelphia: Temple University Press, 1990.

"Life Goes to a Party at an Honor Farm." *Life* 3 (13 September 1937): 108–109.

"Life Goes to a Party at Rosemary Hall." *Life* 2 (15 March 1937): 72–73.

Lindsey, Ben, and Wainwright Evans. *The Revolt of Modern Youth*. New York: Boni and Liverlight, 1925.

Lynd, Robert S., and Helen Merrell Lynd. *Middletown: A Study in American Culture*. New York: Harcourt, Brace and Co., 1929.

———. *Middletown in Transition*. New York: Harcourt, Brace and World, 1937.

Mackenzie, Catherine. "Teen Age Daughters." *New York Times Magazine*, 14 January 1945, 29.

May, Henry. *The End of American Innocence: A Study of the First Years of Our Time, 1912–1917*. London: J. Cape, 1959.

May, Lary. "Making the American Consensus: The Narrative of Conversion and Subversion in World War II Films." In *The War in American Culture: Society and Consciousness during World War II*, ed. Lewis Ehrenberg and Susan E. Hirsch. Chicago: University Chicago Press, 1996.

Maynard, Helen. "Private School Was Our Answer." *Parents* 14 (May 1939): 38–40.

Mazon, Mauricio. *The Zoot-Suit Riots: The Psychology of Symbolic Annihilation*. Austin: University of Texas Press, 1984.

McCarthy, Todd, and Charles Flynn, eds. *King of the B's: Working within the Hollywood System*. New York: E. P. Dutton, 1975.

McClelland, Doug. *The Golden Age of "B" Movies*. Nashville: Charter House Publishers, 1978.

McGee, Mark, and R. J. Robertson. *The J.D. Films: Juvenile Delinquency in the Movies*. Jefferson, NC: McFarland, 1982.

McGovern, James. "The American Women's Pre–World War I Freedom in Manners and Morals." *Journal of American History* (September 1968): 315–333.

McKenzie, Catherine. "Teen-Age Daughters." *New York Times Magazine*, 14 January 1945: 29.

McRobbie, Angela. "Different, Youthful Subjectives: Toward a Cultural Sociology of Youth." In *Postmodernism and Popular Culture*. London: Routledge, 1994.

———. "Post Marxism and Cultural Studies." In *Postmodernism and Popular Culture*. London: Routledge, 1994.

———. Settling Accounts with Subcultures: A Feminist Critique." *Screen Education* 34 (1980): 37–49.

———. "Shut Up and Dance." In *Postmodernism and Popular Culture*. London: Routledge, 1994.

McRobbie, Angela, and Jenny Garber. " "Girls and Subcultures." In *Resistance through Rituals*, ed. Stuart Hall and Tony Jefferson. London: Hutchinson, 1976.

McRobbie, Angela, and Mica Nava. *Gender and Generation*. London: Macmillan, 1984.

Moley, Raymond. *The Hays Office*. Indianapolis: Bobbs-Merrill, 1945.

Moore, Dick. *Twinkle Twinkle Little Star but Don't Have Sex or Take the Car: Child Stars and Hollywood*. New York: Harper and Row, 1984.

Morin, Edgar. *The Stars*. New York: Grove Press, 1960.

"Movies Hit Prosperity Trail." *Business Week* 2 (21 November 1936): 22–24.

Mulvey, Laura. "Visual Pleasure and Narrative Cinema." *Screen* 16 (1975): 6–18.

———. "Afterthought on 'Visual Pleasure and Narrative Cinema' inspired by *Duel in the Sun*." *Framework* 6 (1981): 12–18.

Munden, Kenneth W., ed. *The American Film Institute Catalog of Pictures Produced in the United States: Feature Films 1920–1930*. New York: Bowker, 1971.

Nathanson, Constance. *Dangerous Passage: The Social Control of Sexuality in Women's Adolescence*. Philadelphia: Temple University Press, 1991.

Nava, Mica. *Changing Cultures: Feminism, Youth and Consumerism*. London: Sage, 1992.

"Notes on a Songbird." Undates and unsourced. Deanna Durbin Clipping file. Academy of Motion Picture Arts and Sciences (AMPAS).

O'Connor, John E. "History in Images/Images in History: Reflections on the Importance of Film and Television Study for an Understanding of the Past." *American Historical Review* 93 (December 1988): 1200–1209.

O'Dell, Paul. *Griffith and the Rise of Hollywood*. New York: Castle Books, 1970.

Odem, Mary Ellen. *Delinquent Daughters: Protecting and Policing Adolescent Female Sexuality in the United States 1885–1920*. Chapel Hill: University of North Carolina Press, 1995.

Palladino, Grace. *Teenagers: An American History*. New York: Basic Books, 1996.

Parsons, Talcott. *Essays in Sociological Theory*. Glencoe, IL: Free Press, 1949.

Peiss, Kathy. *Cheap Amusements: Working Women and Leisure in Turn of the Century New York*. Philadelphia: Temple University Press, 1986.

Pipher, Mary. *Reviving Ophelia: Saving the Lives of Adolescent Girls*. New York: Ballantine Books, 1994.

Powdermaker, Hortense. *Hollywood: The Dream Factory*. Boston: Little Brown & Co., 1950.

Prager, Arthur. *Rascals at Large, or the Clue in the Old Nostalgia*. Garden City, NY: Doubleday, 1971.

Purcell, Marion. "Those Fifteen Year Olds." *Scribners* 44 (August 1933): 111–114.

Quigley, Martin. *Decency in Motion Pictures*. New York: Macmillan, 1937.

Ramsaye, Terry. *A Million and One Nights: A History of the Motion Picture*. New York: Simon and Schuster, 1926.

Reinhardt, Aurelia Mary. "The Problem of the Modern Girl." *Woman's Home Companion* 55 (March 1928): 24, 135.

Reuter, E. B. "The Sociology of Adolescence." *American Journal of Sociology* (November 1937): 421–430.

Ringgold, Gene. "Deanna Durbin." *Screen Facts* 5 (1963): 3 22.

Robinson-Hale, Beatrice Forbes. *What's Wrong with Our Girls?: The Environment, Training and Future of American Girls*. New York: Fred A. Stokes Co., 1923.

Rosen, Marjorie. *Popcorn Venus: Women, Movies and the American Dream*. New York: Avon Books, 1973.

Rosten, Leo. *Hollywood: The Movie Colony, The Movie Makers*. New York: Harcourt Brace, 1941.

Royden, Maude. "The Destructive Younger Generation." *Ladies Home Journal* 41 (March 1924): 31,174–175.

Ruiz, Vicki. "Star Struck: Acculturation, Adolescence and Mexican American Women 1920–1950." In *Small Worlds: Children and Adolescents in America 1850–1950*, eds. Paula Petrik and Elliott West, 64–74. Lawrence: University of Kansas Press, 1994.

"The Runaway Girl Problem." *Literary Digest*, 10 May 1924: 31–32.

Ryan, Mary. "The Projection of a New Womanhood: The Movie Moderns of the 1920s." In *Our American Sisters: American Life and Thought*, 2nd ed., ed. Jean Friedman and William Shade, 500–518. Boston: Allyn and Bacon, 1988.

Sanchez, George. *Becoming Mexican American: Ethnicity, Culture and Identity in Chicano Los Angeles, 1900–1945*. Boston: Oxford University Press, 1995.

Schlossman, Steven, and Stephanie Wallach. "The Crime of Precocious Sexuality: Female Juvenile Delinquency in the Progressive Era." *Harvard Educational Review* 48 (February 1978): 65–95.

"The Secret Life of Teens." *Newsweek*, 10 May 1999, 30–59.

Shuler, Marjorie. "Applause by Mail." *Christian Science Monitor* (November 1936): 6.

Shuttleworth, Frank, and Mark May. *The Social Conduct and Attitudes of Movie Fans*. New York: Macmillan, 1933.

Sklar, Robert. *Movie Made America: A Cultural History of American Movies*. New York: Vintage Books, 1975.

Slide, Anthony. "A Tribute to Deanna Durbin." Academy of Motion Picture Arts and Sciences Program. 9 December 1978.

Springer, John and Hamilton, Jack. *They Had Faces Then*. Secaucus, NJ: The Citadel Press, 1974.

Stacey. Jackie. *Star Gazing: Hollywood Cinema and Female Spectatorship*. London: Routledge, 1994.

Staiger, Janet. *Interpreting Films: Studies in the Historical Reception of American Cinema*. Princeton, NJ: Princeton University Press, 1992.

Stoddard, Karen M. *Saints and Shrews: Women and Aging in American Popular Film*. Westport, CT: Greenwood Press, 1983.

"Subdebs Live in a Jolly World of Their Own." *Life* 10 (27 January 1941): 77–79.

"Teen-Age Girls—They Live in a Jolly World of Their Own." *Life* 17 (11 December 1944): 91–99.

Thomas, Bob. *King Cohen: The Life and Times of Harry Cohen*. New York: G. P. Putnam's Sons, 1967.

———. *Joan Crawford: A Biography*. New York: Bantam, 1978.

Thorp, Margaret. *America at the Movies*. New Haven: Yale University Press, 1939; reprint, Arno Press, 1970.

Tuttle, William. *Daddy's Gone to War: The Second World War in the Lives of American Children*. New York: Oxford University Press, 1993.

Umphett, Wiley Lee. *The Movies Go to College: Hollywood and the World of the College-Life Film*. Rutherford, NJ: Farleigh Dickinson University Press, 1984.

Van Waters, Miriam. *Parents on Probation*. New York: Republic, 1927.

———. *Youth in Conflict*. New York: Republic, 1925; reprint, AMS Press, 1970.

Walker, Alexander. *The Celluloid Sacrifice: Aspects of Sex in the Movies*. New York: Hawthorne Books, Inc., 1966.

———. *Stardom: The Hollywood Phenomenon*. London: Michael Joseph Ltd., 1970.

Walsh, Andrea. *Women's Film and Female Experience 1945–1950*. New York: Praeger, 1984.

Warner, Lloyd, and Paul Lunt. *The Social Life of a Modern Community*. New Haven: Yale University Press, 1941.

"A Warning for the Runaway Season." *Literary Digest*, 16 July 1927, 29–30.

Welter, Barbara. *Dimity Convictions: The American Woman in the 19th Century*. Athens: Ohio University Press, 1976.

"What's On the Screen." *The American Girl* (January 1945): 28.

Williams, Carol Traynor. *The Dream Besides Me: The Movies and the Children of the Forties*.

Rutherford, NJ: Farleigh Dickinson University Press, 1980.

Windeler, Robert. *Sweetheart: The Story of Mary Pickford*. New York: Praeger, 1974.

Wolf, Naomi. *Promiscuities: The Secret Struggle for Womanhood*. New York: Random House, 1997.

Zierold, Norman. *The Child Stars*. New York: Coward McCann, 1965.

———. *The Moguls*. New York: Avon Books, 1969.

Index

About the Author

GEORGANNE SCHEINER is Assistant Professor of Women's Studies at Arizona State University. Her research interests include the history of girlhood and adolescence, popular culture, and women and the body. She has published articles on fan clubs and Sandra Dee and currently is coauthoring a book on the history of the Girl Scouts.

ISBN 0-275-96895-2

90000>

EAN

9 780275 968953

HARDCOVER BAR CODE